SOCIOLOGICAL THEORY

SOCIOLOGICAL THEORY

Asha Kiran

ANMOL PUBLICATIONS PVT. LTD.
NEW DELHI-110 002 (INDIA)

ANNMOL PUBLICATIONS PVT. LTD.
Regd. Office: 4360/4, Ansari Road, Daryaganj,
New Delhi-110002 (India)
Tel.: 23278000, 23261597, 23286875, 23255577
Fax: 91-11-23280289
Email: anmolpub@gmail.com
Visit us at: www.anmolpublications.com

Branch Office: No. 1015, Ist Main Road, BSK IIIrd Stage
IIIrd Phase, IIIrd Block, Bangalore-560 085 (India)
Tel.: 080-41723429 • Fax: 080-26723604
Email: anmolpublicationsbangalore@gmail.com

Sociological Theory

First Edition, 2010

ISBN 978-81-261-4562-1

PRINTED IN INDIA

Printed at Mehra Offset Press, Delhi.

Contents

Preface

1. Introduction 1

2. Critical Theory and the Crisis of Social Theory 32

3. Comprehensive Theory of Social Development 65

4. Max Weber: The Fundamental Concepts of Sociology 147

5. Theory of Social Development 191

6. A Historical Sketch of Sociological Theory 243

7. Emile Durkheim: The Science of Society as Moral Order 254

Bibliography 277

Index 278

Preface

Sociological Theory is the definitive source of current perspective and approaches in the field. Organized by theme, the volume includes the most representative material available on topics such as sociology of race and ethnic relations, social differentiation and stratification, social disorganization and deviant behaviour, organizational analysis, general theory in sociology, structure, function and social evolution, problems in social methodology and critical theory. The theories of Auguste Comte, John Stuart Mill, Herbert Spencer, Talcott Parsons, Durkheim, Davis Kingsley, Robert Merton and Karl Marx also appear in longer sections, enabling students and scholars to examine the work in greater depth.

Sociologists develop theories to explain social phenomena. A theory is a proposed relationship between two or more concepts. In other words, a theory is explanation for why a phenomenon occurs. An example of a sociological theory is the work of Robert Putnam on the decline of civic engagement.

The basic insight of sociology is that human behaviour is largely shaped by the groups to which people belong and by the social interaction that takes place within those groups. The main focus of sociology is the group, not the individual. Sociologist is mainly interested in the interaction between people—the ways in which people act towards, respond to, and influence one another. Sociology, does not, however, study everything that happens in society or under social conditions. For example, sociologist study religion only insofar as it affects social relationship, i.e., the relationship of man to man, of one group to another, or of one group to the whole society. This book has several other learning and teaching features-a timeline that gives each theorist's life span, the chapter in which she or he appears in the book, and other important world events occurring during that time.

—Editor

1

Introduction

Sociologists develop theories to explain social phenomena. A theory is a proposed relationship between two or more concepts. In other words, a theory is explanation for why a phenomenon occurs. An example of a sociological theory is the work of Robert Putnam on the decline of civic engagement. Putnam found that Americans involvement in civic life (e.g., community organizations, clubs, voting, religious participation, etc.) has declined over the last 40 to 60 years. While there are a number of factors that contribute to this decline (Putnam's theory is quite complex), one of the prominent factors is the increased consumption of television as a form entertainment. Putnam's theory proposes:

The more television people watch, the lower their involvement in civic life will be.

This element of Putnam's theory clearly illustrates the basic purpose of sociological theory: it proposes a relationship between two or more concepts. In this case, the concepts are *civic engagement* and *television watching*. The relationship is an *inverse* one-as one goes up, the other goes down. What's more, it is an explanation of one phenomenon with another: part of the reason why civic engagement has declined over the last several decades is because people are watching more television. In short, Putnam's theory clearly encapsulates the key ideas of a sociological theory.

Sociological theory is developed at multiple levels, ranging from *grand theory* to highly contextualized and specific *micro-range theories*. There are many *middle-range* and *micro-range* theories in sociology. Because such theories are dependent on context and specific to certain situations, it is beyond the scope of this text to explore each of those theories. The purpose of this chapter is to introduce some of the more well-known and most commonly used grand and middle-range theories in sociology.

Importance of Theory

In the theory proposed above, the astute reader will notice that the theory includes two components: The data, in this case the findings that civic engagement has declined and TV watching has increased, and the proposed relationship, that the increase in television viewing has contributed to the decline in civic engagement. Data alone are not particularly informative. If Putnam had not proposed a relationship between the two elements of social life, we may not have realized that television viewing does, in fact, reduce people's desire to and time for participating in civic life. In order to understand the social world around us, it is necessary to employ theory to draw the connections between seemingly disparate concepts.

Another example of sociological theorizing illustrates this point. In his now classic work, *Suicide*, Emile Durkheim was interested in explaining a social phenomenon, suicide, and employed both data and theory to offer an explanation. By aggregating data for large groups of people in Europe, Durkheim was able to discern patterns in suicide rates and connect those patterns with another concept (or variable): religious affiliation. Durkheim found that Protestants were more likely to commit suicide than were Catholics. At this point, Durkheim's analysis was still in the data stage; he had not proposed an explanation for the different suicide rates of the two groups. It was when Durkheim introduced the ideas of *anomie* and *social solidarity* that he began to explain the difference in suicide rates. Durkheim argued that the looser social ties found in Protestant religions lead to weaker social cohesion and reduced social solidarity. The higher suicide rates were the result of weakening social bonds among Protestants.

While Durkheim's findings have since been criticized, his study is a classic example of the use of theory to explain the relationship between two concepts. Durkheim's work also illustrates the importance of theory: without theories to explain the relationship between concepts, we would not be able to understand cause and effect relationships in social life.

Prominent Sociological Theories

As noted above, there are many theories in sociology. However, there are several broad theoretical perspectives that are prominent in the field (they are arguably paradigms). These theories are prominent because they are quite good at explaining social life. They are not without their problems, but these theories remain widely used and cited precisely because they have withstood a great deal of criticism.

As the dominant theories in sociology are discussed below, you might be inclined to ask, "Which of these theories is *the best*?" As is often the case in sociology, just because things are different doesn't mean one is better than another. In fact, it is probably more useful and informative to view these theories as *complementary*. One theory may explain one element of society better than another. Or, both may be useful for explaining social life. In short, all of the theories are correct in the sense that they offer compelling explanations for social phenomena.

Structural-Functionalism

Structural-Functionalism is a sociological theory that originally attempted to explain social institutions as collective means to meet individual biological needs (originally just *functionalism*). Later it came to focus on the ways social institutions meet social needs (structural-functionalism).

Structural-functionalism draws its inspiration primarily from the ideas of Emile Durkheim. Durkheim was concerned with the question of how societies maintain internal stability and survive over time. He sought to explain social cohesion and stability through the concept of solidarity. In more "primitive" societies it was mechanical solidarity, everyone performing similar tasks, that held society together. Durkheim proposed that such societies tend to be segmentary, being composed of equivalent parts that are held together by shared values, common symbols, or systems of exchanges. In modern, complex societies members perform very different tasks, resulting in a strong interdependence between individuals. Based on the metaphor of an organism in which many parts function together to sustain the whole, Durkheim argued that modern complex societies are held together by organic solidarity (think interdependent *organs*).

The central concern of structural-functionalism is a continuation of the Durkheimian task of explaining the apparent stability and internal cohesion of societies that are necessary to ensure their continued existence over time. Many functionalists argue that social institutions are functionally integrated to form a stable system and that a change in one institution will precipitate a change in other institutions. Societies are seen as coherent, bounded and fundamentally relational constructs that function like organisms, with their various parts (social institutions) working together to maintain and reproduce them. The various parts of society are assumed to work in an unconscious, quasi-automatic fashion towards the maintenance of the overall social *equilibrium*. All social and cultural phenomena are therefore seen as being *functional* in the sense of working together to achieve this state and are effectively deemed to have a *life* of their own. These components are then primarily analysed in terms of the function they play. In other words, to understand a component of society, one can ask the question, "What is the function of this institution?" A *function*, in this sense, is the contribution made by a phenomenon to a larger system of which the phenomenon is a part.

Thus, one can ask of education, "What is the function of education for society?" The answer is actually quite complex and requires a detailed analysis of the history of education, but one obvious answer is that education prepares individuals to enter the workforce. By delineating the functions of elements of society, of the social structure, we can better understand social life.

Durkheim's strongly sociological perspective of society was continued by Radcliffe-Brown. Following Auguste Comte, Radcliffe-Brown believed that the social constituted a separate *level* of reality distinct from both the biological and the inorganic (here *non-living*). Explanations of social phenomena therefore had to be constructed within this social level, with individuals merely being transient occupants of comparatively stable social roles. Thus, in structural-functionalist thought, individuals are not significant in and of themselves but only in terms of their social status: their position in patterns of social relations. The social structure is therefore a network of statuses connected by associated roles.

Limitations

Structural-functionalism has been criticized for being unable to account for social change because it focuses so intently on social order and equilibrium in society. For instance, in the late 19th Century, higher education transitioned from a training centre for clergy and the elite to a centre for the conduct of science and the general education of the masses. In other words, education did not always serve the function of preparing individuals for the labour force (with the exception of the ministry and the elite). As structural-functionalism thinks about elements of social life in relation to their present function and not their past functions, structural-functionalism has a difficult time explaining why a function of some element of society might change or how such change occurs. However, structural-functionalism could, in fact, offer an explanation in this case. Also occurring in the 19th Century (though begun in the 18th) was the industrial revolution. The industrial revolution, facilitated by capitalism, was increasingly demanding technological advances to increase profit. Technological advances and advanced industry both required more educated workforces. Thus, as one aspect of society changed-the economy and production-it required a comparable change in the educational system, bringing social life back into equilibrium.

Another philosophical problem with the structural-functional approach is the ontological argument that society does not have *needs* as a human being does; and even if society does have needs they need not be met. The idea that society has *needs* like humans do is not a tenable position because society is only alive in the sense that it is made up of living individuals. Thus, society cannot have wants and/or needs like humans do. What's more, just because a society has some element in it at the present that does not mean that it must necessarily have that element. For instance, in the United Kingdom, religious service attendance has declined precipitously over the last 100 years. Today, less than 1 in 10 British attend religious service in a given week. Thus, while one might argue that religion has certain functions in British society, it is becoming apparent that it is not necessary for British society to function.

Another criticism often levelled at structural-functionalist theory is that it supports the status quo. According to some opponents, structural-functionalism paints conflict and challenge to the status quo as harmful to society, and therefore tends to be the prominent view among conservative thinkers.

Manifest and Latent Functions

Merton (1957) proposed a distinction between *manifest* and *latent* functions. *Manifest* functions are the intended functions of a phenomenon in a social system. *Latent* functions are the unintended functions of a phenomenon in a social system. An example of manifest and latent functions is education. The manifest purpose of public education is to increase the knowledge and abilities of the citizenry to prepare them to contribute in the workforce. A latent function of the public education system is the development of a hierarchy of *the learned*. The most learned are often also the most affluent. Thus, while education's manifest function is to empower all individuals to contribute to the workforce and society, it also limits some people by creating boundaries of entry into occupations.

Conflict Theory

A prominent sociological theory that is often contrasted with structural-functionalism is conflict theory. Conflict theory argues that society is not best understood as a complex system striving for equilibrium but rather as a competition. Society is made up of individuals competing for limited resources (e.g., money, leisure, sexual partners, etc.). Broader social structures and organizations (e.g., religions, government, etc.) reflect the competition for resources in their inherent inequalities; some people and organizations have more resources (i.e., power and influence) and use those resources to maintain their positions of power in society.

Conflict theory was developed in part to illustrate the limitations of structural-functionalism. The structural-functionalist approach argued that society tends toward equilibrium, focusing on stability at the expense of social change. This is contrasted with the conflict approach, which argues that society is constantly in conflict over resources. One of the primary contributions conflict theory presents over the structural-functional approach is that it is ideally suited for explaining social change, a significant problem in the structural-functional approach.

The following are three primary assumptions of modern conflict theory:

- Competition over scarce resources is at the heart of all social relationships. Competition rather than consensus is characteristic of human relationships.
- Inequalities in power and reward are built into all social structures. Individuals and groups that benefit from any particular structure strive to see it maintained.
- Change occurs as a result of conflict between competing interests rather than through adaptation. Change is often abrupt and revolutionary rather than evolutionary.

A heuristic device to help you think about society from a conflict perspective is to ask, "Who benefits from this element of society?" Using the same example as we did above, we can ask, "Who benefits from the current higher educational system in the U.S.?" The answer, of course, is the wealthy. Why? Because higher education in the U.S. is not free. Thus, the educational system often screens out poorer individuals not because they are unable to compete academically but because they cannot afford to pay for their education. Because the poor are unable to obtain higher education, this means they are also generally unable to get higher paying jobs which means they remain poor. This can easily translate into a vicious cycle of poverty. Thus, while the function of education is to educate the workforce, it also has built into it an element of conflict and inequality, favouring one group (the wealthy) over other groups (the poor). Thinking about education this way helps illustrate why both structural-functionalist and conflict theories are helpful in understanding how society works.

Conflict theory was elaborated in the United Kingdom by Max Gluckman and John Rex, in the United States by Lewis A. Coser and Randall Collins, and in Germany by Ralf Dahrendorf, all of whom were influenced by Karl Marx, Ludwig Gumplovicz,

Vilfredo Pareto, Georg Simmel, and other founding fathers of European sociology.

Limitations

Not surprisingly, the primary limitation of the social-conflict perspective is that it overlooks the stability of societies. While societies are in a constant state of change, much of the change is minor. Many of the broader elements of societies remain remarkably stable over time, indicating the structural-functional perspective has a great deal of merit.

As noted above, sociological theory is often complementary. This is particularly true of structural-functionalism and social-conflict theories. Structural-functionalism focuses on equilibrium and solidarity; conflict-theory focuses on change and conflict. Keep in mind that neither is better than the other; when combined, the two approaches offer a broader and more comprehensive view of society.

Symbolic Interactionism

In contrast to the rather broad approach toward society of structural-functionalism and conflict theory, Symbolic Interactionism is a theoretical approach to understanding the relationship between humans and society. The basic notion of symbolic interactionism is that human action and interaction are understandable only through the exchange of meaningful communication or symbols. In this approach, humans are portrayed as *acting* as opposed to being *acted upon*.

The main principles of symbolic interactionism are:

1. Human beings act toward things on the basis of the meanings that things have for them
2. These meanings arise of out of social interaction
3. Social action results from a fitting together of individual lines of action.

This approach stands in contrast to the strict behaviourism of psychological theories prevalent at the time it was first formulated (in the 1920s and 1930s). According to Symbolic Interactionism, humans are distinct from infrahumans (lower animals) because infrahumans simply respond to their environment (i.e., a stimulus evokes a response or stimulus-> response) whereas humans have the ability to interrupt that process (i.e., stimulus-> cognition-> response). Additionally, infrahumans are unable to conceive of alternative responses to gestures. Humans, however, can. This understanding should not be taken to indicate that humans never behave in a strict *stimulus-> response* fashion, but rather that humans have the capability of not responding in that fashion (and do so much of the time).

This perspective is also rooted in phenomenological thought. According to symbolic interactionism, the objective world has no reality for humans, only subjectively-defined objects have meaning. Meanings are not entities that are bestowed on humans and learned by habituation. Instead, meanings can be altered through the creative capabilities of humans, and individuals may influence the many meanings that form their society. Human society, therefore, is a social product.

Neurological evidence based on EEGs supports the idea that humans have a "social brain," that is, there are components of the human brain that govern social interaction. These parts of the brain begin developing in early childhood (the preschool years) and aid humans in understanding how other people think. In symbolic interactionism, this is known as "reflected appraisals" or "the looking glass self" and refers to our ability to think about how other people will think about us. A good example of this is when people try on clothes before going out with friends. Some people may not think much about how others will think about their clothing choices, but others can spend quite a bit of time considering what they are going to wear. And while they are deciding, the dialogue that is taking place inside their mind is usually a dialogue between their "self" (that portion of their identity that calls itself "I") and that person's internalized understanding of their friends and society (a "generalized other"). An indicator of mature socialization is when an individual quite accurately predicts how other people think about him/her. Such an individual has incorporated the "social" into the "self."

It should also be noted that symbolic interactionists advocate a particular methodology. Because they see *meaning* as the fundamental component of human and society interaction, studying human and society interaction requires *getting at* that meaning. Thus, symbolic interactionists tend to employ more qualitative rather than quantitative methods in their research.

Limitations

The most significant limitation of the symbolic-interactionist perspective relates to its primary contribution: it overlooks macro social structures (e.g., norms, culture) as a result of focusing on micro-level interactions. Some symbolic interactionists, however, would counter that if *role theory* is incorporated into symbolic interactionism-which is now commonplace-this criticism is addressed.

Role Theory

Another more micro-oriented approach to understanding social life that also incorporates the more structural elements of society is Role Theory. Role theory posits that human behaviour is guided by expectations held both by the individual and by other people. The expectations correspond to different roles individuals *perform* or *enact* in their daily lives, such as secretary, father, or friend. For instance, most people hold preconceived notions of the role expectations of a secretary, which might include: answering phones, making and managing appointments, filing paperwork, and typing memos. These role expectations would not be expected of a professional soccer player.

Individuals generally have and manage many roles. Roles consist of a set of rules or norms that function as plans or blueprints to guide behaviour.

Roles specify what goals should be pursued, what tasks must be accomplished, and what performances are required in a given scenario or situation. Role theory holds that a substantial proportion of observable, day-to-day social behaviour is simply persons carrying out their roles, much as actors carry out their roles on the stage or ballplayers theirs on the field. Role theory is, in fact, predictive. It implies that if we have information about the role expectations for a specified status (e.g., sister, fireman, prostitute), a significant portion of the behaviour of the persons occupying that position can be predicted.

What's more, role theory also argues that in order to change behaviour it is necessary to change roles; roles correspond to behaviors and vice versa. In addition to heavily influencing behaviour, roles influence beliefs and attitudes; individuals will change their beliefs and attitudes to correspond with their roles. For instance, someone over-looked for a promotion to a managerial position in a company may change their beliefs about the benefits of management by convincing him/herself that they didn't want the additional responsibility that would have accompanied the position. Many role theorists see *Role Theory* as one of the most compelling theories bridging individual behaviour and social structure. Roles, which are in part dictated by social structure and in part by social interactions, guide the behaviour of the individual. The individual, in turn, influences the norms, expectations, and behaviors associated with roles. The understanding is reciprocal.

Role Theory includes the following propositions:

1. People spend much of their lives participating as members of groups and organizations
2. Within these groups, people occupy distinct positions
3. Each of these positions entails a role, which is a set of functions performed by the person for the group
4. Groups often formalize role expectations as norms or even codified rules, which include what rewards will result when roles are successfully performed and what punishments will result when roles are not successfully performed
5. Individuals usually carry out their roles and perform in accordance with prevailing norms; in other words, role theory assumes that people are primarily conformists who try to live up to the norms that accompany their roles
6. Group members check each individual's performance to determine whether it conforms with the norms; the anticipation that others will apply sanctions ensures role performance.

Limitations

Role theory has a hard time explaining social deviance when it does not correspond to a pre-specified role. For instance, the behaviour of someone who adopts the role of bank robber can be predicted-she will rob banks. But if a bank teller simply begins handing out cash to random people, role theory would be unable to explain why (though *role conflict* could be one possible answer; the secretary may also be a Marxist-Communist who believes the means of production should belong to the masses and not the bourgeoisie).

Another limitation of role theory is that it does not and cannot explain how role expectations came to be what they are. Role theory has no explanation for why it is expected of male soldiers to cut their hair short, but it could predict with a high degree of accuracy that if someone is a male soldier they will have short hair. Additionally, role theory does not explain when and how role expectations change.

Impression Management

An extension of *role theory,* impression management is both a theory and process. The theory argues that people are constantly engaged in controlling how others perceive them. The process refers to the goal-directed conscious or unconscious effort to influence the perceptions other people by regulating and controlling information in social interaction. If a person tries to influence the perception of her or his own image, this activity is called *self-presentation*. Erving Goffman (1959), the person most often credited with formally developing impression management theory, cast the idea in a dramaturgical framework. The basic idea is that individuals in face-to-face situations are like actors on a stage performing roles. Aware of how they are being perceived by their audience, actors manage their behaviour so as to create specific impressions in the minds of the audience. Strategic interpersonal behaviour to shape or influence impressions formed by an audience is not a new idea. Plato spoke of the "great stage of human life" and Shakespeare noted that "All the world is a stage, and all the men and women merely players".

Social Constructionism

Social constructionism is a school of thought introduced into sociology by Peter L. Berger and Thomas Luckmann with their 1966 book *The Social Construction of Reality*. Social constructionism aims to discover the ways that individuals and groups create their perceived reality. Social constructionism focuses on the description of institutions and actions and not on analysing cause and effect. Socially constructed reality is seen as an on-going dynamic process; reality is re-produced by people acting on their interpretations of what they perceive to be the world external to them. Berger and Luckmann argue that social construction describes both subjective and objective reality-that is that no reality exists outside what is produced and reproduced in social interactions.

A clear example of social constructionist thought is, following Sigmund Freud and Émile Durkheim, religion. Religion is seen as a socially constructed concept, the basis for which is rooted in either our psyche (Freud) or man's need to see some purpose in life or worship a higher presence. One of the key theorists of social constructionism, Peter Berger, explored this concept extensively in his book, *The Sacred Canopy*.

Social constructionism is often seen as a source of the postmodern movement, and has been influential in the field of cultural studies.

Integration Theory

Recently, some sociologists have been taking a different approach to sociological theory by employing an integrationist approach-combining micro-and macro-level theories to provide a comprehensive understanding of human social behaviour. Numerous models could be presented in this vein. George Ritzer's Integration Model is a good example.

Ritzer proposes four highly interdependent elements in his sociological model: a macro-objective component (e.g., society, law, bureaucracy), a micro-objective component (e.g., patterns of behaviour and human interaction), a macro-subjective component (e.g., culture, norms, and values), and a micro-subjective component (e.g., perceptions, beliefs). This model is of particular use in understanding society because it uses two axes: one ranging from objective (society) to subjective (culture and cultural interpretation); the other ranging from the macro-level (norms) to the micro-level (individual level beliefs). If used for understanding a specific cultural phenomenon, like the displaying of abstract art in one's home, the integration model depicts the different influences on the decision. For instance, the model depicts that cultural norms can influence individual behaviour. The model also shows that individual level values, beliefs, and behaviors influence macro-level culture. This is, in fact, part of what David Halle finds: while there are art consumption differences based on class, they are not predicted solely by class. Displayers of abstract art tend not only to belong to the upper-class, but also are employed in art-production occupations. This would indicate that there are multiple levels of influence involved in art tastes – both broad cultural norms and smaller level occupational norms in addition to personal preferences.

Theories and Paradigms in Sociology

Sociological Theory Concept and Elements

Investigations in the field of sociological science history are greatly permeated by the analyses of various sociological theories, either old (classical) or newer (modern), conservative or progressive, "mini" or "maxi" ones. The existence of numerous social theories demonstrates not only the development of sociology, but also the complexity and dynamism of social phenomena and inability to establish sharp mathematical relations in a social organism research. At the same time, it helps revealing the positive fact of the openness and developing possibilities of the sociology as a science. The variety of thematic and methodological choices among the sociologists' association members concerning the sociology as a subject supports this tendency. For this reason, the statement of Anthony Giddens (Anthony Giddens: "Social Theory and Modern Sociology", Stanford University Press, Stanford, California, 1987) about multidimensional development directions of the sociology as a science is acceptable, as well as his assertion that during the last two decades of their development the social sciences have been abandoning the ideal that their "aims and logic are more or less the same as the ones in the natural sciences".

The differences in theoretical and methodological approaches to social research are also reflected in the interpretations of sociological theory as a term. The term of theory itself does not cause any significant disagreement, being that the theory encompasses the entirety of systematized knowledge and hypotheses by which the phenomena may be empirically verified and predicted in the sense of their development trends, or by which certain unsolved scientific problems can be unveiled. On the contrary, a great number of various definitions appear in the interpretation of the term of sociological theory and its classification and typology.

In this respect, G. Ritzer points out four meanings of the sociological theory: as a systematic and chronological representation of certain ideas, as different social taxonomies and classifications in the history of social thought, as a form of systematized or partial research hypothesis, and as a form of scientific theory which follows logic laws of scientific attitude establishment. We would rather accept Ritzer's definition of the sociological theory as a form of scientific theory which, along with the scientific research methods application, establishes smaller or greater systems of scientific laws and hypotheses about the society as a whole or about particular societal phenomena. Nicholas C. Mullins defines sociological theories as a kind of "creations (given in any form, most frequently a written one), the aim of which is to analyse and generalize mutual relations among people through the application of certain number of general standpoints and/or variables whose interrelations are determined by specific theory laws". Mullins' definition of sociological theory refers to the need of recognizing basic structural elements of a sociological theory. In addition to this, a sociological theory requires the observation of principles and laws existing in the standard fund of sociological science and science in general, as well as the usage of specific scientific knowledge about the phenomenon related to the theory itself.

Robert Merton has analysed the empirical investigation impact on a sociological theory, outlining the comprehension of the scientific research and theory interaction. Namely, Merton is of the opinion that the function of empirical research is not only to test or verify scientific hypotheses, but it greatly exceeds this passive role of a hypothesis confirmation or refutation. "Research plays an active role: it performs at least four important functions, which help the theory development formation." A scientific theory initiation represents the first basic role of empirical research, being that the research material may be used for the construction of new hypotheses and theoretical attitudes.

The empirical material can undoubtedly contribute to the formation of new theoretical formulations or reformulation of existing ones (a theory resetting). Finally, the creative part of the research lies in the sociological theory psychological and logical comprehension, as well. "For, the main research requirement is that the ideas, variables, be defined with enough clarity to enable the research realization.

This requirement cannot be fulfilled unconsciously and easily in some kind of a discursive presentation often referred to as a sociological theory. The explanation of ideas usually enters an empirical research in the form of the index establishment of variables to be dealt with. Non-research speculations may deal with 'morality' or 'social cohesion' in a very detailed manner but without any clear conception of what is meant by these ideas. Yet, they have to be cleared up if the researcher wants to systematically investigate the cases of low and high morality, social cohesion or social disagreement." Merton's observation of the need for clear formulation of ideas used in a sociological theory is very actual, being that it appears as a problem in disputes in numerous scientific meetings, and it may hence be attributed the significance of a methodological principle in scientific work. Of course, the theoretical opinion in sociology has to be interactively connected to high-standard empirical researches.

A more complete presentation of the sociological theory basic elements is given by Turner in his study. Turner points out four basic sociological theory elements: theory concept, variable, statement and form. As a sociological theory element, concept represents the author's fundamental idea about certain social phenomenon, this idea having a unique meaning regardless of the context in which it is presented. The sociological theory variable shows the theoretical concept development. The theoretical statements represent sociological conclusions about the social phenomenon structure or about their interrelations. The sociological theory form refers to the level of its exactness. So-called "firm" theories are more abstract and they allow deductive conclusion, while the "loose" sociological theories are closer to scientific hypotheses (assumptions).

Sociological Paradigm

The concept of scientific paradigm, and particularly the sociological paradigm, is closely connected to sociological theories. If we assume that a scientific paradigm represents a general hypothesis of scientific knowledge, a general knowledge which can be presented both as a practical one and as a specific matrix of scientific research, then we can talk about a wider and more exact system of views, attitudes and theories concerning the scientific explanation of objective reality. In its widest meaning, a scientific paradigm is "a set of facts and convictions which is systematically presented, that is presented as a theory whose function is to initiate theoretical productions, and practical research in certain fields thereafter, so that it appears in this sense as a source of some future or already existing theoretical composition". In accordance with that, a sociological paradigm represents a fundamental illustration of the society (the definition of its concept, the comprehension of its structure and dynamics) which has been more or less accepted in the association of sociologists during certain periods of this science development.

The sociological paradigm performs significant functions in a qualitative sociological analysis. According to Merton, at least five functions of a paradigm in sociology may be specified: a) the function of defining concepts, b) the function of decreasing the probability of unconscious introduction of latent assumptions and concepts, c) the function of cumulating theoretical interpretations, d) the function of concept systematization, and, e) the function of qualitative analysis codification 8.

The first function of the paradigm in sociology is to provide precision in designating the central concepts of a sociological analysis, and it can almost be compared to the significance and functions of mathematical symbols in natural sciences. Moreover, the paradigm implies logical concept derivation from previously clearly defined concepts. The cumulation of theoretical interpretations in a sociological paradigm enables new theoretical attitudes to be derived from and supported by the previous ones, producing a coherent theoretical structure. In case the fundamental paradigm assumptions are weak, new theoretical statements cannot withstand theoretical and empirical verification. Paradigms may initiate the systematization of significant concepts, as well as point out the need of empirical and theoretical investigation of certain problems. Paradigms also contribute to certain codification and unification of procedures in partial and global researches.

In this respect, in the frame of sociology we may find the old sociological paradigm and the new sociological paradigm, which mutually differ with regard to the theories, methods and instruments applied in learning about the social totality. Professor Miroslav Peèujliæ is of the opinion that the old (classical) sociological paradigm pervaded classical sociological theories and so-called objectivistic theories (positivism, functionalism, system theories, structuralism).

The statements and attitudes of a classical sociological paradigm are predominant in them, particularly the conceptions of: linear progress and historical determinism, mechanical comprehension of the universe, idealized image of the society in the centre of which are order, harmony, nonconflicting, and in which the conflicts, social struggles, force and domination, social changes, discontinuity, great obsession of theory by apology and governing system preservation, dominance of system over personality, limited picture of historical actors, are either excluded or less discussed.

A new sociological paradigm is created on completely new assumptions and knowledge, such as: the openness of history, entropic comprehension of the world (a danger of the planet destruction), the beginning of an era of great cultural transformations, mutual permeance of social processes of continuity and discontinuity, the necessity of free human actions development, the appearance of new agents of social changes, the beginning of social movements, the outset of new factors of social dynamics. Alongside with that, a new sociological paradigm organically originates from the critical and creative meditation of previous systems of thought in the science of sociology. "The first step in a large revitalization of sociology lies, then, in the synthesis, in supplementation of mutually exclusive streams: a modern system theory, critical theories of the society, theories of radical changes (dialectics), as well as in the apprehension of social phenomena as the phenomena with certain meanings. Comparative investigation of objective circumstances and subjective motives, observation of the phenomenon in the system frame, but of more profound changes as well, critical examination of the existent and also of the desirable and possible future (alternative)-all of that provides incomparably more powerful intellectual instruments for the understanding of the new, more complex world that is being formed.

Yet, it gives much more, in fact. A new sociological paradigm, critical interpretation and comprehension of existing and search for more rational social life forms, and a desirable and possible future, have become a decisive factor of great cultural transformations brought into focus by history". In this manner, sociology is actively included into the modern civilization courses, it observes and analyses contemporary society and establishes itself as a modern science.

"A true history of sociological theory has to exceed by evidence the chronologically arranged disquisition set; it has to deal with interrelations between the theory and other items, like the social origin and status of its exponents, a variable social organization of sociology, changes of the ideas brought about by their expanding, and the relations of ideas toward the surrounding social and cultural structure".

Being that sociology is a multi-paradigmatic science (Ritzer), and we can agree with that, in a sociological explanation we should also take into consideration the verified data of various theories and paradigms developed in its scope.

In this respect, the research of the social structure in modern society, for example, demands the application of both social-class and stratification theories, which may cover the research subject more complexly if combined in use. Ritzer's paradigms may in this sense be understood as complementary and not exclusive and mutually independent paradigms. Namely, although the paradigm of social facts, paradigm of social definitions and social-behavioural paradigm differ in their contents, their statements are respected in modern sociology.

Typology and Classification

The complexity and numerousness of sociological theories produce difficulties in formulating firmer criteria for their categorization and classification. According to the level of generality, sociological theories may be classified into general theories of society (so-called "great theories") and particular theories of society (so-called "small" sociological theories). The well-known sociological theory historian J. Gorièar is of the opinion that general theories of society include the sociological systems of Auguste Comte, Herbert Spencer, Max Weber, as well as the Marxist theory of society.

Particular sociological theories are characteristic for modern sociological orientation which is, through complex theoretical and empirical research, trying to give adequate sociological picture of certain social phenomena (town, village, labour, family, social groups, social structure, social changes, etc.). Robert Merton, an American, with his middle range theory, is a typical representative of such theoretical determination. According to the middle range theories, sociological research is aimed at revealing the structure and development laws of certain social phenomena in certain periods of time. Apart from the polarized opinion of sociologists about the middle range theory validity, Merton points out significant features of these theories which do not divide sociological knowledge up, as often asserted, but consolidate them by reconciling theory oriented empirical research and sociological generalizations. In this sense, according to Merton, the middle range theories:

- consist of limited sets of assumptions out of which specific hypotheses are derived and confirmed by empirical research,
- get united into wider theoretical networks, as illustrated by the theory of aspiration level, referential groups and structure of circumstances,
- are abstract enough to deal with different spheres of social behaviour and social structure, so that they exceed pure description or empirical generalization (theory of social conflict is applied to ethnic and racial conflicts, class conflicts and international conflicts),

- abolish the distinctions between micro-sociological problems, appearing in a small group research, and macro-sociological problems, occurring in a comparative investigation of social mobility and formal organization, as well as the interdependence of social institutions,
- are in harmony with various systems of sociological thought (Durkheim, Weber, Marx, Sorokin, Parsons, etc.),
- also include the specification of ignorance, orienting toward the problems which can be nowadays cleared up in the light of the accessible knowledge. The appearance of these theories represents to a certain extent a response to the uncritical acceptance of the theory of social development as a form of linear and automatic social progress. Contrary to the tendency of sociologists to develop allinclusive theories, which was the characteristic of the sociological systems established in the 19th and beginning of 20th centuries, and to a certain degree in agreement with the philosophical system of thought, contemporary sociological researches, according to Merton, have to thoroughly and theoretically-empirically investigate each and every segment of the society.

Sociological theories may be classified according to the country (state) in which they appear most frequently (American sociological theories, German, French, English, etc.), according to the time of their origin (the 19th century sociological theories, the 20th century sociological theories, old and new theories), according to the ideological factor (middle-class theories of society and Marxist theory of society), scientific concept and contents of a sociological theory (biologist theory, psychologist theory, formalistic theory, Marxist theory of society, etc.).

Several types of sociological theories may be recognized, depending on the sociological theory level of development and consistency. The types are: concepts, empirical generalization, social taxonomies and models. According to J. H. Turner, "the 'concepts' are only appropriate, non-verifiable theories, the 'ideas', or 'perspectives' which cannot be treated as theories in any serious systematization; empirical generalizations are most often only empirical descriptions or generalizations of some partial phenomena, social taxonomies are most frequently only the elements and efforts of systematization of certain phenomena (usually mere biographies and bibliographies of important persons in sociology), and only models and tendencies toward modelled construction represent the genuine way for the development of a sociological theory".

Difficulties in determining the sociological theory types are also occurring due to different concepts of sociologists with regard to the social order, social changes, comprehension of subjective-objective relations, the role of an individual in the society, system of values, social functions, social development. The dependence of sociological theories and ideological connotation on the society complicates the typology and classification of sociological theories likewise (the examples of functionalism and Marxist theory of society). One may find in them the analyses of social system nature and structure, the distribution of economic, political and spiritual power, various definitions of social changes and laws of social trends. The sociological theory classification has also been presented in the most popular sociology textbooks in USA and Great Britain. In the mentioned textbooks, the authors try to offer relevant information to the readers about the main theories and courses of sociological science development. In this sense, basic sociological theories are presented in scholarly circles in the form of tripartite classification into the Marxist theory of society, functionalism and interaction theory. According to these authors, they are at the same time the predominant scientifically-theoretical and empirical orientations in the modern sociology.

Apart from the relatively simplified classification of sociological theories in the academic sociology, much more complex and developed systems of sociological theory classification may be found in the modern sociological literature. W. L. Wallace classifies sociological theories into eleven groups:

1) ecological school,
2) demographic school,
3) materialism,
4) psychological school,
5) technological school,

6) functional structuralism,
7) interchanging structuralism,
8) conflict structuralism,
9) symbolical interaction school,
10) social action school,
11) functional imperativeness.

The criteria of this classification are polyvalent-social life factors, the place of structure in a social system and the role of individuals and smaller social groups in the society as a whole. One of the significant sociological theory classifications in the modern sociology has also been derived by J. H. Turner. Turner classifies sociological theories into:

1) functional theories,
2) conflict theories,
3) interactional theories,
4) the theory of interchange, and
5) ethno-methodology.

Turner obviously combines several criteria in his classification, particularly the functional analysis and individualistic sociology.

Several attitudes have been singled out in the discussions about the contents of the modern sociology concept. One of the attitudes determines the modern sociology as the sociology in the transition of centuries (passing from the 19th to the 20th century), when great socio-economical and political changes emerged, especially the consolidation of imperialism and societal industrialization. The opinion of the others is that modern sociology begins with the works of Emile Durkheim (1858-1917), Max Weber (1864-1920) and Charles Cooley (1864-1929). American sociologist Talcott Parsons states that the generation of sociologists acting during the period of 1890-1935 laid the foundations of modern sociology. In this sense, particular significance is attributed to Durkheim's definition of concepts, such as structure, function and social institution. Paul Lazarsfeld claims that modern sociology begins with the application of contemporary methods for social phenomena investigating (at the end of the World War II), that is with data codification and systematization. Regardless of different comprehension of the modern sociology concept, we consider the definition of Lj. Sloviæ acceptable. Under this term she understands a synthetical expression for the sociological science development phase in which great structural social changes are generated on the basis of industrial and post industrial development, and in which the sociology tends to reveal the principles and laws of social phenomena and changes, including the criteria for their evaluation.

Starting from the above presented, more or less complex typologies and classifications of sociological theories, as well as from the necessity of clear presentation of former and contemporary sociological orientations, we think that sociological theories can be divided into classical and modern sociological theories. Besides the fact that the temporal, content-subject and validity criteria were combined in this case, the traditional academic presentation of the problems in our sociological literature was also given importance to a great extent. The following are included into the classical sociological theories: the positivistic theory of Auguste Comte, mechanistic theories, biologist theories, psychologist theories, Marxist theory of society, formal-sociological theories and cyclic theories of society. Modern sociological theories are presented by: behavioural theories in sociology, functionalism, structuralist theory of society and critical societal theory.

Discipline of Social Theory

Social theory is the use of theoretical frameworks to study and interpret social phenomena within a particular school of thought. An essential tool used by social scientists, theories relate to historical debates over the most valid and reliable methodologies (e.g. positivism and antipositivism), as well as the primacy of either structure or agency. Certain social theories attempt to remain strictly scientific, descriptive, and objective. Conflict theories, by contrast, present ostensibly normative positions, and often critique the ideological aspects inherent in conventional, traditional thought.

Òhe origins of social theory are difficult to pinpoint, but debates frequently return to Ancient Greece. From these foundations in Western philosophy arose.Enlightenment social contract theory, sociological positivism, and modern social science. Today, 'social science' is used as an umbrella term to refer, not just to sociology, but also to economics, political science, jurisprudence, and other disciplines. Social theory is accordingly interdisciplinary; drawing upon ideas from fields as diverse as anthropology and media studies. Social theory of an informal nature, or authorship based outside of academic social and political science, may be referred to instead as "social criticism" or "social commentary". Similarly, "cultural criticism" may be associated both with formal cultural and literary scholarship, as well as other non-academic or journalistic forms of writing.

Harrington discusses the etymology of social theory, stating that while the term did not exist in any language before the twentieth century, its origins are ancient and lie in two words; 'social' from the Latin *socius* and 'theory' from the Greek *theoria* (Harrington 2005). Social theorising aided the Greeks in making sense of their lives, and in questioning the value and meaning of things around them.

Social theory as a distinct discipline emerged in the 20th century and was largely equated with an attitude of critical thinking, based on rationality, logic and objectivity, and the desire for knowledge through aposteriori methods of discovery, rather than apriori methods of tradition. With this in mind it is easy to link social theory to deeper seated philosophical discussions.

Relation to the Natural Sciences

Compared to disciplines within the objective natural sciences — such as physics or chemistry — social theorists may make less use of the scientific method, and their conclusions and data can be interpreted more subjectively. While standards of rigor do exist within quantitative social science methodologies, their precision is bounded by a degree of uncertainty inherent in human behaviour. However, because experiments in the natural sciences are necessarily social artifacts, and social theory treats social artifacts as being constructed, social theorists posit that even experiments in the natural sciences and their concomitant results are social constructions. Social theories can complement research in the natural sciences and vice-versa.

The concept that social theory may supersede certain aspects of the natural sciences is called the social construction of reality. Social theory takes knowledge, the manner in which we acquire knowledge, and the institutions by which knowledge is reified and disseminated among a human collectivity to be socially constructed. In effect, the laws of nature can only be derived using social tools within a social context. According to social theory, the understanding of natural phenomena is predicated on the understanding of social phenomena, as the interpretation of natural phenomena is a social activity.

This interpretation of the natural sciences leads to some deeper epistemological questions. By questioning the methods by which we deem knowledge to be "objective," we necessarily put into question any scientific knowledge whatsoever. Social theory does not exist in mutual exclusion to the natural sciences; one is often complementary to the other. Rather, social theory calls for natural scientists to examine their methodologies with a critical eye by situating said methodologies within a social context.

History of Sociological Theory

Pre-enlightenment Social Theory

The earliest proto-social scientific observations are to be found in the founding texts of Western philosophy, as well as in the non-European thought of figures such as Confucius. Prior to the enlightenment, social theory took largely narrative and normative form. Expressed as stories and fables, it may be assumed the pre-socratic philosophers and religious teachers were the precursors to social theory proper.

Saint Augustine (354-430) and St. Thomas Aquinas (*circa* 1225-1274) concerned themselves exclusively with the idea of the *just society*. St. Augustine describes late Ancient Roman society but through a lens of hatred and contempt for what he saw as false Gods, and in reaction theorized The City of God. Similarly, in China, Master Kong (otherwise known as Confucius) (551-479 BCE) envisaged a just society that went beyond his contemporary society of the Warring States. Later on, also in China, Mozi (*circa* 470-*circa* 390 BCE) recommended a more pragmatic sociology, but ethical at base.

Sociology in Medieval Islam

There is evidence of early Muslim sociology from the 14th century: Ibn Khaldun, in his *Muqaddimah* (later translated as *Prolegomena* in Latin), the introduction to a seven volume analysis of universal history, was the first to advance social philosophy and social science in formulating theories of social cohesion and social conflict. He is thus considered by many to be the forerunner of sociology.

Political Philosophy and Social Contract Theory

During the Age of Enlightenment, political entities expanded from basic systems of self-governance and monarchy to the complex democratic and communist systems that exist of the Industrialied and the Modern Era. In the 18th century, after Montesquieu's The Spirit of Law established that social elements influences human nature, pre-classical period of social theories have changed to a new form that provide the basic ideas for social theory. Such as: evolution, philosophy of history, social life and social contract, public and general will, competition in social space, organistic pattern for social description and... Jean-Jacques Rousseau in this time played a significant role in social theory. He revealed the origin of inequality, analysed the social contract (and social compact) that forms social integration and defined the social sphere or civil society. He also emphasized that man has the liberty to change his world, a revolutionary assertion that made it possible to program and change society.

Classical Social Theory

The first "modern" social theories (known as classical theories) that begin to resemble the analytic social theory of today developed almost simultaneously with the birth of the science of sociology. Auguste Comte (1798-1857), known as the "father of sociology" and regarded by some as the first philosopher of science, laid the groundwork for positivism-as well as structural functionalism and social evolutionism. In the 19th century three great classical theories of social and historical change emerged: the social evolutionism theory (of which Social Darwinism forms a part), the social cycle theory and the Marxist historical materialism theory.

Another early modern theorist, Herbert Spencer (1820-1903), coined the term "survival of the fittest". Some Post-Modern social theorists like Shepard Humphries, draw heavily upon Spencer's work and argue that many of his observations are timeless (just as relevant in 2008 as 1898). Vilfredo Pareto (1848-1923) and Pitirim A. Sorokin argued that 'history goes in cycles', and presented the social cycle theory to illustrate their point. Ferdinand Tönnies (1855-1936) made *community* and *society* (*Gemeinschaft and Gesellschaft*, 1887) the special topics of the new science of "sociology", both of them based on different modes of will of social actors. Most of the 19th century pioneers of social theory and sociology, like Saint-Simon, Comte, Marx, John Stuart Mill or Spencer, never held university posts. In this sense they were broadly regarded as philosophers. Emile Durkheim, however, endeavoured to formally established academic sociology, and did so at the University of Bordeaux in 1895, publishing his *Rules of the Sociological Method*. In 1896, he established the journal *L'Année Sociologique*. Durkheim's seminal monograph, *Suicide* (1897), a case study of suicide rates amongst Catholic and Protestant populations, distinguished sociological analysis from psychology or philosophy.

Many of the classical theories had one common factor: they all agreed that the history of humanity is pursuing a certain fixed path. They differed on where that path would lead: social progress, technological progress, decline or even fall, etc. Social cycle theorists were much more skeptical of the Western achievements and technological progress, however, arguing that progress is but an illusion in of the ups and downs of the historical cycles. The classical approach has been criticized by many modern sociologists and theorists, among them Karl Popper, Robert Nisbet, Charles Tilly and Immanuel Wallerstein.

Karl Marx rejected Comtean positivism but nevertheless aimed to establish a *science of society* based on historical materialism, becoming recognised as a founding figure of sociology posthumously. At the turn of the 20th century, the first wave of German sociologists, including Max Weber and Georg Simmel, developed sociological antipositivism. The field may be broadly recognised as an amalgam of three modes of social scientific thought in particular; Durkheimian sociological positivism and structural functionalism, Marxist historical materialism and conflict theory, and Weberian antipositivism and verstehen critique.

Modern Social Theory

Much of 19th-century classical social theory has been expanded upon to create newer, more contemporary social theories such as Multilineal theories of evolution (neoevolutionism, sociobiology, theory of modernization, theory of post-industrial society) and various strains of Neo-Marxism.

In the late 19th and early 20th centuries, social theory became most closely related to academic sociology while other related studies such as anthropology, philosophy, and social work branched out into their own disciplines. Such subjects as "philosophy of history" and other such multi-disciplinary subject matter became part of social theory as taught under sociology.

Attempts to recapture a space for discussion free of disciplines began in earnest in the late 1920s and early 1930s. The Frankfurt Institute for Social Research provides the most successful historical example. The Committee on Social Thought at the University of Chicago followed in the 1940s. In the 1970s, programs in Social and Political Thought were established at Sussex and York. Others followed, with various different emphases and structures, such as Social Theory and History. Cultural Studies programs, notably that of Birmingham University, extended the concerns of social theory into the domain of culture and thus anthropology. A chair and undergraduate program in social theory was established at the University of Melbourne and a number of universities now specialize in social theory. Social theory at present seems to be gaining more acceptance as a classical academic discipline.

In modern times, generally speaking, social theory began to stress free will, individual choice, subjective reasoning, and the importance of unpredictable events in place of the classic determinism – thus social theory become much more complex. Rational Choice Theory and Symbolic Interactionism furnish two examples. Most modern sociologists deem there are no great unifying 'laws of history', but rather smaller, more specific, and more complex laws that govern society.

Post-modern Social Theory

Scholars and historians most commonly hold postmodernism to be a movement of ideas arising from, but also critical of elements of modernism. Because of the wide range of uses of the term, different elements of modernity are chosen as being continuous, and different elements of modernity are held to be critiqued. Each of the different uses also is rooted in some argument about the nature of knowledge, known in philosophy as epistemology. Individuals who use the term are arguing that either there is something fundamentally different about the transmission of meaning, or that modernism has fundamental flaws in its system of knowledge.

The argument for the necessity of the term states that economic and technological conditions of our age have given rise to a decentralized, media-dominated society in which ideas are simulacra and only inter-referential representations and copies of each other, with no real original, stable or objective source for communication and meaning. Globalization, brought on by innovations in communication, manufacturing and transportation, is often cited as one force which has driven the decentralized modern life, creating a culturally pluralistic and interconnected global society lacking any single dominant centre of political power, communication, or intellectual production. The postmodern view is that inter-subjective knowledge, and not objective knowledge is the dominant form of discourse under such conditions, and the ubiquity of copies and dissemination fundamentally alters the relationship between reader and what is read, between observer and the observed, between those who consume and those who produce. Not all people who use the term postmodern or postmodernism see these developments as positive. Users of the term often argue that their ideals have arisen as the result of particular economic and social conditions, including what is described as "late capitalism" and the growth of broadcast media, and that such conditions have pushed society into a new historical period.

The term "postmodernism" was brought into social theory in 1971 by the Arab American Theorist Ihab Hassan in his book: The Dismemberment of Orpheus: Toward a Postmodern Literature. In

1979 Jean-François Lyotard wrote a short but influential work *The Postmodern Condition: A report on knowledge*. Jean Baudrillard, Michel Foucault, and Roland Barthes were influential in 1970s in developing postmodern theory.

Theory Construction

Almost all good research is guided by theory. Selecting or creating appropriate theory for use in examining an issue is thus an important skill for any researcher. Important distinctions: a theoretical orientation (or paradigm) is a worldview, the lens through which one organizes experience (i.e. thinking of human interaction in terms of power or exchange); a theory is an attempt to explain and predict behaviour in particular contexts. A theoretical orientation cannot be proven or disproven; a theory can. Having a theoretical orientation that sees the world in terms of power and control, I could create a theory about violent human behaviour which includes specific causal statements (e.g. being the victim of physical abuse leads to psychological problems). This could lead to an hypothesis (prediction) about what I expect to see in a particular sample, e.g. "a battered child will grow up to be shy or violent." I can then test my hypothesis by looking to see if it is consistent with data in the real world. I might, for instance, review hospital records to find children who were abused, then track them down and administer a personality test to see if they show signs of being violent or shy. The selection of an appropriate (i.e. useful) theoretical orientation within which to develop a potentially helpful theory is the bedrock of social science.

2

Critical Theory and the Crisis of Social Theory

Recent Sociological and Theoretical Paradigms

Social theory today is in crisis. During the 1960s, a variety of new theoretical paradigms emerged which put in question the prevailing quantitative, empiricist, and positivist conceptions of social theory and social research. Growing dissatisfaction with the dominant methodologies and theories produced by the mainstream promoted a search for alternative methodologies and conceptions of social theory and research. The new paradigms of phenomenology, enthno-methodology, structuralism, Marxism, feminism, and other critical theories offered new conceptions which claimed to be more adequate in characterizing contemporary society and in providing inspiration and guidance for transforming it. These theories have caused much ferment in the field of social theory and have inspired heated debates over the nature, methods, and goals of critical social theory.

More recently, poststructuralist and postmodern social theory have further challenged mainstream social theory and science, attacking their basic presuppositions. In addition, these new critical discourses have sharply criticized Marxism, structuralism, phenomenology, and other critical paradigms for participating too staunchly in the premises and methods of modern, enlightenment rationality and traditional social theory. While debates have emerged between advocates of critical theory and the newer, postmodern approaches which I shall discuss later in the paper, there are also common positions. Like some of the new

French theories, the critical theory of the so-called Frankfurt school offers a multi-disciplinary approach for social theory which combines perspectives drawn from political economy, sociology, cultural theory, philosophy, anthropology, and history. It thus overcomes the fragmentation endemic to established academic disciplines in order to address issues of broader interest.

Both new French theory and critical theory therefore put in question the boundaries established by the academic division of labour which separates social theory from other disciplines. Both claim that there are epistemological and metaphysical problems with abstracting from the interconnectedness of phenomena in the world, or from our experience of it. On this view, philosophy, for example, that abstracts from sociology and economics, or political science that excludes, say, economics or culture from its conceptual boundaries, is by nature one-sided, limited, and flawed. Both critical theory and new French theory therefore transgress established disciplinary boundaries and create new theories and discourses that avoid the deficiencies of the traditional academic division of labour.

In this chapter, I shall argue that as an antidote to the frequently non-critical quantitative approaches within mainstream social science and theory, critical theory provides a potentially more useful and politically relevant alternative than poststructuralist and postmodernist theory. In opposition to the subjectivism and relativism, often bordering on nihilism, advanced by some of these postmodernist perspectives, critical theory, by contrast, advances the conception of a critical and normative theory which is committed to emancipation from all forms of oppression, as well as to freedom, happiness, and a rational ordering of society. In contrast to the often hypertheoretical and apolitical discourse of postmodern theory, critical theory seeks a connection with empirical analysis of the contemporary world and social movements which are attempting to transform society in progressive ways.

To highlight the contributions of critical theory to contemporary social theory, I shall therefore, first, present the conception of dialectical social theory contained in the notion of a critical theory of society. Next, I articulate what I consider to be among its most substantive contributions to contemporary social theory, and then I shall criticize some of its limitations and provide some new perspectives for critical theory today. To begin, however, I wish to briefly describe the origins and development of critical theory.

Historical Background

Critical theory is often associated with the so-called "Frankfurt School," a term which refers to the work of members of the *Institut fur Sozialforschung*. The Institute was established in Frankfurt, Germany during 1923 as the first Marxist-oriented research centre affiliated with a major German university. The Institute's work in the 1920's was directed by Carl Grunberg, and tended to be empirical, historical, and oriented toward problems of the European working class movement, although theoretical works by Karl Korsch, Georg Lukacs, and others were also published in its journal, *Archiv fur die Geschichte des Sozialismus und der Arbeiterbewegung*.

After Grunberg's retirement in 1930, Max Horkheimer became Director of the Instutute. Horkheimer gathered around him such talented theorists as Leo Lowenthal, Friedrich Pollock, Erich Fromm, Henryk Grossman, and Herbert Marcuse. Later T.W. Adorno, Otto Kirchheimer, Franz Neumann and others joined the Institute, which also supported theorists like Korsch and Walter Benjamin. Under Horkheimer's directorship, the Institute sought to develop an interdisciplinary social theory which could serve as an instrument of social transformation. During the Horkheimer era, Institute work was characterized by a synthesis of philosophy and social theory and research. The results of Institute work were published in its journal, *Zeitschrift fur Sozialforschung* (1932-1941), which contains a rich collection of articles and book reviews still worth reading.

Upon assuming the position of Director, Horkheimer delivered an inaugural address on January 24, 1931, entitled "The State of Social Philosophy and the Tasks of an Institute for Social Research". In this text, Horkheimer defines social philosophy as an attempt to elucidate the "fate of human beings, insofar as they are parts of a community, and not mere individuals. It concerns itself above all with the social life of people: state, law, economy, religion, in short, with the entire material and spiritual culture of humanity". Horkheimer's lecture provides the first major conception of his view of critical social theory as a synthesis of social science and philosophy, and therefore provides a useful introduction to the Institute's project.

Horkheimer begins by pointing to the limitations of the classical German social theories of Kant and Hegel, and the limitations of contemporary metaphysical and positivist philosophies. This exercise typifies Horkheimer's method of clarifying his own position through criticism of opposing positions. Kant is criticized for grounding social philosophy in the experience and faculties of the particular individual. Hegel's attempt to situate philosophy within society and history is presented as an improvement over Kant, yet Hegel's idealism and tendency to justify the existing order is rejected. Then Horkheimer criticizes the current forms of idealism in the neo-Kantian, neo-Hegelian, phenomenological, and existential philosophies for their questionable speculative metaphysics and for their tendencies to celebrate a higher transcendental sphere of Being (*Sein*) and meaning (*Sinn*) over concrete existence. The positivist schools which root their theories in isolated facts are also criticized for their unsupportable metaphysical presuppositions and methodological limitations. Horkheimer concludes that none of the dominant philosophical schools contain an adequate social philosophy. He assumes that social philosophy encompasses "the entire material and spiritual culture of humanity." Consequently, he rejects the claims of the specific social sciences such as "material sociology" to provide adequate knowledge since the specialized sciences abstract from the structure and organization of society as a whole to describe limited domains of social experience. In opposing the separation between social theory, science, and philosophy which was dominant at the time, and which continues to be dominant today, Horkheimer calls for a new sort of *synthesis* between philosophy and the specialized sciences.

Consequently, while Comte, Durkheim, positivists, and others want to purge philosophy from social theory, Horkheimer defends its importance for critical social theory. He claims that the positivist conception that philosophy "is perhaps beautiful, but scientifically fruitless because it is not subject to controls," verification, experiments and the like, must be rejected, as must as well the philosopher's prejudice that he or she is dealing with the essential while the scientist is dealing with bare, trival facts. These conflicting claims to the primacy of science and philosophy must be overcome in favor of a "dialectical penetration and development of philosophical theory and the praxis of the individual disciplines". For Horkheimer, the philosophical drive toward the universal and essential should be the animating spirit for social research, but philosophy must be at the same time "sufficiently open to the world to allow itself to be impressed with, and transformed by, progress in concrete studies".

To fulfill these goals, Horkheimer envisaged a program of supradisciplinary research which would investigate current social and political problems. This project would unite "philosophers, sociologists, economists, historians, and psychologists in an ongoing research community who would do together what in other disciplines one individual does alone in the laboratory, — which is what genuine scientists have always done: namely, to pursue the great philosophical questions using the most refined scientific methods; to reformulate and to make more precise the questions in the course of work as demanded by the object; and to develop new methods without losing sight of the universal".

After praising his predecessor Carl Grundberg's legacy and contributions, Horkheimer stresses that the Institute will now undertake a "new start" directed at "new tasks". He claims that the Institute's new multidisciplinary program will allow its members to raise the question of "the interconnections between the economic life of society, the psychic development of the individual and transformations in the realm of culture... including not only the so-called spiritual contents of science, art and religion, but also law, ethics, fashion, public opinion, sport, amusement, life style, etc.". This research program is somewhat unorthodox for a Marxian social theory which in the past tended to neglect the dimension of individual and social psychology, and which also downplayed the study of culture and leisure. Attention to these topics would eventually produce many of the distinctive contributions of critical theory. In his inaugural address, Horkheimer distances his conception of social theory from a crude Marxian materialism. He proclaims that the Institute will not subscribe to any metaphysical theses, such as idealism or materialism, on the relation between the economy, society, culture, and consciousness. Horkheimer notes that the attempt to derive all forms of life from one metaphysical substance is "bad Spinozaism." From the very beginning, therefore, Horkheimer rejects all metaphysical absolutism and all philosophical reductionism. He argues that an illusory idealism that derives everything from the Idea is "an abstract and therefore badly understood Hegel," just as the attempt to derive everything from an economy which is understood merely as material being is "an abstract and therefore badly understood Marx". Such theses posit an "uncritical, obsolete and highly problematic cleavage of spirit and reality into naive absolutes" and must be dialectically overcome.

Critical social philosophy, by contrast, describes the complex set of *mediations* that interconnect consciousness and society, culture and economy, state and citizens. These relations can best be clarified and developed in concrete historical contexts in which one asks: "which interconnections exist in a definite social group, in a definite period of time and in a definite country, between the role of this group in the economic process, the transformation of the psychic structures of its individual members, and the totality of the system that affects and produces its thoughts and mechanism".

To begin this task, the Institute proposed to study technically qualified workers and employees in Germany by gathering empirical material on their psychological, social, and political attitudes which would be interpreted in a theoretical framework that encompasses economic theory, sociology, and psychology. Horkheimer illustrated the project of the Institute's social theory by indicating that an empirical study of the white-collar working class would be its first research project. In addition, he indicated that his colleagues would predominantly undertake studies in "theoretical economics, economic history, and the history of the working class movement". Thus, at least during the early Horkheimer years, the Institute sought to continue many of

Grunberg's projects with regard to topics central to classical Marxism and socialist politics, but from a more comprehensive theoretical vantage point.

Materialism and Dialectics

The Institute began publishing its research and studies in its journal *Zeitschrift fur Sozialforschung*. In the first issue, Horkheimer described the goal of their work as developing a "theory of contemporary society as a whole," aiming at "the entirety of the social process. It presupposes that beneath the chaotic surface of events one can grasp and conceptualize a structure of the effective powers". This theory would be based on the results of historical studies and the individual sciences and would therefore strive for the status of "science". Yet these investigations would not exclude philosophy, "for it is not affiliation to a specific discipline but its importance for the theory of society which determines the choice of material". Although Horkheimer and his colleagues were basically inspired by Marxism, from 1930 through 1936, members of the Institute used code words like "materialism" and the "economic theory of society" for their version of the Marxian theory. The Institute developed a supradisciplinary, materialist social theory as a response both to inadequacies within classical Marxism and within the dominant forms of bourgeois science and philosophy. Orthodox Marxism had congealed into a dogmatic, reductionist, and objectivist metaphysical materialism, while bourgeois social science was characterized by a fragmentation of the sciences, each cut off from the other and pursuing its own investigations isolated from other disciplines. Both bourgeois science and scientistic Marxism utilized excessively objectivist methods, and thus were not able to conceptualize current problems such as the ways that social and cultural conditions were inclining strata of the working class and other social groups toward fascism. Lacking a theory of the subject, orthodox Marxism could not really explain why revolutionary consciousness failed to develop, and could not point to how revolutionary consciousness and struggle could be produced.

The Institute theorists created a new variety of *materialism* against all idealist modes of thought. Rejecting both the mechanistic metaphysical materialism already criticized by Marx and Engels in *The Holy Family*, as well as the current positivist forms of materialism, Horkheimer and his colleagues defined the objects of materialist theory in terms of material conditions, human needs, and social struggles against oppression. Furthermore, materialism did not signify for the Institute a specific metaphysical doctrine but stood instead for a whole series of ideas and practical attitudes, taking different forms in different contexts. Their materialist social theory during the early 1930s developed a particular style of "ideology critique" which analyzes the social interests ideologies serve by exposing their historical roots and assumptions, including the distortions and mystifications which they perpetuate. The Institute also developed a materialist approach to "cultural critiqu and produced one of the first systematic critical theories of mass culture. In "Materialism and Metaphysics," Horkheimer spells out what is involved for him in a materialist view of the world, and what sort of thought, research, and action it involves. He begins by criticizing metaphysical materialism which attempts to capture the totality of being in a universal philosophical system. In these remarks, Horkheimer makes evident his hostility to metaphysical systems, absolutism, and all foundationalist theories that attempt to discover a metaphysical foundation for knowledge. He then argues that the specific views that a materialist holds at a given moment are not dictated by any unchanging metaphysical theses, but rather by the:

> "tasks which at any given period are to be mastered with the help of the theory. Thus, for example, criticism of a dogma of religious faith may, at a particular time and place, play a decisive role within the complex of materialist views, while under other circumstances such criticism may be unimportant. Today the knowledge of movements and tendencies affecting society as a whole is immensely important for materialist theory, but in the eighteenth century the need for knowledge of the social totality was overshadowed by questions of epistemology, of natural science, and of politics".

Horkheimer claims that while idealist views generally aim at *justification*, and are advanced by ruling class ideologues to affirm dominant class interests, materialist theories aim at *explanation* with references to material conditions, classes, and specific historical situations. He especially objects to notions of metaphysical·cognition and absolute truth, and argues that there is "an irreducible tension between concept and being". Horkheimer here rejects metaphysical theses of the identity of thought and being, of knowledge and the known. He argues, instead, that concepts are not organs of absolute knowledge, but are simply instruments for achieving certain goals which are to be constantly developed and modified in the course of experience.

Horkheimer thus proposes a post-metaphysical conception of materialism, and stresses the different content that materialist theories have in different contexts. He and his colleagues rejected both Hegel's identity theory which posits an identity between thought and being within an idealist ontology, as well as the forms of epistemological realism held by many positivist materialists then and now which maintained that correct thought simply mirrors or reflects the object of thought. In addition, the Institute stressed the historical nature of all theories and their subject matter: "The theoretical activity of humans, like the practical, is not the independent knowledge of a fixed object, but a product of ever-changing reality". As historical conditions change, concepts and theories must also change; thus, there is no stable foundation for absolutist metaphysical views.

For Horkheimer, concepts and theories therefore provide representations of the socio-material world and not any absolute or indubitable knowledge. Horkheimer also criticizes theories which operate with a subject/object model that rigidly distinguishes between subject and object, arguing that "the subject-object relation is not accurately described by the picture of two fixed realities which are conceptually fully transparent and move towards each other. Rather, in what we call objective, subjective factors are at work; and in what we call subjective, objective factors are at work". Horkheimer's materialism is thus *dialectical*, utilizing a subject/object dialectic in which objective conditions help constitute the subject, while the subject in turn helps constitute objective (material, historical) conditions. For Horkheimer: "A dialectical process is negatively characterized by the fact that it is not to be conceived as the result of individual unchanging factors. To put it positively, its elements continuously change in relation to each other within the process, so that they are not even to be radically distinguished from each other. Thus the development of human character, for example, is conditioned both by the economic situation and by the individual powers of the person in question. But both these elements determine each other continuously, so that in the total development neither of them is to be prsented as an effective factor without giving the other its role".

Horkheimer and his colleagues consistently followed this dialectical conception which stressed the relative autonomy of thought, culture, and all other "superstructural" phenomena in a process of reciprocal interaction with a socioeconomic "base." They thereby rejected all versions of economic determinism and reductionism and provided conceptual space for analysing the often important causal role of cultural factors in history and society. A dialectical social theory thus analyzes the relationships between different aspects of society rather than providing a unidimensional determinist model that appeals to the economic dimension of society as the sole causal factor in explaining social development and structure.

Furthermore, the Institute's version of "dialectical materialism" is thoroughly *historical* because it stresses that our experience, views of the world, and concepts change in relation to historical development, and that therefore both our theories and perceptual apparatuses, as well as the objects of knowledge, are historical: "Materialism, unlike idealism, always understands thinking to be the thinking of particular men within a particular period of time. It challenges every claim to the autonomy of thought".

In sum, for Horkheimer, "materialism is not interested in a worldview or in the souls of men. It is concerned with changing the concrete conditions under which humans suffer and in which, of course, their souls must become stunted. This concern may be comprehended historically and psychologically; it cannot be grounded in general principles". Horkheimer believes that it is primarily materialist theories which are currently concerned with human suffering, and with transforming the material conditions which produce human suffering to produce a more rational society and a more humane form of existence. This analysis assumes that "the wretchedness of our own time is connected with the structure of society; social theory therefore forms the main content of contemporary materialism". In particular, "the fundamental historical role of economic relations is characteristic of the materialist position... Understanding of the present becomes more idealist, the more it avoids the economic causes of material need and looks to a psychologically naive elaboration of so-called 'basic elements of human existence'". Horkheimer's materialist social theory thus focuses on human needs and suffering, the ways that economic conditions produce suffering, and the changes necessary to eliminate human suffering and to increase human well-being. Such a project requires a critical social theory which confronts the social problems of the present age: "If materialist theory is an aspect of efforts to improve the human situation, it inevitably opposes every attempt to reduce social problems to second place". The social theory in turn is produced by a synthesis of philosophy and the sciences.

For the Institute, philosophy without empirical scientific research is empty, just as science without philosophy is blind. In the mid-1930s, Horkheimer's unification of science and philosophy seemed to involve a dialectical interpenetration and mediation of science and philosophy, without making one superordinate to the other. Consequently, Horkheimer rejects both metaphysics and positivist concepts of science which profess "'the dogma of the invariability of natural laws'". Dominant positivist conceptions of science, according to Horkheimer, are "unhistorical," and "science" for critical theory will not be privileged above philosophy and social theory.

Yet Horkheimer maintains that: "materialism has in common with positivism that it acknowledges as real only what is given in sense experience, and it has done so since its beginnings". Sense experience, however, is mediated through concepts, and both sense perception and cognition are subject to social conditions and historical change. Thus, notions of absolute intuition, whether through the senses or cognition, are to be rejected. Horkheimer and his colleagues therefore subscribe to a non-transcendental materialist theory of knowledge which acknowledges, with Kant and the idealists, that forms of cognition and theories determine our experience of the external world, but which acknowledges as well that objective material conditions in turn condition forms of thought and knowledge. The results of post-metaphysical, materialist social theory are thus always provisional, contextual, and subject to revision.

Critical Theory

The term "critical theory" was first coined in 1937 after the majority of the Institute's members had already emigrated to the United States following the triumph of Hitler. For many years, "critical theory" stood as a codeword for the Institute's Marxism and for its attempt to found a radical supradisciplinary social theory rooted in Hegelian-Marxian dialectics, historical materialism, and the Marxian critique of political economy and theory of revolution. Note that I said *supradisciplinary* and not "interdisciplinary." The critical theory project initially involved attempts of individuals from various disciplines to work together collectively to develop a historical and systematic theory of contemporary society rather than just bringing individuals from separate disciplines together to chat, or assigning various specialists different topics for research and inquiry. As Lowenthal (1980:109) put it: the term "interdisciplinary work" simply "means nothing more than to leave the disciplines as they are while developing certain techniques which foster a kind of acquaintance between them without forcing them to give up their self-sufficiency or individual claims." Critical theory, on the contrary, criticized the validity claims of the separate disciplines and attempted to create a new kind of social theory.

Critical theorists privileged Marxian categories in their supradisciplinary discourse, arguing that Marx's concepts of commodity, money, value, exchange, and fetishism characterize not only the capitalist economy but also social relations under capitalism where human relations and all forms of life are governed by commodity and exchange relations and values. Building on Lukacs' theory of reification (1971), they argued that capitalist society produced a rigid, reified structure wherein human beings were transformed into things. On this theory, through the process of reification, the unnatural conditions of the capitalist economy and labour process, the commodification of all goods, services, and objects, and the new modes of thought promoted by the mass media and positivist science appear to be "natural" and to form a system impervious to human control or intervention.

Horkheimer's essay "Traditional and Critical Theory" (1972) provides the most systematic and comprehensive presentation of the Institute's conception of social theory, while spelling out the presuppositions of their project and its relation to traditional theory. Traditional theory from Descartes through positivism is characterized by what is now called "foundationalism" i.e the attempt to ground theory in theoretical postulates which form the foundation of its theory upon which the traditional theorist builds its theoretical constructions. Traditional theory tends to be deductive, privileging natural science and mathematics; its goal, Horkheimer claims, is unity and harmony, with mathematics as its model (1972:190).

Horkheimer suggests that traditional theory is thus a projection of the bourgeois ideal of the harmonious capitalist market unified by calculable laws of supply and demand. Critical theory frequently shows the relationships between ideas and theoretical positions and their social environment, and thus attempts to contextualize or historicize ideas in terms of their roots within social processes. Following this line of inquiry, Horkheimer suggests that traditional theory is itself part of the social practices that constituted capitalism and bourgeois society. Its tendencies toward mechanistic materialism reproduced the mechanistic thought and practice of the industrial revolution according to which the world was conceptualized as a machine during an era in which machines came to dominate human beings. The dominant bourgeois trends of abstract and quantitative thought which informed traditional theory reproduced the tendencies toward abstraction and a mode of quantification that was based on exchange in the capitalist market where value was expressed in abstract, quantitative terms. Just as a bourgeois society governed by exchange value abstracted from values, goals, sentiments, and qualities, so too did traditional theory. And, finally, the fragmentation and division of the sciences reproduces the bourgeois division of labour under capitalism whereby specialization and fragmentation are dominant features of the structure of society.

Social theories, for critical theory, are thus forms of social practice which reproduce dominant forms of social activity. Traditional theory is, Horkheimer claims, unaware of the ways in which it is bound together with social processes and thus fails to see its lack of autonomy and social determination. As it became increasingly involved in social processes of production and reproduction, it became increasingly conformist, uncritically submitting to the dominant instrumental, quantitative, and capitalist values. Unaware of its social determination, "theory was absolutized...and became a reified, ideological category". Consequently, "The scholar and his science are incorporated into the apparatus of society; his achievements are a factor in the conservation and continuous renewal of the existing state of affairs, no matter what fine names he gives to what he does".

Traditional theory uncritically reproduces the existing society, while critical theory articulates activity striving to transform society. As Horkheimer put it:

> "There is a human activity that has society itself for its object. The aim of this activity is not simply to eliminate one or another abuse, for it regards such abuses as necessarily connected with the way in which the social structure is organized. Although it itself emerges from the social structure, its purpose is not, either in its conscious intention, or in its objective significance, the better functioning of any element in the structure. On the contrary, it is suspicious of the very categories of better, useful, appropriate, productive, and valuable, as these are understood in the present order".

Critical theory is thus rooted in "critical activity" which is oppositional and which is involved in a struggle for social change and the unification of theory and practice. "Critique," in this context, therefore involves criticism of oppression and exploitation and the struggle for a better society. Yet, in addition to its critique of vulgarized Marxian mechanistic materialism and economic reductionism and determinism, critical theory also rejects the efforts to ground Marxism in proletarian class-consciousness and its embodiment in a communist party —a concept that governed Lukacs' earlier work. Horkheimer argues that "even the situation of the proletariat is, in this society, no guarantee of correct knowledge". While the proletariat may have knowledge of its exploitation and wretchedness, the fragmentation of the working class and the fact that many of its members are brutalized and undereducated indicates that some workers will fall prey to conservative or reformist tendencies; thus, there is no guarantee that its consciousness will be either theoretically correct or revolutionary.

Nonetheless, a careful reading of Horkheimer's "manifesto" makes it clear that the Institute conceived of itself at the time as part of the tradition of Hegelian Marxism, and grounded its theory in the Marxian critique of political economy. Horkheimer and his associates firmly adhere to the Marxian standpoint that the economy is the crucial determining factor for all social life and individual activity. Moreover, critical theory accepts the Marxian critique of capitalism which sees all social problems as ultimately rooted in the irrationality and contradictions of the capitalist mode of production. For example, Horkheimer writes: "The categories which have arisen under its influence criticize the present. The Marxian categories of class, exploitation, surplus value, profit, impoverishment and collapse are moments of a conceptual whole whose meaning is to be sought, not in the reproduction of the present society, but in its transformation to a correct society".

System, Totality, and Critical Global Theory

Critical theory insists that one needs a theory of society grounded in a theory of capitalism to make sense of socio-historical processes and developments because the dynamics of capitalism play such a constitutive role in social life. Furthermore, to understand and explain social phenomena, one needs to contextualize one's topic of inquiry within a comprehensive theoretical framework for social analysis and critique in order to avoid illegitimate abstraction which would, for instance, analyse a political or cultural phenomena apart from its constitution in socioeconomic processes. Yet while critics of totalizing modes of thought often attack critical theory's use of Hegelian-Marxian concepts of totality, I would argue that critical theory does not operate with either a fetishized or reified concept of totality. Indeed, polemics against the concept of totality, or totalizing modes of thought, generally do not distinguish between varying senses and types of "totality." Often "totality" is identified with a harmonizing metaphysical mode of thought which stresses coherence, unity, and order in which all parts are seen as elements of a whole in which holistic harmony is posited as a normative value. The Institute sharply rejected such metaphysical concepts of totality, and they use the term "totality" in different ways in different contexts.

Frequently, critical theorists use the term "totality" in a synchronic sense to refer to the structure of society, defined by the Marxian critique of political economy, which provides the framework and context of inquiry, and which constitutes many social facts. For the Marxian theory, the relations of production provide the framework for development of a capitalist system; the economy thus constitutes a form of society. The critical theorists begin with the categories of economics and the Marxian critique of political economy precisely because the economy continues to play a constitutive role within all areas of social life and thus provides the framework for developing a theory of society. Marx's concepts of commodity, money, value, and exchange characterize not only economics, but also social relations because social relations and everyday life are governed by commodity and exchange relations and values. In this sense, critical theory utilizes totalizing concepts to describe a totalizing capitalist system which attempts to impose its values, structures, and practices throughout social life.

The concept of totality refers in other contexts to the diachronic, or historical, perspectives of critical theory which both characterize the historical conditions which have produced the existing capitalist society, and which conceptualize the vicissitudes of capitalist development and the (hoped for) transition to socialism. Thus, rather than operating with a static or metaphysical notion of totality, the Institute utilized dynamic and historical modes of totalizing thought. The Institute's justifications for its macro, or global, theory of society were thus: 1) capitalist society is organized as a system and requires systemic theory to grasp its social organization; 2) the logic and social processes of capitalism penetrate into ever more domains of social life requiring a theory of capitalist society as a whole to explain developments and processes in every domain of social reality. Consequently, since capitalist society is totalizing, so too must social theory; 3) capitalist society constantly changes and develops, and requires global historical analysis of its various stages and transformations; and 4) social critique and transformation require delineation of historical alternatives and normative values which can be used to criticize existing states of affairs and to argue for alternative values and organization of society.

Critical theory is thus intrinsically global and historical, and attempts to provide the "Big Picture" that sketches the fundamental outlines of socioeconomic development and the ways in which capitalism structures social life, as well as the dynamics through which a capitalist society can be replaced by a socialist one. Yet the Institute was constantly on the alert to avoid any sort of economic reductionism and was especially concerned to trace the linkages between the economy and the political, social, cultural, and psychic realms while stressing the relative autonomy of the superstructures. The critical theorists thus described the *mediations*, or interconnections, between these spheres as well as the contradictions, and thus produced what might be called a "*mediated totality*." That is, the critical theorists believed that the boundaries between the various realms of existence reproduced in the fragmentation of the disciplinary sciences are artificial and abstract.

Consequently, to intelligently pursue theoretical and political issues requires supradisciplinary research and a dialectical method of presentation that demonstrates in concrete detail the interconnections and conflicts between the primary areas of the socio-historical system that constitutes the context and framework for thought and action. Dialectics for the Institute involved model-building and the making of connections or mediations. Social theory therefore involves construction of a model of the current society and a demonstration of the fundamental connections — as well as of the contradictions and conflicts — among the various domains of the current social system. Consequently, critical theory provides analyses of a mediated social totality that describe various relations among spheres of reality, rather than reducing all of society to the dynamics of the economy.

Critical theory is thus systemic, totalizing, integrating, and global. Social theory therefore has a mediating function for the critical theorists, integrating science and philosophy and mediating between research (*Forschung*) and theoretical construction and presentation (*Darstellung*) (Dubiel 1985). Critical theory mediates between various domains of reality, between parts and whole, between appearance and essence, and between theory and practice. The now "classical" 1930s model of critical theory thus synthesizes social theory, research, and radical politics in a critical global theory of the present age. Critical theory today, as I shall argue in the remainder of this essay, confronts the challenge of reconstructing its theory of capitalist society in the light of new social conditions and developments.

Conflicting Paradigms and the Critical Theory of Society

In discussions within the Institute, Marcuse argued that Horkheimer's "manifesto" underplayed the importance of philosophy and consequently he wrote a systematic essay on "Philosophy and Critical Theory" (1968). Horkheimer seemed to agree with this position and himself contributed a "Postscript" which highlighted the role of philosophy (1972:244ff). Critical theory's goal of helping to create a rational society, Horkheimer suggests, follows rationalist philosophy's demand that reason should shape the totality of life and follows as well its activist concept of rational/critical activity. Yet critical theory "never aims simply at an increase of knowledge as such. Its goal is man's emancipation from slavery".

Philosophy's role in critical theory is to analyse the presuppositions of a critical social theory and to criticize the presuppositions and effects of competing theories. For the Institute, philosophy provided a critical perspective on the nature and social function of social theories that was constitutive for the development of a critical theory of society. Rejecting dichotomies between fact and values and the Weberian/positivist notion of a value-free social science, critical theory urged reflection on the values and interests underlying any specific social theory and urged scrutiny and defence of its presuppositions. Critical theory is thus deeply self-reflexive and self-critical, forcing critical theorists to continually concern themselves with reflections on method and the nature and effects of a critical social theory.

Horkheimer and Marcuse generally agreed on the project of developing a synthesis of philosophy, social theory, and research in a supradisciplinary project. There were some differences, however, with the models developed by Adorno and Benjamin. While Horkheimer believed that critical social sciences would provide indispensible material for the theory, Adorno and Benjamin put more faith in philosophy and cultural theory as providing privileged sources of knowledge of contemporary society. For both, constellations of certain cultural artifacts contained "dialectical images" which would illuminate contemporary social conditions. They were more mistrustful of the social sciences than Horkheimer and tended to focus on cultural and philosophical criticism and ideology critique-emphases that would increasingly come to dominate the Institute's work and which would frequently displace their project of developing a social theory of the contemporary era. During the 1930s and early 1940s, the Institute attempted to develop a theory of capitalist society which would build upon, update, and go beyond classical Marxism. Thus, it is important to discern that critical theory strives to provide both a substantive social theory of the present age and a meta-theory of its theoretical presuppositions and method.

On one hand, critical theory contains a set of ways of looking at theory and at the world and a set of investigative, research, textual, and political practices. Yet, critical theory also provides a substantive, comprehensive theory of the present age in addition to its methodological orientation for doing social theory and research and for relating theoretical work to radical politics. Its substantive theory contains one of the first attempts to develop a synthesis of Marx and Freud and to incorporate psychoanalytic perspectives into its research. The critical theorists undertook projects which attempted to discern why individuals submitted to irrational authority and what psychological conditions produced authoritarian personalities who would submit to fascism. Later, the critical theorists analysed changes in socialization processes which were producing a weakness of the ego and "the decline of the individual." They also analysed the new relationships between the state and economy, the role of new technologies and mass communication as new modes of social control, and new class stratifications and the integration of the proletariat which was diminishing class conflict in a new consumer society.

In general, the critical theorists hoped to produce aspects of a theory of the transformation of competitive capitalism into monopoly capitalism and fascism, and hoped to be part of a historical process through which capitalism would be replaced by socialism. Their categories were intended to criticize the existing organization of society and to provide utopian sketches of a better society. Critical theory is thus motivated by an interest in emancipation from capitalism and provides a philosophy of social practice engaged in "the struggle for the future." Critical theory, Horkheimer argued, must remain loyal to the "idea of a future society as the community of free human beings, insofar as such a society is possible, given the present technical means" (1972:245).

Pollock's "State Capitalism" established a framework for the Institute's later analysis of the new relations between the state and the economy during the postwar era. Pollock claims that state capitalism — in both its "democratic" and "totalitarian" forms — produces a "command economy" exhibiting a "primacy of the political" whereby the state comes to manage the economy. Against Neumann's analysis of fascism in *Behemoth* (1941), Pollock maintained that "the profit motive is superseded by the power motive." Indeed, the Institute members never agreed about whether economic or political imperatives were primary for the new fascist state. Building on the Austrian Social Democrat Rudolf's Hilferding's *Finance Capital* (1910), Pollock's essay laid the foundation for later claims regarding the integration of the economy, the state, and the public sphere. It also maintained that capitalism had discovered new strategies to avoid economic crisis and provided the basis for the burgeoning belief that capitalism could henceforth stabilize itself and prevent the realization of socialism. Thus, it raised new doubts concerning the revolutionary role of the working class which was so central to the classical Marxian theory.

For Marx, the industrial proletariat was to serve as the agent of socialist revolution because it was the largest, most exploited, and the most militant class. Bearing the burden of industrial production, the working class was seen as the logical subject of revolution due to its crucial position in the production process and its potential for organization in highly centralized, large-scale industries. The Marxian theory of revolution also predicted severe capitalist economic crises which would lead the working class to revolt against poverty-stricken conditions where it had "nothing to lose but its chains." Even as capitalism was undergoing one of its most intense crises in the 1930s, however, the powerful parties and unions of the European working classes were defeated by the forces of fascism. Indeed, following that defeat, the prospects for socialist revolution looked ever bleaker to the Institute theorists.

As a consequence, the critical theorists increasingly distanced themselves from the traditional Marxist position which claimed that socialist revolution was inevitable and that historical progress would necessarily lead from capitalism to socialism. Henceforth, their relation to Marxism would become more ambivalent and complex. While individuals like Horkheimer would eventually abandon Marxism altogether for a form of mystical irrationalism derived from Schopenhauer and Nietzsche, Marcuse and others would continue to develop their own particular versions of the Marxian theory.

Crisis of Critical Theory

One of the key Institute positions was that the "culture industries" were now playing an increasingly important role in managing consciousness and obscuring social conflict. First sketched out in Horkheimer and Adorno's *Dialectic of Enlightenment* (1972), originally written during the early 1940s, this standpoint became an essential component of critical theory and inaugurated a new discourse about the role of mass communication and culture in the constitution of contemporary societies. According to Adorno and Horkheimer, the culture industries were organs of mass deception which manipulated individuals into accepting the current organization of society. In their view, the culture industries were engaging in sophisticated forms of ideological indoctrination, using "entertainment" to sugarcoat oppression while eroding cultural standards in order to quell any forms of expression which might contest the given order.

During World War II, the Institute split up due to pressures of the war. Horkheimer and Adorno moved to California, while Lowenthal, Marcuse, Neumann, and others worked for the U.S. government as their contribution in the fight against fascism. Horkheimer and Adorno worked on their book, *Dialectic of Enlightenment*, which contains implicit critiques of Marxism, as well as of fascism and consumer capitalism. Departing from the Marxian theory of history, they presented a philosophy of history that traced the fate of the Enlightenment from the beginnings of scientific thought among the Greeks to fascist concentration camps and the cultural industries of U.S. capitalism. They showed how Western rationality served as an instrument of domination and how "enlightenment" turned into its opposite: mystification and oppression. The book criticized enlightenment scientism and rationalism, and implicitly implicated Marxism within the "dialectic of Enlightenment."

After World War II, Adorno, Horkheimer, and Pollock returned to Frankfurt to reestablish the Institute in Germany, while Lowenthal, Marcuse, and others remained in the United States. In Germany, Adorno, Horkheimer, and their associates published a series of books and became a major intellectual force in their native land. At this time, the term "Frankfurt School" became widespread as a characterization of its version of supradisciplinary social research and of the particular social theory developed by Adorno, Horkheimer, and their associates. The Frankfurt school engaged in frequent methodological and substantive debates with other social theorists, most notably, in the "positivist dispute" in which they criticized more empirical and quantatitive approaches to social theory and defended their own more speculative and critical brand of social theory. The German group around Horkheimer and Adorno was also increasingly hostile toward orthodox Marxism and in turn were criticized by a variety of "Marxist-Leninists" and "scientific Marxists" for their alleged surrender of revolutionary and scientific Marxian perspectives.

The Frankfurt School eventually became best known for its theories of "the totally administered society," or "one-dimensional society," which theorized the increasing power of capitalism over all aspects of social life and the development of new forms of social control. This theory included analyses of working class integration within contemporary capitalist societies and new techniques of capitalist stabilization which severely questioned the Marxian theory of revolution. According to many critical theorists, new forms of technology, new modes of organizing production, new configurations of class, and new methods of social control were producing a "one-dimensional" society without opposition. It also seemed that new forms of political, social, and especially cultural conformity, were becoming institutionalized.

The development of a "totally administered society" led Adorno and Horkheimer to theorize "the end of the individual" and to stress the importance of preserving subjectivity in order to fulfill the goals of liberalism and socialism alike. The erosion of subjectivity, they believed, betrayed the promise of modernity which was itself predicated on the belief that the augmentation of science and technology would improve human control over nature and produce greater freedom, individuality, and happiness. Instead, the critical theorists argued, the institutions and practices of "advanced industrial society" were producing ever greater conformity and social domination.

Ultimately, in his highly esoteric *Negative Dialectics and Aesthetic Theory* this situation led Adorno to attempt the resurrection of a repressed subjectivity against mass society and its philosophical expressions like existentialism and positivism. It was ultimately Marcuse who provided the most comprehensive formulation of the theory of one-dimensional society in *One Dimensional Man* (1964). In his now-classic analysis, advanced industrial society integrates and absorbs all forces of opposition so that the "subjective" conditions for conflict between classes, as well as between the individual and society vanish at the very time that the "objective" reality of exploitation and injustice intensifies. Marcuse analyzes the new forms of social control in "one-dimensional society" and the diminution of the "other dimension" of social critique, rebellion, and utopian thinking, which presents alternatives to the existing order. Against "one-dimensionality," he advocated the "power of negative thinking" and the "great refusal." These slogans found empirical referents duringthe 1960s in the New Left and the counterculture which, to some extent, embraced Marcuse as a theoretical spokesperson.

During the 1950s, however, there were divergences between the work of the Institute relocated in Frankfurt and Fromm, Lowenthal, Marcuse, and others who did not return to Germany and who frequently developed theories that were at odds with both the current and earlier work of Horkheimer and Adorno. Thus, it is misleading to consider the work of various critical theorists during the postWar period as members of a monolithic "Frankfurt School." Whereas there was both a shared sense of purpose and collective work on supradisciplinary social theory from 1930 to the early 1940s, thereafter critical theorists frequently diverge and during the 1950s and 1960s the term the "Frankfurt School" can really only be applied to the work of those associated with the Institute in Germany.

It is therefore impossible to characterize the "Frankfurt School" as a whole since its work spanned several decades and involved a variety of thinkers who later engaged in sharp debates with each other. Rather, one should perceive various phases of Institute work: 1) the empirical-historical studies of the Grunberg era; 2) the attempts in the early to mid-1930s to establish a materialist supradisciplinary social theory under Horkheimer's directorship; 3) the attempts to develop a critical theory of society during the exile period from about 1937 to the early 1940s; 4) the dispersion of Institute members in the 1940s and the new directions sketched out by Horkheimer and Adorno; 5) the return of the Institute to Germany and its work in Frankfurt during the 1950s and 1960s; 6) the development of critical theory in various directions by Fromm, Lowenthal, Marcuse, and others who remained in the U.S.; 7) the continuation of Institute projects and development of critical theory in Germany by Jurgen Habermas, Oskar Negt, Alfred Schmidt, and others in the 1970s and 1980s; and, finally, 8) contributions to critical theory by a variety of younger theorists and scholars currently active in Europe and the United States.

In retrospect, one can see that a crisis of critical theory emerged with its fragmentation after World War II. In effect, its social theory stopped developing, despite some empirical research projects and sustained metatheoretical analyses by certain of its members, especially Adorno. Consequently, while I believe that critical theory provides the most advanced theoretical perspectives within contemporary social theory from the 1930s through the early 1960s new socio-cultural developments since then have rendered obsolete some of its theses concerning one-dimensional society, the media, technology, and so on. In particular, critical theory has not continued to theorize new technologies, new developments in the media, changes in socialization practices, and new cultural developments. This is somewhat surprising since its earlier contributions were precisely in these areas.

The reasons for the failure of most critical theorists to update and develop their substantive social theory are many and complex. Horkheimer seems to have burned out by the 1950s and provided few important contributions during his later years. Adorno did a great deal of work in social theory in the 1950s and 1960s, as well as turning out an incredible profusion of texts in the areas of literary criticism, cultural critique, philosophy, and aesthetics. But his work turned more and more from supradisciplinary research to philosophical reflections. Habermas also tended to focus his attention increasingly on philosophical theorizing, although his book *Legitimation Crisis* (1975) provides some important new perspectives for critical social theory, as do many of his later texts, especially *Theory of Communicative Action* and *The Philosophical Discourse of Modernity* (1987).

In Germany and the United States, most of the work in critical theory during the last decade has followed Habermas in attempting to develop more adequate philosophical foundations for critical theory, or to delineate philosophical aspects of critical theory. Thus, there has been a deficit of social research and elaboration of new theoretical perspectives in the domain of social theory. Contributions of this sort have come, by contrast, from members of the postmodern camp who have attempted to theorize the impact of new technologies, new media, and other socio-cultural developments. The response of critical theory has been by and large to polemicize against postmodern theory as a new form of irrationalism. Yet if critical theory wishes to meet the postmodern challenge and win back its role as the cutting edge of radical social theory, it must seek new directions and provide theoretical accounts of contemporary developments in a wide range of domains.

New Directions; New Perspectives of Fragmentation

With its fragmentation, trivialization, and academicization, social theory today is in acute crisis and needs new directions and new perspectives to which critical theory can contribute. While critical theory stopped developing and articulating new social conditions and developments, postmodern social theory and theories of postindustrial society lack the sustained commitment to social research, social critique, and political practice found in the best contributors to critical theory. While both schools provide a powerful challenge to mainstream theory, I believe that critical theory's sustained criticism of mainstream theory's presuppositions, methodologies, and lack of critical reflexivity, provides a more sustained critique than postmodern theory. Moreover, I believe that critical theory's traditional goal of providing a theory of the present age and radical politics provides superior perspectives to the often corrosive skepticism and nihilism found in much postmodern theory which disables both theoretical inquiry and political practice.

But if critical theory seeks to contribute to finding the way out of the contemporary crisis of social theory, it must itself develop new perspectives. In opposition to the previous model of "one-dimensional society," critical theorists today should focus on the contradictions, conflicts, and crisis tendencies within contemporary capitalist societies. To the neglect of political economy and empirical research found in much critical theory, we should respond with theoretical analyses of developments within the capitalist economy and of changes in class stratification, the labour process, new technologies, the media, and politics. In opposition to the apolitical and even depoliticized versions of critical theory that continue to circulate, those who wish to revitalize critical theory should attempt to politicize it, to connect it with new social movements and existing political struggles. As we move into the 1990s and toward the end of the century, many theoretical and political tasks stand before us. If critical theory wishes to participate in the Left Turn needed to eliminate the current hegemony of the Right and to help to build a better society, it needs to develop both its analysis of the present situation and a new politics in order to become once again the cutting edge of radical social theory.

Critical Theory in Sociological Context

Critical theory is the examination and critique of society and culture, drawing from knowledge across the social sciences and humanities. The term has two different meanings with different origins and histories: one originating in sociology and the other in literary criticism. This has led to the very literal use of 'critical theory' as an umbrella term to describe theoretical critique.

Critical theory, in the sociological context, refers to a style of Marxist theory with a tendency to engage with non-Marxist influences. This tendency has been referred to pejoratively by stricter Marxists as 'revisionism'. Modern critical theory arose from a trajectory extending from the nonpositivist sociology of Weber and Simmel, the neo-Marxist theory of Lukács and Gramsci, toward the milieu associated with Frankfurt Institute of Social Research. It is with the so-called 'Frankfurt School' of theorists that the term is most commonly associated: Herbert Marcuse, Theodor Adorno, Max Horkheimer, Walter Benjamin, and Jürgen Habermas. With the latter, critical theory shed further its roots in German Idealism and moved closer to American Pragmatism. The theoretical concern for a cultural 'superstructure' derived from a material 'base' often remains as the only central Marxist tenet in contemporary critical theory.

Two Primary Definitions

The two meanings of critical theory—from different intellectual traditions associated with the meaning of criticism and critique—derive ultimately from the Greek word *kritikos* meaning judgment or discernment, and in their present forms go back to the 18th century. While they can be considered completely independent intellectual pursuits, increasingly scholars are interested in the areas of critique where the two overlap.

To use an epistemological distinction introduced by Jürgen Habermas in *Erkenntnis und Interesse* [1968] (*Knowledge and Human Interests*), critical theory in literary studies is ultimately a form of hermeneutics, i.e. knowledge via interpretation to understand the meaning of human texts and symbolic expressions — including the interpretation of texts which are themselves implicitly or explicitly the interpretation of other texts. Critical social theory is, in contrast, a form of self-reflective knowledge involving both understanding and theoretical explanation to reduce entrapment in systems of domination or dependence, obeying the emancipatory interest in expanding the scope of autonomy and reducing the scope of domination. From this perspective, much literary critical theory, since it is focused on interpretation and explanation rather than on social transformation, would be regarded as positivistic or traditional rather than critical theory in the Kantian or Marxian sense. Critical theory in literature and the humanities in general does not necessarily involve a normative dimension, whereas critical social theory does, either through criticizing society from some general theory of values, norms, or "oughts," or through criticizing it in terms of its own espoused values.

In Social Theory

Critical theory was first defined by Max Horkheimer of the Frankfurt School of sociology in his 1937 essay *Traditional and Critical Theory*: Critical theory is a social theory oriented toward critiquing and changing society as a whole, in contrast to traditional theory oriented only to understanding or explaining it. Horkheimer wanted to distinguish critical theory as a radical, emancipatory form of Marxian theory, critiquing both the model of science put forward by logical positivism and what he and his colleagues saw as the covert positivism and authoritarianism of orthodox Marxism and Communism. Core concepts are: (1) That critical social theory should be directed at the totality of society in its historical specificity (i.e. how it came to be configured at a specific point in time), and (2) That critical theory should improve understanding of society by integrating all the major social sciences, including geography, economics, sociology, history, political science, anthropology, and psychology.

This version of "critical" theory derives from Kant's (18th-century) and Marx's (19th Century) use of the term "critique", as in Kant's *Critique of Pure Reason* and Marx's concept that his work *Das Kapital* (*Capital*) forms a "critique of political economy". For Kant's transcendental idealism, "critique" means examining and establishing the limits of the validity of a faculty, type, or body of knowledge, especially through accounting for the limitations imposed by the fundamental, irreducible concepts in use in that knowledge system. Early on, Kant's notion associated critique with the disestablishment of false, unprovable, or dogmatic philosophical, social, and political beliefs, because Kant's critique of reason involved the critique of dogmatic theological and metaphysical ideas and was intertwined with the enhancement of ethical autonomy and the Enlightenment critique of superstition and irrational authority. Marx explicitly developed this notion into the critique of ideology and linked it with the practice of social revolution, as in the famous 11th of his "Theses on Feuerbach," "Philosophers have only interpreted the world in certain ways; the point is to change it".

One of the distinguishing characteristics critical theory, as Adorno and Horkheimer elaborated in their *Dialectic of Enlightenment* (1947), is a certain ambivalence concerning the ultimate source or foundation of social domination, an ambivalence which gave rise to the "pessimism" of the new critical theory over the possibility of human emancipation and freedom. This ambivalence was rooted, of course, in the historical circumstances in which the work was originally produced, in particular, the rise of National Socialism, state capitalism, and mass culture as entirely new forms of social domination that could not be adequately explained within the terms of traditional Marxist sociology. For Adorno and Horkheimer state intervention in the economy had effectively abolished the tension in capitalism between the "relations of production" and "material productive forces of society," a tension which, according to traditional critical theory, constituted the primary contradiction within capitalism. The market (as an "unconscious" mechanism for the distribution of goods) and private property had been replaced by centralized planning and socialized ownership of the means of production. Yet, contrary to Marx's famous prediction in the *Preface to a Contribution to the Critique of Political Economy*, this shift did not lead to "an era of social revolution," but rather to fascism and totalitarianism. As such, critical theory was left, in Jürgen Habermas' words, without "anything in reserve to which it might appeal; and when the forces of production enter into a baneful symbiosis with the relations of production that they were supposed to blow wide open, there is no longer any dynamism upon which critique could base its hope." For Adorno and Horkheimer, this posed the problem of how to account for the apparent persistence of domination in the absence of the very contradiction that, according to traditional critical theory, was the source of domination itself.

In the 1960s, Jürgen Habermas raised the epistemological discussion to a new level in his *Knowledge and Human Interests*, by identifying critical knowledge as based on principles that differentiated it either from the natural sciences or the humanities, through its orientation to self-reflection and emancipation. Though unsatisfied with Adorno and Horkeimer's thought presented in *Dialectic of Enlightenment*, Habermas shares the view that, in the form of instrumental rationality, the era of modernity marks a move away from the liberation of enlightenment and toward a new form of enslavement. His ideas regarding the relationship between modernity and rationalization are in this sense strongly influenced by Max Weber. Habermas dissolved further the elements of critical theory derived from Hegelian German Idealism, though his thought remains broadly Marxist in its epistemological approach. Perhaps his two most influential ideas are the concepts of the public sphere and communicative action; the latter arriving partly as a reaction to new post-structural or so-called 'post-modern' challenges to the discourse of modernity. Habermas engaged in regular correspondence with Richard Rorty and a strong sense of philosophical pragmatism may be felt in his theory; thought which frequently traverses the boundaries between sociology and philosophy.

Postmodern Critical Theory

While modernist critical theory (as described above) concerns itself with "forms of authority and injustice that accompanied the evolution of industrial and corporate capitalism as a political-economic system," postmodern critical theory politicizes social problems "by situating them in historical and cultural contexts, to implicate themselves in the process of collecting and analysing data, and to relativize their findings". Meaning itself is seen as unstable due to the rapid transformation in social structures and as a result the focus of research is centred on local manifestations rather than broad generalizations. Postmodern critical research is also characterized by what is called, the *crisis of representation*, which rejects the idea that a researcher's work is considered an "objective depiction of a stable other". Instead, in their research and writing, many postmodern scholars have adopted "alternatives that encourage reflection about the 'politics and poetics' of their work. In these accounts, the embodied, collaborative, dialogic, and improvisational aspects of qualitative research are clarified".

Often, the term 'critical theory' is appropriated when an author (perhaps most notably Michel Foucault) works within sociological terms yet attacks the social or human sciences (thus attempting to remain 'outside' those frames of enquiry). Jean Baudrillard has also been described as a critical theorist to the extent that he was an unconventional and critical sociologist; this appropriation is similarly casual, holding little or no relation to the Frankfurt School.

Critical Ethnography

Critical ethnography is "a type of reflection that examines culture, knowledge, and action...Critical ethnographers describe, analyse, and open to scrutiny otherwise hidden agendas, power centers, and assumptions that inhibit, repress, and constrain". While "conventional ethnography" "describes what is", critical ethnography "asks what could be"....Conventional ethnographers study culture for the purposes of describing it; critical ethnographers do so to change it".

In Literary Criticism

The second meaning of *critical theory* is that of theory used in literary criticism ("critical theory") and in the analysis and understanding of literature. This is discussed in greater detail under literary theory. This form of critical theory is not necessarily oriented toward radical social change or even toward the analysis of society, but instead specializes on the analysis of texts. It originated among literary scholars and in the discipline of literature in the 1960s and 1970s, and has really only come into broad use since the 1980s, especially as theory used in literary studies has increasingly been influenced by European philosophy and social theory.

This version of "critical" theory derives from the notion of literary criticism as establishing and enhancing the understanding and evaluation of literature in the search for truth. Some consider literary theory merely an aesthetic concern, as articulated, for example, in Joseph Addison's notion of a critic as one who helps understand and interpret literary works: "A true critic ought to dwell rather upon excellencies than imperfections, to discover the concealed beauties of a writer, and communicate to the world such things as are worth their observation." This notion of criticism ultimately goes back to Aristotle's *Poetics* as a theory of literature.

From the literary side, starting in the 1960s literary scholars, reacting especially against the New Criticism of the previous decades, which tried to analyse literary texts purely internally, began to incorporate into their analyses and interpretations of literary works initially semiotic, linguistic, and interpretive theory, then structuralism, Lacanian psychoanalysis, post-structuralism, and deconstruction as well as Continental philosophy, especially phenomenology and hermeneutics, and critical social theory and various other forms of neo-Marxian theory. Thus literary criticism became highly theoretical and some of those practicing it began referring to the theoretical dimension of their work as "critical theory", i.e. philosophically inspired theory of literary criticism. And thus incidentally critical theory in the sociological sense also became, especially among literary scholars of left-wing sympathies, one of a number of influences upon and streams within critical theory in the literary sense.

Furthermore, along with the expansion of the mass media and mass/popular culture in the 1960s and 1970s and the blending of social and cultural criticism and literary criticism, the methods of both kinds of critical theory sometimes intertwined in the analysis of phenomena of popular culture, as in the emerging field of cultural studies, in which concepts deriving from Marxian theory, post-structuralism, semiology, psychoanalysis and feminist theory would be found in the same interpretive work. Both strands were often present in the various modalities of postmodern theory.

Language : Construction Communication

The two points at which there is the greatest overlap or mutual impingement of the two versions of critical theory are in their interrelated foci on language, symbolism, and communication and in their focus on construction. From the 1960s and 1970s onward, language, symbolism, text, and meaning became foundational to theory in the humanities and social sciences, through the short-term and long-term influences of Ludwig Wittgenstein, Ferdinand de Saussure, George Herbert Mead, Noam Chomsky, Hans-Georg Gadamer, Roland Barthes, Jacques Derrida and other thinkers in the traditions of linguistic and analytic philosophy, structural linguistics, symbolic interactionism, hermeneutics, semiology, linguistically oriented psychoanalysis, and deconstruction. When, in the 1970s and 1980s, Jürgen Habermas also redefined critical social theory as a theory of communication, i.e. communicative competence and communicative rationality on the one hand, distorted communication on the other, the two versions of critical theory began to overlap or intertwine to a much greater degree than before.

Both versions of critical theory have focused on the processes of synthesis, production, or construction by which the phenomena and objects of human communication, culture, and political consciousness come about. Whether it is through the transformational rules by which the deep structure of language becomes its surface structure (Chomsky), the universal pragmatic principles through which mutual understanding is generated (Habermas), the semiotic rules by which objects of daily usage or of fashion obtain their meanings (Barthes), the psychological processes by which the phenomena of everyday consciousness are generated (psychoanalytic thinkers), the *episteme* that underlies our cognitive formations (Foucault), and so on, there is a common interest in the processes (often of a linguistic or symbolic kind) that give rise to observable phenomena. Here there is significant mutual influence among aspects of the different versions of critical theory. Ultimately this emphasis on production and construction goes back to the revolution wrought by Kant in philosophy, namely his focus in the *Critique of Pure Reason* on synthesis according to rules as the fundamental activity of the mind that creates the order of our experience.

3

Comprehensive Theory of Social Development

Recent Development Experience

From the perspective of 10,000 years of history, human progress over the past 200 years has been extraordinary and the achievements of the past five decades are nothing short of miraculous. In two centuries social productivity has increased to the extent that the global community is now able to sustain a population 12 times as large as in 1800. From a rural-based, agrarian society in which less than three percent of the people lived in towns and cities, the human community has evolved into an urban-centred, industrial society in which the urban population now exceeds 40 percent of the total. This change has brought with it and aggravated a host of problems – overcrowding, pollution, crime, etc.—but it has also brought political freedom, economic security, education and modern conveniences to billions of people.

What is more remarkable is that this social movement continues to expand and accelerate. The 1997 UNDP Human Development Report observes that over the past 50 years the world has made greater progress in eradicating poverty than during the previous 500. Around the globe, life expectancy is climbing, infant mortality is declining, epidemic diseases are receding, famine is becoming extinct and education is becoming more widespread. Since 1950 average per capita income has tripled, in spite of unprecedented population growth, and average real per capita consumption in developing countries has doubled. These achievements raise the possibility and the hope that unprecedented levels of prosperity could soon spread to all humanity. These accomplishments still leave more than one billion people in poverty. But there is growing evidence to suggest that today's least developed countries could match and perhaps even exceed the achievements of the most advanced industrial nations within a much shorter time than it took for the original achievements. Beginning in 1780, it took the United Kingdom 58 years to double output per capita. The United States did it in 47 years, beginning in 1839. Japan accomplished the feat in only 24 years, beginning in the 1880s. But after the Second World War, Indonesia did it in 17 years, South Korea in 11, and China in 10. From 1960 to 1990 real per capita standards of living based on purchasing power parity multiplied twelve-fold in South Korea, seven-fold in Japan, more than six-fold in Egypt and Portugal, and well above five-fold in Indonesia and Thailand.

While the possibilities for increasing the velocity and expanding the scope of development to all countries are encouraging, it is by no means clear how quickly or to what extent they will be realized. Nor is there consensus regarding the policies, strategies and actions most conducive for that realization. Regardless of whether we consider developing countries, nations in the process of transition to market economies, or those moving from the industrial into the post-industrial phase, countries and regions are distinguished by vast differences in performance that are not easily explained or eliminated.

Among developing countries, between 1965 and 1990 per capita GDP rose by 5.5 percent annually in high performing East Asian countries compared to less than 2 percent in South Asia and about.25 percent in Sub-Saharan Africa. Much thought has gone into analysis of the Asian Tigers' success, but no generally accepted formula has emerged from their experience that is applicable to countries at different stages of development and faced with differing conditions than those prevalent in East Asia during the past few decades.

The experience in Eastern Europe since 1990 suggests that our understanding of the development process is far from complete. The transition strategies implemented by 25 East European countries were unable to prevent widespread economic decline and social distress. Production in all 25 countries fell significantly, from a minimum of 18 percent in Poland to 45 percent in Russia, 60 percent in Ukraine and 75 percent in Armenia. Even in East Germany, where the German government and industry have pumped in more than $1.1 trillion since reunification, the expected results have not been achieved. Unemployment in East Germany has grown from very low levels to more than 25 percent, while productivity remains at one-fifth the level prevalent in the western part of the country.

Questions regarding strategy and wide disparities in performance are also found among advanced industrial nations, particularly with reference to the issue of employment. In 1990 the people of the Western world shared a powerful common anxiety about the future of work. Since then unemployment has been increasing throughout most of Europe to reach the highest levels in half a century. At the same time, it has been falling in the USA, where the employment rate has reached peak historical levels and is projected to continue rising through the coming decade. Technological development, which people everywhere feared would devour more and more jobs in the coming years, appears to be associated with opposite effects on different sides of the Atlantic.

The experience of the past two centuries has given rise to at least five major categories of development theory. Applying these theories to explain the development of 23 countries during the period 1850-1914, Morris and Adelman found that each major theory adequately explains the experience of a range of countries and periods, but none of the theories applies universally to the 19th Century experience of all the countries. These findings suggest the need for a more comprehensive approach. Realization of this need prompted then Secretary General of the United Nations, Boutros Boutros-Ghali, to call for thoughtful reflection on development "as the most important intellectual challenge of the coming years."

Theory as a Revealer of Potential

Why focus on theory when there are so many pressing practical problems that warrant attention? Because awareness of a theoretical possibility can help us discover real opportunities and potentials that might otherwise go unrecognized and untapped. The recent acceleration of social development is an observable and measurable fact. But in the absence of a theoretical framework, it is difficult to discern, for instance, whether the astonishing accomplishments of East Asian countries over the past two decades are a temporary aberration in an otherwise very gradual process or the forerunner of even higher growth rates in future.

The power of comprehensive theoretical knowledge is dramatically illustrated by the efficacy of modern medical physiology. The human body is a highly complex organism in which multiple systems and subsystems work together as a seamless unity to maintain health and support growth and development. Each physiological function can be reduced to basic principles of physics and biochemistry that are common not only to all human systems, but all life systems as well. Hundreds of major or minor factors enter into the equations that support health. An excess or shortage of even a single factor can disturb the balance, retard growth or threaten life. Treatment may concentrate on one errant factor, but it is based on knowledge of the greater whole in which this factor operates. Medical knowledge has become so precise that analysis of the chemical composition of the blood can be used to ascertain overall health and accurately diagnose a wide variety of disorders in people of different ages and physical condition.

Society is also a complex organism in which multiple systems and subsystems work together to maintain the health of the community and support growth and development. But here the similarity ends. For when it comes to development, there is no agreement on the fundamental principles that govern social functions. Many partial theories have been put forth that help us explain specific phenomena and formulate successful strategies based on a few key factors in conditions which are stable and fall within the familiar boundaries of economic growth. But when we try to extend the theory to new and rapidly changing circumstances, such as those prevalent in Eastern Europe during the recent transition period, we find that explanations and strategies based on one or a small group of factors are insufficient to account for the variety of different results or to formulate policies appropriate for each particular circumstance. Development is a complex, multidimensional phenomenon that touches every major strand of social activity, applies to a very wide range of circumstances and passes through many different stages in its progression. An adequate theory must be sufficiently comprehensive to address this breadth of activity, circumstances and stages. Ultimately it should lead to the development of diagnostic capabilities that approach the precision achieved by medical science.

Experience from other fields demonstrates that a conscious knowledge can increase the speed and efficiency of any activity by a factor of 10 or even more. A trained mechanic or engineer easily repairs a defective machine, while an untrained user may flounder for long periods and very possibly make the problem worse. A clearer theoretical understanding of development will not only reveal opportunities that presently are unrecognized. It can also lead to the formulation of more effective strategies capable of increasing the speed and efficiency of development by a factor of ten or more.

Untapped Opportunities

Humanity has progressed very far from its modest origins. It has already created what must appear from a historical perspective almost infinite plentitude. Development theory should enable us to understand what productive power or powers have made this great accomplishment possible and what further achievements still lay in potential that can be attained through further exercise of this same or other powers. We observe today a confluence of conditions that seem to indicate that a further acceleration of social progress is possible. They include a broad range of political, economic, technological and social factors that have direct or indirect impact on development.

Each in itself can support higher rates of social advancement. Taken together, their contribution could lead to accomplishments at least as far beyond present levels as society has already advanced since the beginning of the Industrial Revolution. Development theory should not only confirm or deny this possibility, but also show the precise relationship between these conditions and the greater results society seeks to obtain.

Peace: Any evaluation of development potentials needs to take into account the influence of internal and external social stability on social progress. The end of the Cold War has dramatically reduced the threat of armed international conflicts and the catastrophic consequences of nuclear war, providing a far more stable and secure climate for worldwide economic expansion. War is a destroyer of development. It physically demolishes what society has accomplished. The Cold War limited the physical destruction to regional conflicts, but it directed a substantial portion of the energies and talents of the world community into an unproductive arms race. Since 1988, world military expenditure has fallen by about a third, $400 billion. If the current peaceful status is sustained, it could free up even more capital for investment and reducing the inflationary pressure of burgeoning government deficits. The long feared negative impact of reduced military expenditure on economic growth has been much less than anticipated. Falling defence spending has been followed by a surprisingly rapid recovery in defence-dependent states such as California and an unexpectedly long period of national economic expansion in the USA. This experience should help reduce the resistance to further cuts.

Democracy: Since 1980, a democratic revolution has been spreading through Latin America, Eastern Europe and, most recently, Africa, freeing hundreds of millions of people from repression by authoritarian regimes. As peace provides a secure external environment for international development, democracy provides a stable and conducive environment within countries for more rapid social progress. Democracy raises human aspirations. It encourages individuals to take active initiative for their own advancement. It facilitates freer and wider social interactions. It releases greater social energy. It vastly increases the dissemination of information and the multiplication of new organizations. As the transition from monarchy to democracy was a catalyst for rapid economic advancement of Western countries over the past three centuries, the spread of democratic institutions today opens up greater possibilities for global expansion. Development theory needs to explain the dynamics of the process by which political and social conditions impact economic performance.

Social Velocity: Development is a function of the velocity of social transactions. The speed of movement of information, ideas, decisions, technology, people, goods and money has significant impact on the productivity of the society and its further advancement. The 'shrinking of the world' through better transportation and communication opens up commercial opportunities inconceivable just a few years ago. During the past two decades the volume of international travelers, freight, telephone and other forms of electronic communication have increased by more than an order of magnitude. Between 1980 and 1994, overseas telephone traffic to and from the USA increased from 200 million to 3.4 billion calls. New technologies such as satellite-based wireless phones are reducing the cost of expanding the communications infrastructure. Electronic mail has drastically reduced the cost and increased the speed of written communications. The meteoric growth of the Internet provides instantaneous low cost access to global sources of information and commercial markets. The speed of technology diffusion is also accelerating. The Xerox machine was not introduced into India until the late 1970s, more than 15 years after its use became widespread in the USA. Three years ago, Windows 95 was launched in New Delhi just weeks after its release in the USA. Last year Intel announced its latest microprocessor simultaneously in USA, India and Beijing. A comprehensive theory needs to account for the contribution of the increasing velocity of social transactions on development in the past and its potential for accelerating social progress in the future.

Technological Application: The rate of technological innovation and diffusion is one thing, the extent of technology application is quite another. Technological development far outpaces technological applications and accomplishments in even the most advanced societies. Adoption and full utilization of already proven technologies can dramatically elevate performance in every country and in every field. To cite a single example, the average yield of tomatoes in India is 8 tons per acre, yet more advanced farmers achieve yields as high as 20 tons. The average yield of tomato in California is 35 tons in California, but one of California's leading tomato farmers with 1200 acres under cultivation routinely obtains average yields of 55 tons or more by applying advanced systems for micro-nutrient management applicable to all crops and climates. Applying more sophisticated and capital intensive technology, Israeli farmers achieve yields of 250 tons or more of tomato per acre.

This wide variation in the application of technology within and between countries is nothing new. But it is a significant determinant of development and a factor that is at least partially responsive to social policies. The theory needs to explain these variations and show how they act as determinants of the development process.

Global Growth Engines: The global economy is developing multiple centers and engines of growth. The impact of these factors is compounded by the globalization of economic growth. In the past, the growth of the world economy has been driven by a single country or at best by a few localized centers, while the vast majority of nations benefited only peripherally or not at all.

The emergence of multiple growth centers acts as a self-generating engine that increases the overall momentum of the world economy. Valid development theory cannot limit its purview to national level policies and economic environment. It is becoming more and more necessary to consider development as a movement of global society, in which individual nations may move in different directions and advance at different rates, but remain aspects of a common movement.

Today virtually all of the known factors that support and stimulate development are more accessible and more prevalent than ever before.

Education, the most essential resource for development, is far more widespread than at any time in history. Technology is far more available and so are trained people to operate it. Information, that most powerful catalyst of human initiative, is more easily obtainable through the very rapid expansion of the press, journals, telephones and fax machines, satellite television and data linkages. Investment, once thought to be a critical constraint, is pouring into developing countries and pouring from household savings into new productive enterprises. Management know-how, a traditional weakness in most developing countries, has also improved dramatically.

Barriers to Development

Development theory needs to explain the process by which these potentials are created and their role in development. It needs to explain how they combine and interact to determine the direction and speed of social progress. At the same time it should be able to account for the fact that in most instances the actual exploitation of opportunities falls far short of the potential and lags far behind the maximum pace achievable or already achieved by some other societies. Solutions are known for many of the most severe problems of development, yet these problems persist. If the unseen potentials are far more prevalent than most people conceive, the unseen barriers to progress also seem to be much more obstructive. Observation of social progress reveals three recurring types of obstacles to development – limited perception, out-dated attitudes and anachronistic behaviors.

Perceptual Walls and Apparent Dead Ends

One of the most striking characteristics of development discernible in all periods, countries and fields of activity has been the inability of society to envision or foresee its own future destiny. This attribute is usually accompanied by the contrary tendency to perceive opportunities as insurmountable obstacles. Innumerable times in history, humanity has come face to face with what it believed was a dead end to progress, only to discover sooner or later a way around or through the dead end to open up a wider field of opportunities. This description is literally applicable to the search by European seafarers for a sea route to Asia. In the 15th Century, a great number of Portuguese vessels were dispatched in search of a route around Africa, but all of them were repelled by an impenetrable barrier when they reached the tiny Cape Bojador midway down the Western coast of the continent.

The barrier was the widespread belief that Bojador represented the edge of the world and that to sail beyond it was certain death. It took persistent efforts by Prince Henry, 12 expeditions, and a very large purse to persuade one bold captain to skirt the cape and break the perceptual wall. Once done, Portugal soon discovered the Southern route to India and became a leading mercantile power.

Today humanity no longer fears the end of the earth, but powerful perceptual barriers still exist with regard to employment, technology, trade, environment, corruption, inflation and population that represent very real barriers to development the world over. Malthus was not the only one to foresee imminent doom where in fact there was enormous opportunity. In 1950 Holland's population exceeded 5 million, reaching a density that many believed approached the ultimate limits that this tiny landmass could support. Today the Netherlands has 15 million people, almost three times the population density, yet it ranks among the most prosperous nations in the world and is a major food exporter. In the mid 1960s, India suffered from two successive years of drought and was on the verge of severe famine. An expert team sent to India by the Food and Agricultural Organization estimated that the country's food grain production would rise by a maximum of 10% before 1970. Many Indian scientists shared this pessimistic view. Actually grain production rose 50 percent during this period and doubled within a decade to make the country self-sufficient in food grains. Had India's leaders shared the view of the experts, the Green Revolution may never have been attempted.

Errors in assessment of future possibilities occur when we make projections of future performance on the basis of historical trends, even though changing circumstances have radically altered the environment. The development of the high yielding varieties of wheat and rice dramatically altered the equation for food production, yet was not factored into the assessment of what could be achieved. Looking forward, we often see apparently insurmountable obstacles to future progress. Looking backwards, we discover continuity and progress. History has shown time and again that there are no dead ends, only people who are unable to see the opportunities and solutions concealed behind the immediate obstacles.

Outmoded Attitudes

The most persistent obstacles to human development are not physical barriers, but out-dated attitudes. The original Iron Curtain across Europe was not established by the Soviet Government after World War II. It was put up by Turkish Muslims during the

Middle Ages to prevent Christian infidels from establishing a direct overland trade route to Asia. This impenetrable barrier to land transit through the Middle East forced the Europeans to seek a sea route, eventually leading to the Portuguese discovery. Once found, direct sea trade developed and the Middle East lost the opportunity to be the central trade route between Europe and the Far East.

For a brief period in the 13th Century Korea led the world in printing technology, introducing the use of metal for making printing blocks. This distinguished position was short-lived because Korean scholars refused to accept a 25 character phonetic alphabet that King Sejong developed to replace the thousands of Chinese ideographic characters then in use. A human attitude barred the way to a nation's progress. Korea's printers were soon left behind by developments elsewhere.

Fifteenth century China possessed a navy unparalleled in size, skills and technology, but their expeditions led only to dead ends. The purpose of these expeditions was to display the splendor and prowess of the Chinese emperors. They obstinately resisted foreign ways of life and discouraged trade. The Chinese developed a traditional immunity to world experience. Confucian teachings would accommodate and sequester the most astonishing novelties that mariners found. A Great Wall of the mind separated China from the rest of the planet. Ultimately, threats from the Mongols made the Chinese emperors ban all marine ventures. Fully equipped with technology, intelligence and national resources to become great discoverers, an attitude doomed them to become the discovered.

The science of medicine developed very slowly in Europe due to the reluctance of physicians to share their successful remedies, until the establishment of the Royal Society of Physicians in the 18th Century led to more open exchange of information, support for research and medical education. One of the deepest and the most widespread of human prejudices has been faith in the unaided, unmediated human senses. When the telescope was invented for seeing at a distance, prudent people were reluctant to allow the firsthand evidence of their sight to be overruled by some dubious novel device. The eminent geographer Cremonini refused to waste his time looking through Galileo's contraption just to see what "no one but Galileo had seen.... and besides, looking through those spectacles gives me a headache." A famous mathematician, Father Clarius, said Galileo first built satellite and star-like objects into the telescope glass and then pretended to see them in the sky. Distrust of the new was for long an obstacle to the development of science. Four centuries later, Charles Darwin railed against the superstitious resistance of elder scientists to ideas that contradicted established theory, going so far as to suggest an age limit on membership in scientific associations.

The absence of roads in many parts of rural France kept the population isolated, poor, uneducated and culturally backward until late in the last century. A proposal for construction of roads in rural Gascony met with strong popular resistance because people feared that it would make them vulnerable to theft. Only after the roads were finally built did the rural population come to understand the enormous practical benefits roads provided by opening markets for farm produce and bringing modern medicine, education and manufactured goods to the countryside. The resistance of French peasants to efforts by the Government to spread education arose from the belief that reading and writing were totally irrelevant to their lives.

Today outmoded attitudes bar social advancement in every field. The expansion of world trade after 1950 has been a tremendous force for stimulating job creation and raising living standards around the world. Yet fear and resistance to expansion of trade persists among Americans and Canadians to the North American Free Trade Association, among Europeans to closer economic and monetary union, and among people in every country to freer international trade under the World Trade Organization.

Anachronisms

Development is also retarded by a plethora of anachronisms which have no other raison d'être than the momentum of past habits that refuse to die. High rates of childbirth have been traditionally practiced by the poor all over the world to compensate for high rates of infant mortality. Yet even after the introduction of modern medical technology in developing countries drastically reduced infant mortality rates in the 1950s, rates of child birth remained at high levels and have taken decades to decline to a degree commensurate with improved infant survival rates. Traditional behaviors have been slow to change until the population became more educated.

Clock makers' guilds were begun in Paris (1544) and London (1630) to enforce monopolies against foreign goods. The French guilds excluded new talent, imposed exorbitant dues on their members, and restricted the number of apprentices. The English guilds were less constricting and more favorable to development of the clock makers' crafts. When demand surged for seafaring clocks and better scientific instruments of all sorts by the mercantile powers, English clock-makers were free to respond to the opportunity and prosper.

Gold was a popular form for saving personal wealth and a hedge against inflation in many countries prior to the establishment of reliable banking systems. The safety of banks and the higher returns available from other forms of investment have gradually diminished the importance of gold as a form of savings. In some Asian countries, the traditional habit of saving and paying dowry in the form of gold jewelry has continued unabated, even after more secure and financially attractive forms of savings became widely available. The people of India possess nearly 30,000 metric tons of gold valued at $300 billion, an amount roughly twice the value of the public deposits held by Indian banks. Because India must import gold for conversion into jewelry, this form of savings removes liquidity from the national economy and prevents the reinvestment of personal savings in productive activities within the country. At a time when hundreds of billions of dollars are desperately needed for investment in roads, power plants and telecommunications infrastructure, an anachronistic habit forces the nation to depend on foreign investors while it sits on a huge hoard of untapped wealth.

UNDP has calculated that $40 billion a year would be sufficient to eradicate global poverty within ten years. Yet long after the end of the Cold War and at a time when there is not even a serious potential enemy in sight, world military expenditure remains at $850 billion a year. The war is over, but a costly, wasteful, unproductive anachronism persists.

It is possible to cite instances in which perceptual blind spots, unwarranted fears, provincial attitudes and anachronistic habits limit development in every country and every field of life. The rare few that are willing to concede that physical resources may not impose severe limits on human progress are very likely to insist that the fixed character of human nature does. History contains a record of infinite potentials discovered and countless opportunities missed due to a lack of perception, tradition-bound attitudes and insistence on anachronistic behaviors. But history also reports innumerable instances in which humanity has demonstrated the capacity to draw appropriate knowledge from its experience, overcome its limited vision and fixed behaviors and take major developmental leaps forward. In his introduction to the Brandt Commission Report, Former German Chancellor Willy Brandt expressed his hope that the problems created by men can be solved by men. Any attempt to formulate a comprehensive theory of social development must reflect the central role of human beings in both determining and overcoming self-imposed limits on social progress.

Central Thesis

Current debate in the field of development often focuses on the importance that should be given to different economic and social outcomes and the most effective policies to achieve them. Although this discussion has importance, it tends to distract attention from more fundamental issues that need to be addressed, regardless of which goals are accorded the highest priority.

A theory of development needs to begin not with goals and policies to promote development, but with knowledge of the essential nature and characteristics of development itself, for development is not a set of policies or programs or results. It is a *process*. This process has been taking place in societies since time immemorial, but it has acquired greater intensity and velocity during the past five hundred years and has accelerated rapidly over the past five decades. In the broadest terms applicable to all societies and historical periods, *development can be defined as an upward directional movement of society from lesser to greater levels of energy, efficiency, quality, productivity, complexity, comprehension, creativity, mastery, enjoyment and accomplishment.*

Although the term development is most commonly applied to economic advancement, the term applies equally to political, social and technological progress as well. Indeed, it is extremely difficult to extricate any of these fields of change entirely from the others, for they are all various expressions or dimensions of the wider development of the human collective. However, for the purposes of this discussion, we propose to focus on the field of economic development and consider other fields only at the points where they most directly interact with and influence economic progress. At the same time, we will try to establish that the same process and the same principles are applicable to all other fields of social life as well.

Many factors influence and determine the outcome of this process. There must be a motive force that drives social change, some essential preconditions for that change to occur, barriers that obstruct the process, a variety of resources such as capital and technology which contribute to the process, along with several types and levels of infrastructure that support it. All of these factors need to find an appropriate place in a comprehensive theory. However, there is one central characteristic that most clearly distinguishes development from other forms of social change, but whose importance may not always be appreciated because it is largely non-material in nature. That characteristic is organization. *The essential nature of the process is the progressive development of social organizations and institutions that harness and direct the social energies for higher levels of accomplishment. Society develops by organizing all the knowledge, human energies and material resources at its disposal to fulfill its aspirations.*

Human Centred Approach

Recent thought places emphasis on human development as something distinct and different from economic growth. In establishing priorities and strategies, this distinction can be useful. There is abundant evidence to show that high rates of economic growth do not necessarily lead to rapid improvements in living standards for poorer sections of the population and that greater improvement in these living standards can be achieved by strategies that do not focus exclusively on growth. This distinction focuses on development priorities and the strategies, not on the essential nature of the development process itself. A comprehensive theory must be human centred, but not just in the sense of insisting that human beings are the rightful beneficiaries of social progress. It has also to view human beings as the source and primary motive force for development. Development is the process of human beings developing. It is the energy of people seeking to fulfill their aspirations that serves as its driving force. People's awareness and comprehension determines the direction of the social movement. The efficiency, productivity, innovation, creativity and organizational capacities of people determine the level of accomplishment and enjoyment. Society progresses by developing and bringing forth into expression the higher potentialities of its members. The extent of people's education, the intensity of their aspirations and energy, the quality of their attitudes and values, skills and information are crucial determinants of the process. For this reason, *we conclude that the same principles of development are applicable to the development of all levels and units of human existence — individuals, organizations, social sectors, nations and the international community.* They are all expressions of the same process by which human beings acquire greater capacities and express these capacities in more productive activities.

In earlier millennia the human resource was primarily a physical instrument for manual labour, much like other work animals. Society has now developed to the point that the individual's mental capabilities are called more and more into play. By this process, the productivity of the human being has already risen a thousand-fold. The individual who drove a bullock cart now flies an airplane or steers a ship capable of carrying huge payloads. What an individual could or could not produce in a lifetime, he or she now produces in a month or a week or a day. This process of increasing productivity is still going on. A study of this process suggests that it could continue indefinitely and without limit. As we presently utilize only a tiny fraction of the sunlight that shines upon the earth, people presently utilize only a tiny portion of their individual potentials and social opportunities. Societies also utilize only a tiny portion of their potentials. The most limiting barriers to human development are not physical. They are limitations in knowledge, vision, attitudes and aspiration for higher accomplishment. A valid theory must be able to explain the central role of these intangible factors in the development process.

Survival, Growth and Development

Our definition of development distinguishes it from two other social processes, survival and growth. Survival is the process by which a community sustains itself at the minimum level needed for its existence without any manifest tendencies for horizontal expansion or vertical advancement. A society existing at the level of survival has sufficient energy to meet the most basic human needs, but no surplus available to enhance life at the present level or to direct toward higher levels of achievement.

At the next level are societies that have grown beyond the minimum level needed for survival, but remain organized along the same lines as in the past. People in these societies may be spurred by the availability of improved technology or the example of other communities to increase their level of effort, expand the scope of their activities, and adopt modified methods or techniques, but life remains organized essentially the same as before. A quadrupling of oil prices in the mid 1970s enabled oil exporting countries in the Middle East to dramatically increase GDP and per capita incomes with little change in the organization or productivity of the society. Since Okinawa was returned to Japan by the USA in 1972, the heavy dependence of the island economy on US military bases has been replaced by dependence on transfer payments and investments in infrastructure by the Japanese Government, resulting in higher incomes and improved living standards. But the basic organization of economic activities remains the same.

Development is distinguished from survival and growth by the emergence of new or higher levels of organization. In this case there is not merely a quantitative increase in the level of activity or accomplishment but a qualitative change in the way the activity is carried out in society. Prior to the development of standing armies, the entire society was called upon to defend the community in times of war. The division of society into military and civilian components enabled the community to develop economically at the same time as it expanded or defended itself militarily. The shift from nomadic grazing to sedentary agriculture marks a major development in agriculture. Not only do the techniques differ. The organization of the activity is far more sophisticated. Instead of going out in search for harvestable crops and then migrating on to greener pastures, the farmer gathers all the necessary resources, selects and cultivates appropriate crops and sets aside a portion of the produce as seed material for the following season. The transition from a rural agrarian to an urban commercial economy, from commercial to industrial and from industrial to service economy are major developmental changes in the structure and organization of society. Similar transitions occur within each field of social activity as well.

Growth is the process of expansion or proliferation of activities at any established level of development in the continuum from primitive tribal and agrarian societies to technologically advanced industrial societies. Growth and development are distinct processes, but they are also closely interrelated, complementary and mutually supportive. Development of the society to a higher level may be preceded, accompanied or followed by significant growth in different fields. Development in narrower fields also leads to growth of the society as a whole. In either case *we apply the term development to connote the qualitative vertical movement to a higher level of performance and the term growth to connote the quantitative horizontal expansion of activities at whatever level of organization the society has reached in a particular field.*

The phenomenal achievements of the Marshall Plan in promoting rapid economic recovery and growth in Europe after the Second World War may have blurred the distinction between growth and development. Based on West Germany's post war experience, it was easy to conclude that a large infusion of capital could achieve rapid advancement in the eastern part of the country. In reality, the two cases are very different. Germany's remarkable recovery after the war is primarily an expression of growth. The physical infrastructure and industrial capacity that had been destroyed during the war were quickly rebuilt. The productive skills and social attitudes of the population were already prepared by the country's past experience and accomplishments. They did not have to be created. In contrast, the task in East Germany since

1990 has been to rapidly establish new political, administrative and economic systems. The infusion of enormous amounts of fresh capital stimulated the growth of construction and commerce, but it has not and cannot by itself bring about these structural changes. Inadvertently it may even have aggravated the task of development by raising high expectations among the population in East Germany that their living standards would be lifted to the level of their western countrymen by central government aid and programs, rather than by their own initiative to acquire more progressive attitudes, more productive skills and more efficient social organizations.

The remainder of this paper focuses on the required conditions, essential ingredients and stages of the process of development at many different levels of society and in many different fields. Except in this context, it will not be concerned with the process of growth as it is governed and described by basic principles of economics.

Conscious Development

Human development proceeds from experience to comprehension. In the course of development, society accumulates the experience derived from the initiative of countless individuals and gradually formulates from it a conscious understanding of the secrets of success in different fields of activity. Experience comes first and full comprehension usually comes long afterwards. In this sense, we can say that the normal process of development is subconscious in that it is carried out before this conscious understanding has been fully acquired. We use the term *subconscious* to refer to those instances in which human beings pursue a new line of activity in any field without a conscious knowledge of the end results toward which they are moving, the obstacles and essential conditions for success, and the stages and principles governing the process of accomplishment.

Societies progress through the combined efforts of countless individuals and small groups, most of whom are only aware of and motivated to achieve their own limited goals. Yet the adoption of shared goals and common or similar strategies by these individuals and groups is utilized to elevate the society and fulfill the underlying intentions of the social collective. That which develops is the society. The society consists of diverse and divergent groups of individuals. The accomplishments of the society are the subconscious outcome and resultant expression of the combined aspirations and efforts of this heterogeneous collective.

Natural versus Planned Development

A further distinction needs to be made between the natural process of social development and planned development initiatives by governments. Natural development is the spontaneous, subconscious progression of society; planned development is the effort of governments to accelerate social progress through special policies and programs. Natural development is always subconscious. Planned development is mostly subconscious, but has the potential of becoming conscious, if the country's leaders are able to acquire a comprehensive knowledge and apply it in the formulation and implementation of development strategies.

The theory needs to make clear the precise nature of the differences and similarities between planned and spontaneous development. In the case of planned development, government is the initiator of the process utilizing its capacity to set direction and policy for the society. In the case of natural development, individuals, groups of individuals and organizations are the initiators. But apart from this, is there really a fundamental distinction between the process of development in these two instances? Our conclusion is that there is not. The principles governing the process remain the same, regardless of who initiates or how it is initiated. This implies that the success of any planned development effort will depend on the degree to which it succeeds in fulfilling the conditions and imitating the stages of natural development.

Green Revolution

One of the most dramatic illustrations of a conscious, planned development initiative by government was the Green Revolution in India. Until the mid 1960s, agriculture in India did not differ significantly from the way it was carried out during the two centuries of British colonial rule that ended in 1947. The Green Revolution involved the introduction of new hybrid varieties of wheat developed in Mexico and the term is commonly used as a synonym for the introduction of new technology in agriculture. But the most significant characteristic of Green Revolution was not technological. It was a planned initiative by the Indian Government to raise the organization of agriculture in Indian society to a higher level.

Prior to Green Revolution, the structure of Indian agriculture consisted of subsistence level farming by isolated individual producers, primarily for their own consumption. This structure generated inadequate overall production to meet the needs of an expanding population, periodic shortages and recurring threats of famine, which had only been avoided after 1947 by imports of increasingly large quantities of food grains. Green Revolution was a comprehensive and integrated strategy to transform the organization of Indian agriculture into a closely coordinated national system capable of producing sufficient surpluses to meet the needs of the entire population and to achieve national self-sufficiency in food grains.

The Indian Government recognized that to be successful, it would be necessary to convince the farmer that the new technology could generate significantly higher yields, to ensure that the higher yields would be readily purchased without a drastic fall in farm prices, to provide for large scale import and domestic production of hybrid seeds, fertilizers and pesticides, to establish sufficient warehouse capacity to store larger volumes of food grain, to undertake research and extension activities to adapt the varieties to Indian conditions, and to educate farmers, extension workers and scientists on the new agricultural practices.

The Green Revolution strategy accomplished these multiple objectives through the establishment of a number of new quasi-governmental organizations. The Food Corporation of India was set up and empowered to purchase surplus grains from production centers and distribute them for marketing in food deficit areas, effectively establishing a national market for food grains for the first time. The Agricultural Pricing Commission was constituted to guarantee farmers a remunerative price for their produce. Other agencies were established to import and expand production of essential inputs, expand warehousing facilities, coordinate agricultural research and educational activities. This comprehensive strategy provided economic incentives to the farmer for increased production as well as financial and social incentives to agricultural scientists to embrace the new technology. A national program was conducted involving 100,000 demonstration plots in farmers' fields to convince the farmers that the new varieties would be remunerative.

Green Revolution was not only a planned initiative of the government. It was also a conscious initiative, conceived and implemented according to a time-bound plan to achieve well-defined goals and objectives very rapidly. Unlike many other planned development initiatives, it was based on a full and correct understanding of the real needs, aspirations, and preparedness of the society and on a knowledge of what was needed to release the energy and elicit the active participation of the society. The program succeeded because it was able to create a higher level of social organization and it was able to mobilize the energy, enthusiasm and capacities of scientists and farmers.

Planned development differs from natural development in that it is an attempt by government to initiate and accelerate a process of change that would otherwise take place more slowly or perhaps not at all. The success of any planned development effort depends on its ability to provide the necessary conditions and elements required for natural development. The stages that both processes must traverse and the principles that govern them are otherwise the same.

Many planned development efforts fail because they are initiated with insufficient understanding of the essential conditions and the steps necessary to mimic the natural social process. In the early years, the organizational innovations launched to support the Green Revolution were primarily controlled and managed by governments. But that fact is only incidental. The important point is that these organizations were effectively integrated with the activities of the society and attuned to support its development. During the 1960s, only government in India possessed the necessary resources and organizational capabilities to bring about such a massive organizational change so rapidly. Were comparable programs to be introduced today, the private sector could be called upon to play a much more active role. The achievement of national food self-sufficiency within five years and a doubling of total food grain production within a decade confounded the expectations of the experts and exceeded even the most optimistic projections. But the ultimate accomplishment of India's Green Revolution was to elevate the entire social organization of agricultural production and marketing in the country to a far higher level. This remarkable achievement illustrates the power of planned development when it is undertaken with conscious knowledge

New Activities in Society

If the emergence of more complex and efficient levels of organization is the essential characteristic of development, then we must ask what is the process that stimulates the emergence of new organizations, what are the stages through which it proceeds and the agents that determine its direction. The theory must be able to adequately explain the conditions that determine the onset of new activities, the response of society to the activities, and the speed of their propagation.

It is our view that *development occurs when the subconscious preparedness of society leads to generates new ideas and conscious initiatives by individuals. The accumulated surplus energy of society releases the initiative of pioneers who apply new ideas, acquire new skills and introduce new types of activities. Imitation of successful pioneers eventually attracts the attention and overcomes the resistance of conservative forces in society, leading the society to accept and embrace the new activity by establishing customs, laws, and other organizational mechanisms to actively support its propagation. At a further stage the activity is promoted through education and family until it becomes a social institution and is assimilated into the social culture.* This process can be described in terms of three phases: social preparedness, the initiative of pioneers, and assimilation by the society.

Social Preparedness for Development

The potentials for development always far exceed the initiative of society to exploit them. The actual achievements of society depend on the measure that it is ready to actively respond to new opportunities and challenges. That response is the real determinant of development. Three fundamental conditions determine a society's level of preparedness: energy, awareness and aspiration.

Energy

The first condition is the availability of surplus energy. Development is an expression of social creativity. It requires an immense investment of creative energy for society to experiment with new modes of activity, take the risks associated with change, break the active resistance and passive inertia of fixed habits, raise standards of functioning to higher levels, acquire new skills and build higher order organizations. Moving from one level of social organization to another requires the accumulation of surplus energy as in the conversion of matter from a liquid to a gaseous state. Development is the result of surplus energy moving vertically and being organized at a higher level, rather than merely being expended in horizontal expansion at the same level. The higher level organization is able to utilize the energy more productively.

Surplus energy is available only when the society is not fully absorbed in meeting the challenges of existence at the current level. The production of material surpluses and high levels of movement and exchange are indices that surplus energy is available for development. Surpluses are a measure of accomplishment and mastery at the previous level of development. The accumulation of surpluses has been a stimulus for growth of civilizations throughout history. The production of agricultural surpluses by Athenian farmers prompted Athens to open up trade routes and become a major commercial power in the ancient world. Arthur Lewis noted the central role played in the Industrial Revolution by the growing prosperity of English farmers resulting from the commercialization of English agriculture in the previous century.

The generation of new ideas, scientific experimentation and technical innovation are also symptomatic of surplus energy. When material needs are met and social activities have become highly organized, the mind becomes increasingly active and creative. People conceive of new possibilities and mentally explore new opportunities. The breakdown of feudalism and waning of Church authority in Western Europe unleashed an explosion of new ideas and creativity during the Renaissance. The energy liberated by greater political, social and intellectual freedom ushered in the great mercantile age.

Energy is the fuel for growth in individuals, organizations and societies. Highly creative and accomplished people are often characterized by the high levels of energy they exude and by their capacity for non-stop work. Indomitable energy has been an outstanding trait of great political leaders such as Napoleon, Churchill and Gandhi and business leaders such as Andrew Carnegie, Henry Ford, and Tom Watson of IBM. Inventor Thomas Alva Edison was known to work for days on end without sleep in the process of developing 1,100 patentable inventions and founding the General Electric Company. Organizations that are growing rapidly share the same characteristic, which is apparent even to casual visitors to high tech companies in Silicon Valley. Energy is highly visible in progressive urban centers around the globe, from New York and London to Hong Kong and Tokyo. It is, therefore, not surprising that this characteristic is found abundant in societies that have achieved high levels of development or that it becomes increasingly pervasive as societies enter the take-off phase.

The importance of surplus energy is most dramatically illustrated by two conditions under which it is unable to accumulate or express itself – war and dictatorship. War destroys infrastructure and interferes with production and trade. It physically saps the energy and resources of a country. The threat of war keeps those energies perpetually directed toward self-defence, rather than self-development. Dictatorship, on the other hand, can spur development efforts up to a point, using the threat or pressure of coercion to channel initiative in desired directions. But dictatorship also blocks the free emergence of new ideas and fresh initiatives, which are the seeds of social innovation. It can ensure obedience to authority but does not spur entrepreneurship and innovation. The end of feudalism in Western Europe was an important contributor to the onset of the mercantile era and the founding of the great European commercial empires. The further transition from monarchy to democracy stabilized the internal order and provided the social foundations for the Industrial Revolution. It stimulated innovation by encouraging the free exchange of ideas and provided incentives for greater individual effort by legally safeguarding property from arbitrary confiscation.

Awareness

Surplus social energy collects as potential beneath the surface, accumulating until it acquires sufficient force to burst out in new activities. It expresses initially in society as increasing thought and discussion about new possibilities, an urge for innovation and improvement, and growing dissatisfaction with the status quo. But the mobilization of this energy for action depends on fulfillment of a second essential condition — awareness of new development opportunities and challenges. Societies that are fully consumed by the struggle for survival have little time or inclination to direct their attention outward to observe what other societies are accomplishing or forward to envision new possibilities. When life reaches a certain level of stable comfort, societies become increasingly interested in and aware of what is going on in the world around them. This awareness may also be thrust on a society by the unwanted intrusion of an external influence. The influx of English manufactured goods into the pre-industrial economies of Europe and the arrival of a modern armed American fleet in Tokyo harbor in the 19th Century both had the effect of awakening societies to the opportunities and challenges of development and stimulating them to respond.

The increasing pace of development over the past five centuries is directly linked to an increase in the speed and reliability of information about what is taking place in other parts of the country, region and world due to improvements in communication and transportation. The proliferation of books and newspapers following the invention and diffusion of the printing press and the growth of international shipping following the invention of navigation aids beginning in the 15th Century, the growth of railways, telegraph, and telephones in the 19th Century, and the impact of radio, film, television, computers and satellite technology in the 20th Century have exponentially multiplied the dissemination of information and the general level of social awareness. Today more than 60,000 newspapers are published around the globe, including 8000 dailies, with a combined circulation of 500 million and an estimated readership of 1.5 billion people.

Aspiration

Energy provides the fuel and awareness helps to set the direction for social progress, but one other condition must be met to unleash the development process. The society must feel a strong aspiration or felt need for achievement at a higher level that spurs efforts to convert a perceived possibility into a material reality. Social development is an expression of social will seeking to elevate the performance of the collective. As the society becomes more conscious of the external environment and its own internal potentials, its aspiration and will for progress increase. The greater the knowledge of its potentials, the greater the aspiration.

History tells us of many accomplished societies in the past that generated surplus wealth and leisure time and yet chose not to respond to opportunities, even when presented with information about the successful accomplishments of other societies. Many development workers have encountered communities in which the aspiration for further development appeared to be absent. Such incidences contradict prevalent assumptions about human motivation and are often dismissed as bizarre or primitive exceptions.

A closer observation reveals that this phenomenon is far more common than we may assume in societies, organizations and individuals. The theory needs to explain the circumstances under which the motivation for development is released as well as those under which it may be curtailed by accomplishment.

Castes, classes and communities within countries respond differently to achievements and new ways of life adopted by those whom they view as socially or culturally inferior. Thus, the aristocracy of France refused to engage in commerce as an activity beneath their station. Successful French businessmen made haste to purchase royal patents of nobility and withdraw from commercial activity. Their counterparts in England invested in commercial ventures resulting in a fusion of the landed nobility and merchant class, facilitating the remarkable economic growth of Britain in the 17th and 18th Centuries. The educated classes in some countries respond in similar fashion to opportunities that are viewed as beneath their social station, even when the financial rewards are substantial.

Awareness of a development opportunity also fails to evoke a response from the population when it is perceived to be beyond their means to accomplish. This explains why poorer individuals and societies sometimes do not respond to the accomplishments of the rich, even when the same opportunity is open to all, why the less educated assume they cannot emulate the achievements of the more educated, and why rural communities may ignore the achievements of urban centers.

Failures to respond to opportunities arising out of a sense of social superiority or social inferiority are expressions of a common principle. People respond to the example of those with whom they identify socially. *When there is awareness of a developmental achievement by one belonging to the same social and cultural context, it can evoke a powerful urge for accomplishment in society.* When the achievement is by one who lies outside the context, it is often ignored. Thus, the adoption of new crops and cultivation practices by a wealthy farmer may not lead to similar behaviour by smaller farmers in the same community. Age, social status, class, caste, wealth, occupation and other factors help define social identity.

There was a time when different societies, classes and groups within societies differed widely in the extent to which they manifested an aspiration for development. This is no longer as true. Over the past five decades both awareness of the possibility and the release of the aspiration for development have been spreading rapidly from one country and level of society to another. Harlan Cleveland coined the phrase "revolution of rising expectations" to describe this phenomenon which he observed in Eastern Asia in the early 1950s. Spurred by the end of colonialism and the diffusion of democracy, since then this revolution has circled the globe and ignited a clamor for education, higher levels of consumption and opportunities for advancement among billions of people. The universal awakening of this urge for progress is another compelling reason why the speed of development is increasing so rapidly.

This principle has important implications for planned development efforts. It implies that efforts by government to initiate development will only be successful in areas where the necessary social urge and preparedness already exist. Many well-conceived development initiatives fail to catch on or go awry because the leaders try to accomplish what the population has not yet come to aspire for. In these instances, the planned initiative can only contribute to preparing the society for readiness at some future date, but will not generate immediate results.

Surplus energy, awareness of opportunities and aspiration for advancement are pre-conditions that prepare society for new development initiatives. This is not a linear process. The three factors interact with one another in complex ways to generate a growing pressure and ground swell of new activities. Accomplishment at a previous level helps release energy and aspiration for further accomplishment. Energy makes for greater alertness and awareness. Awareness of what others are doing evokes greater aspirations and provokes energetic responses. The process spirals back on itself, constantly reinforcing the forward momentum, while at the same time each new level of achievement brings a certain measure of satisfaction and security that relieve the pressure for further effort. Alternations between rising urge and rising satisfaction are one reason for the modulating rhythm of progress and stagnation that is often observed.

Role of the Pioneer in Development

When these three factors are present in requisite measure, the society is subconsciously prepared for change. But it still needs an agent through which to express this preparedness in action. In natural development, that is the role of pioneering individuals. Once the society is prepared, sooner or later it gives rise to the initiative of one or more pioneering individuals who break out from the existing mold and attempt something new. Although exceptional and eccentric individuals may initiate new activities in any society, these activities usually disappear with passing of their founder or give rise to isolated imitation that never acquires significant momentum. The development pioneer is a conscious product of the society whose aspiration and initiative give expression to the subconscious aspiration of the society in which he lives.

Every new developmental activity is initially conceived and introduced by one or a few pioneers. The pioneer is one who sees, believes in and acts upon an opportunity which others fail to see or believe in or lack the energy or courage to pursue. The pioneer exhibits a new understanding, new attitudes, new skills and behaviors different from those prevalent in the community at the time. If the pioneer's initiative is in tune with the social aspiration and social preparedness, it inspires and encourages other dynamic individuals to imitate or improve upon the new initiative.

Pioneers play a crucial role wherever a new activity needs to be seeded in the community for the first time. The first farmer in a village to shift from rice cultivation or sugarcane to growing fruits or flowers for export; the first teacher in a rural town to leave the security of a salaried job to establish a private tutorial institute, and the first industrialist to acquire a new manufacturing technology from overseas all serve as role models and catalysts for development in their respective fields of activity. Viewed from the perspective of the individual, it is the pioneer who initiates the collective process. But *viewed from the perspective of the society, it is the collective that expresses its intention and aspiration through the initiative of the pioneer.*

The role of the pioneer is vital to development, because the next stage of social progress almost always remains unseen by the collective. It is the free thinking, far seeking individual who dares to imagine or conceive what the popular mind is unaware of and then translates that vague possibility into a reality which all can see. Henry Ford became a pioneer and model for American industry early in this century by popularizing methods for mass production. Fred Smith, founder of Federal Express, pioneered creation of a new industry, the overnight parcel delivery business. The pioneer is usually not a rare exception or anomaly in society. He shares to a large degree its aspirations, knowledge and values. By acquiring one new or different attribute or behaviour, he charts a new course and reveals a new possibility, all the time basing himself on the society's present accomplishments and in most cases moving in a direction which the society has already indicated.

Multiplier Effect

It does not really matter whether pioneers come forward on their own internal prompting or in response to an opportunity or demonstration created by government. In either case, the individual embodies and represents the social initiative. What does matter is the response of the society to the pioneer. Often the early pioneer meets with a response of indifference, resistance, contempt or hostility from the community around him, especially when his actions represent a radical departure from the status quo. This usually occurs when the pioneer comes too much before his time, before the society is fully ready to act on its urge for something new. At other times the successful pioneer is actively admired and respected, yet no one else comes forward to imitate his success. In either case, the pioneer's initiative fails to catch on. *If the pioneer pushes through change before the society is fully prepared, the change comes abruptly in the form of a revolution. If the society is fully prepared to accept and follow the pioneer, then the change occurs by a smooth evolution. Revolution is premature evolution.*

Under appropriate conditions, the success of the pioneer leads to active imitation by other adventurous individuals who in turn serve as models for still others to imitate. In this case, the initiative of the pioneer gets multiplied over and over, rippling through the society and unleashing a development movement. The establishment of the first retail photocopy shop at a prominent location in New Delhi in the late 1970s by the owner of a typing service was an initiative whose time was right. Competing typing companies in the city quickly imitated the pioneer. Within three years the new business had spread like wildfire throughout the country. The adventurous farmer who dug the first successful borewell in a poor, backward South Indian village was initially an isolated example that others refused to follow. But when other farmers in the village saw how the pioneer's social position was elevated by his new-found wealth, every other farmer in the village rushed to emulate him. Within two years, 440 new wells had been dug in ten surrounding villages. When India's first software export company was founded in the 1970s, it was difficult for anyone to conceive that within a short span of time hundreds of companies would follow its example. Today India has become a world class competitor in software services with exports projected to exceed $6 billion by year 2000. Knowing how to create the appropriate conditions for unleashing the multiplier effect is essential for formulating effective planned development strategies.

Organizing New Social Activities

The surplus energy accumulated by the society and given expression through the initiative of pioneers and their followers does not gain momentum until it becomes accepted and organized by the society. The process of organization may take many different forms. It may occur by the enactment of new laws or regulations that support the activity or it may be in the form of a new system or accepted set of practices. Each development advance of the society ushers in new and higher levels of organization. Rapid expansion of commerce in Europe during the 16th and 17th Centuries necessitated development of the banking system throughout Europe, as well as commercial laws and courts for civil arbitration. The huge sums required for investment in international trade gave rise to the creation of new legal entities, such as the joint stock company, which enabled individual investors to pool resources.

Each significant developmental advance leads to the emergence of a host of new organizations designed to support it and puts pressure on existing organizations to elevate their functioning to meet the higher demands of the new phase. Since 1950, country after country has been introducing organizational systems and structures to support modern business and international trade, such as business directories, franchising, lease purchase financing for industrial and consumer products, courier delivery services, credit rating and collection agencies, industrial estates, free trade zones, credit card and ATM banking services, cellular and pager communication systems, and most recently a completely new range of Internet services. Each of these organizational innovations increases the range, scope, quality, convenience, productivity or efficiency with which the available social energies can be utilized for productive purposes. The role of these organizations is most apparent in instances when they are absent. When the countries of Eastern Europe began the transition from centrally planned to market economies, they lacked many of supporting structures and practices needed for a market system to operate effectively.

One of the most effective ways in which society actively supports the organization of new activities is through the organization of formal educational and vocational training programs.

Organization Matures into Institution

At a further stage, the society accepts and assimilates the new way of functioning to such an extent that it no longer requires the support of specialized organizations, policies or laws to promote it. The activity becomes a part of the normal way the society functions. It becomes a way of life. It matures from the stage of organization to institution. An organization matures into an institution when the social acceptance becomes total. An organization is maintained by human or social agencies. An institution is self-existent. It is supported by the customs, beliefs and social tradition. It does not require agents to support and maintain it. Law is an organization upheld by the power and authority of the legislature and legislative systems, police and penal systems, courts and judicial systems. Competition is an institution upheld by the weight of social tradition that is imparted to the individual by the family, fostered through the educational system and embodied in the free enterprise system, but not dependent on any of these agencies for its existence and expression. Organizations at one stage of development give rise to institutions at a later stage. The maturation of a new activity does not necessarily mean that the formal organizations established to support it disappear, but rather they are no longer an essential support for its existence.

Cultural Transmission by the Family

At an advanced stage in the maturation of a new social activity, the family assumes an active role in its propagation. Family is a miniature of the society. The basic organization of society comes from the organization of family. Family imparts essential social training to its members in self-restraint, responsibility, human relations and goal-directed behaviors. Once a new activity has been accepted as desirable by wide sections of the population, families assume an increasing role in equipping the next generation with knowledge, skills and attitudes supportive of the activity. The hereditary transmission of occupation from father to son has taken place for millennia. Today children are no longer as likely to enter the same field as their parents, but they still acquire basic skills and attitudes that influence their occupation. When an activity has matured to the point that family plays a very active role in its transmission, the activity has become a part of the culture of the society.

The Powers of Organization

Viewed from a historical perspective, the process of development appears as an unlimited cornucopia perpetually spilling forth an astonishingly lavish array of new riches. A theory of development must be able to account for this phenomenal capacity of the society and reveal the source of its creative powers. This theory identifies organization as the principle source of this prodigious social creativity.

Organization is the thread out of which the fabric of development is woven. Every step of social advancement involves an elevation in the way acts are carried out. Organization is a tremendous creative power. Henry Ford's organization of manufacturing operations enabled him to increase automobile production 500-fold, with a small amount of capital and without any significant advancement in technology. When Ford introduced the system of mass production, the average US car-maker produced 1000 to 2000 cars a year. Ford raised production to over one million cars a year. Between 1908 and 1927, his company produced more than 15 million automobiles. In the process, he reduced the time required for assembling a chassis from 728 minutes of one worker's time to 93 minutes and brought down the price of the cars he sold from $950 to $290. Starting out with a cash base of $28,000 in 1903, by 1927 the company had accumulated a cash surplus of nearly $700 million – a 25,000-fold increase in 24 years! In the 21st Century organization will fully emerge as the primary source of productivity and wealth.

What then is the source of the vast productive power of organization? Action or work is physical. Organization is a power of the human mind. Mind has the capacity to relate and combine individual acts to form systems that can be repeated over and over again to accomplish the maximum results with the least investment of time, energy and resources. Systems are miniature organizations. Social organizations are collections of systems coordinated in space and time to achieve specific results. The introduction of organization elevates action from the physical to the mental level.

A market is a simple form of organization to bring together buyers and sellers at a particular place and specific time for purchase or exchange of goods with less expenditure of time and energy. The more advanced the organization, the greater its capacity to channel social energies efficiently to achieve greater results. The development of retailing from the small family-owned corner store to the modern department store to the mail order catalogue and the Internet illustrate the impact of increasingly sophisticated organization on any field of activity.

The development of organization in society takes place both in the horizontal and vertical plane. It spreads horizontally at each level to cover the entire society with its systems. It rises vertically to achieve higher levels of complexity and higher standards of performance. The horizontal expansion of organization increases its reach and extends its access. The vertical elevation of organization raises its skills, efficiency and productivity.

Education is a mental system for organizing facts. It is also a social organization for transmitting the essence of society's cumulative experience to future generations in a concentrated and abridged form. It combines systems for the collection and categorization of knowledge, for presentation, preparation and guidance of teachers, and for instruction and evaluation of students. Over the past few centuries the organization of education in different countries has been expanding horizontally to cover the entire population at the level of primary and secondary school level. It has also been rising vertically to attain higher levels of quality, making available a greater depth and breadth of knowledge in more fields. As an advanced manufacturing system is capable of producing enormous quantities of high quality products with minimum cost and wastage, an advanced educational system imparts the maximum knowledge and develops the mental abilities of the population to the maximum extent in the minimum time.

In a similar manner, advanced commercial organizations expand horizontally and vertically to promote the maximum volume of business and wealth generation. They acquire the ability to mobilize the energies and capacities of large numbers of people, to master and apply a wide array of sophisticated production technologies, to mobilize large amounts of capital, to utilize a wide range of resources and infrastructure facilities to achieve higher levels of efficiency and productivity. The horizontal expansion of the banking system enables the society to mobilize household savings and lend funds to qualified borrowers. In India a fivefold multiplication of bank branches throughout the country between 1966 and 1979 contributed to a fivefold increase in bank deposits within a 13-year period. At the same time, the establishment of higher order specialized financial agencies with expertise in specific sectors has supported growth of investment in fields such as agriculture, industry and exports. Computerization has recently begun to improve the efficiency, quality and range of banking services.

The stock exchange is an organization that enables those with surplus savings to invest in productive enterprises that require capital for their growth and that can utilize it profitability to create greater wealth. Access for investors is made possible by a system of brokers who are authorized by the exchange to buy and sell securities. Originally brokers had to be physically situated at the exchange in order to monitor performance of different stocks and perform transactions. Technology now enables brokers to access information and conduct trades from anywhere in the world. It is even permits investors to by-pass the broker and conduct transactions for themselves, thereby changing the nature of the organization. The creation of more sophisticated investment products such as mutual funds, futures and derivatives has elevated the organization of investment to a higher level that incorporates more variables and can be used to reduce the risk of specific events. As a result of these advances, the process of raising money, trading securities and investing surplus funds has been made far more productive than ever before.

Skills of Society

The emphasis of development theory on social organizations and institutions is certainly not new. In the study cited earlier, Morris and Adelman identified five major categories of development theory that recognize the central role of institutional changes in development. These theories differ as to which institutional changes are most significant and as to the motive force that brings about these changes. None of the theories adequately explains the relationship between the social organizations that drive the development process and the underlying society that undergoes this process. Organization is simply presented as an important factor with no organic relationship to the society in which it arises. *This theory attempts to show that social organizations are a natural outgrowth and projection of emerging energy, knowledge, skills and values in the society. They are at once the means and the expression of society's development.*

We have explained earlier how the initiative of the pioneer can lead to imitation by other pioneers and eventual acceptance of a new activity in society. What we are actually describing is the process by which the society acquires new skills. Individuals or organized group of individuals attempt a new activity one or more times until they discover a way to conduct the activity successfully. In the process, they acquire the knowledge, skills and values necessary for the new activity. Those who imitate the pioneers also acquire these knowledge, skills and values. At a later stage the society learns how to encourage and support the new activity on a wider scale. It does this by disseminating the knowledge, skills and values acquired by individuals in the past and by institutionalizing them in the form of social systems. The activity matures into an organization. The acquisition by the society of the capacity to propagate the new activity is the acquisition of a new skill by the society.

Society is a developing organization of activities. A crucial determinant of social productivity is society's capacity for coordinated, systematic functioning. Individuals increase their productivity and effectiveness by acquiring and applying higher and higher levels of physical, social and mental skills to carry out their activities. Skills enable the individual to channel and control physical movements and nervous energies to achieve mental objectives. In the absence of skills, energy is wasted and results are poor. The difference in productivity between the untrained two-fingered typist and the professional secretary may be tenfold or more. The difference in quality between the amateur violinist and the accomplished maestro is immeasurable.

The same differences exist in the quality and productivity of work in organizations and societies. Commercial organizations rise in effectiveness by elevating the quality of the systems they employ to perform routine functions. Systems are the skills of an organization that channel and direct its energies for maximum results. The remarkable growth of the Ford Motor Company was achieved by introducing a complex arrangement of physical and administrative systems designed to control the flow of materials, parts and finished products through 50,000 square feet of chutes, conveyors, tubes, hoists and assembly lines and to track purchases, inventory, job routing, labour productivity, shipping and accounting transactions with great precision. So elaborate and impressive was the organization that it prompted a reporter for a local newspaper to sum up his impression of the new factory in three words, "System, System, System."

Like the individual and the organization, societies develop by effectively directing and channelling their energies by continuously increasing the organizational efficiency with which they execute every type of activity. As skills direct the energies of the individual and systems direct the energies of the organization, organizations direct the energies of the society. Organizations constitute the skills of society. These social systems are of many types, both formal and informal. They cover the actions and interactions within and between every field of social activity. A comparison of any two countries at different levels of development will reveal significant differences in the level and sophistication of the systems they employ to carry out activities. The effectiveness of organization is determined by its authority, complexity, and capacity for coordination and integration with social needs.

Organization with Society

Organization is the mechanism by which the surplus energy in society is harnessed, mobilized, directed and channeled to produce greater results. Organization derives energy from being integrated with the society in which it functions. The energy of the society comes from its needs and aspirations. This energy pervades the social organizations established to meet these needs. The more finely the organization is tuned to fulfill underlying social aspirations, the greater the energy flowing through it. Development does not occur by the mere importation and superimposition of foreign institutions. The organization of East

India Companies by several European powers expressed the competitive urge of these countries for imperial expansion overseas. These companies were backed by the political, military and productive energies of the nations they represented. The organizations they established in the colonies were integrated with the needs and aspirations of the homeland, not those of the colonies.

The will of the society changes over time as old attitudes and goals are replaced with new ones. Organizations that adapt to these changes continue to thrive. Those that remain fixed in the past mold decline, become ineffective and are eventually discarded or fade away as the East India Companies faded in the light of more civilized values in the 20th Century. When India gained Independence, the Indian military was able to survive and make a smooth transition from functioning under the British colonial administration to functioning under a democratically elected government because its essential task remained maintenance of national security. In contrast the Indian banking system had to undergo radical change from serving the interests of a few large exporters and importers to financing agricultural and industrial activities of millions of small producers. Since the banks were nationalized in 1970, bank deposits have increased more than 100 times, because their policies and practices were drastically reoriented to serve the changing priorities of the country.

Development involves the emergence in society of organizations that reflect the aspirations of the society and are fashioned in consonance with its cultural values and ways of life. The imposition or blind imitation of external models of organization may result in artificial forms of organization that at best partially channel the social energies for development. Japan developed rapidly because it possessed the knack for adapting and moulding Western institutions to its own social and cultural context. East European countries have encountered seriously difficulties and achieved disappointing results by wholesale import of Western models.

Authority of Organizations

Organization derives productive power from authority. What distinguishes an organized social collective from a mob? The organized collective mobilizes and directs the energies and capacities of people in a controlled manner to carry out purposeful activities, whereas the mob unleashes pent-up energies in an uncontrolled manner for destruction. The capacity to control and govern human energies is an essential characteristic of all organizations.

The first human collectives most probably consisted of bands of hunters working together to obtain food and protect the members of the group. Formation of a hunting collective required the identification of a leader who could direct the actions of the group, give instructions and enforce discipline. The primary qualifications for leadership were physical strength and fighting prowess, that is, the capacity to physically enforce authority over other members of the group. Authority was essential to maintain order and discipline within the group regarding the sharing of food and work responsibilities as well as to demand courageous self-sacrifice of members in times of war. The greater the strength of the leader, the greater the stability, internal order and fighting capacity of the group. The maturation of the hunting group into an army involved a further development of organization. The military leader appointed a hierarchy of officers, each empowered with specific limits of authority. Strict obedience to those in command and unquestioned execution of instructions endowed the organized army with far greater strength.

Organizations derive power from internal authority and discipline. Western society's reverence for freedom and individual liberty has sometimes eclipsed the vital role of authority in social organization. Without it, no organization and no society can exist or function for a moment. The greater the authority under which individuals function, the greater the accomplishment. As society progressed from the primitive fighting group to more advanced forms of human collective, the centre of authority gradually shifted from the military to other centers in society. Religious, academic, administrative, political and commercial centers of power became increasingly important. The distribution of authority may have diluted the absolute authority of the military leader, but it enormously enhanced the overall exercise of authority in society. Whereas the military leader was primarily concerned with the exercise of authority to preserve peace and to conquer in war, these new centers of power exercised authority over what people believed, worshipped, taught their children, grew, produced, consumed, how they worked together and settled disputes, where they traded or travelled, what they could own, buy or sell. This more organized society acquired infinitely greater capacity to increase the productivity of its members.

During the last millennium, the evolution of authority in Western society moved from feudalism to absolute monarchy to democracy and rule of law. Power shifted from the landed aristocrat to the hereditary monarch and finally to the electorate. Each stage of this transition has brought with it a tremendous enhancement in the authority of society and in its overall development. The feudal lord was king unto himself within the limited confines of his own fiefdom, able to command the loyalty of his serfs in return for the barest subsistence existence but subject always to the threat of attack from other feudal lords or foreign invaders. Under feudalism, the society as a whole was organized at the level of survival and capable only of the lowest levels of productivity and development. The emergence of strong central monarchs greatly enhanced the power and productivity of society. The king was able to mobilize large armies for defence or conquest, to raise large sums as taxes to build roads or finance naval explorations, to issue money and protect property, to regulate crafts and promote trade to enhance the wealth of the country.

The further transition from monarchy to democracy has shifted power from concentration in a tiny aristocratic elite to distribute it over a large number of elected political leaders and administrative officials and through a increasingly complex system of laws and judicial mechanisms. At the same time democracy has extended the authority of the state enormously. In addition to maintenance of law and order and national defence, governments today exercise extensive and detailed authority over almost every aspect of life, including all forms of transportation and communication, manufacturing, export and import, banking, investment, employment, health, insurance, zoning, construction, broadcasting and preservation of the environment. Government in most countries today is the single largest employer and most of these employees exercise a measure of authority over some aspect of social life.

Contemporary thought emphasizes the limits of authority as a means for accomplishment. Under certain circumstances and up to a certain point, the imposition of authority from outside in the form of discipline and compulsion can be effective, as it was in propelling the remarkable economic and scientific achievements of Soviet Russia after the devastating effects of World War II. However, external authority is limited in its efficacy to what can be demanded of the individual or compelled by threat of punishment. It cannot produce the individual initiative, dynamism, spirit of innovation and creativity which are the driving forces for higher levels of human achievement. These forces flourish only in the measure individuals internalize the authority of society and freely accept its goals, aspirations and standards of behaviour as their own. The physical man responds to external compulsion. The mental man is guided by the authority of his knowledge, opinions, attitudes and values. The transition of society from monarchy to democracy marks the replacement of external authority by internal motivation as the driving force for social development. Wherever this change has taken firm root, the productivity and development of society have increased enormously.

The central importance of authority for social development is strikingly apparent in some of the countries of the former Soviet Union today, where the authority of the state and the society have been seriously eroded. In implementing transition strategies, many people in these countries had the mistaken impression that democracy and market economies thrived in the absence of regulatory authorities, so that sweeping away the old bureaucracy would dramatically improve economic performance. They failed to understand that free markets depend as much on authority as other economic systems. Eliminate the authority that prevents price collusion, the formation of monopolies, securities fraud, tax evasion, quality standards, and arbitrary confiscation of property, then markets are no longer free or efficient. The methods of enforcement may differ in a democracy, but the importance of conformity to the rules is the same. The breakdown of law and order, the rise of monopolistic conglomerates, and spread of organized crime in Eastern Europe during the last decade is clear testimony to the necessity of authority in social development.

Corruption in many developing societies today channels huge sums of money from public service to private benefit and influences policy decisions for the advantage of the few at the expense of the many. Most governments, including those of many industrialized nations, lack the capacity to fully enforce such basic measures as tax collections. However, all authority for development does not rest with governments. The assessment of a company's financial prospects by investment bankers and public accountants, ratings of product and service quality by independent consumer groups or scientific bodies, the certification of practitioners by organizations of professionals are also expressions of authority in the society. In the absence of these agencies, consumers hesitate to purchase new products, investors are reluctant to invest, clients have no way to determine the qualifications of lawyers and doctors, and so forth.

The ultimate source of organizational authority is the social will of the collective. To the extent that organizations are tuned to fulfill the aspirations of the society, they acquire authority. This authority may come by informal consent of those who participate in or benefit from the activities of the organization or by formal legal enactment. The right of consumers to protection from dishonest trade practices began as a social aspiration that was reflected in the consumer oriented policies of progressive retailers such as Sears. Later what the society had informally accepted as proper was augmented by specific laws defining the rights of consumers.

Complexity of Organization

One of the primary powers of organization that make it so productive is the division of labour. The division of labour did not begin with Ford's production line. It is as old as society. It is the capacity of society to divide up the activities essential for its functioning and assign different specialized tasks to different individuals. The establishment of a permanent standing army separate from the rest of the population enabled a portion of the population to focus exclusively on productive activities while others focused on maintaining law and order and defence. Specialization of function enables people with specific endowments to do what they do best. It also enables individuals to acquire a narrow set of skills rather than trying to learn how to perform every activity for themselves. Whether for a family, a company or a society, the result of this specialization is an enormous enhancement in overall efficiency. In Ford's factory, the combination of systems and specialization multiplied worker productivity eight times and total production 500 times.

Division of labour enables organizations to carry out vast numbers of different activities simultaneously. The greater the number of individual functions it performs, the more complex the organization. The more complex the organization, the greater its productive potential. Complexity is also enhanced by increasing the number of levels in the organizational hierarchy and the extent of coordination and integration it achieves with other organizations and activities in the same field and in other fields. Organizational complexity is powerfully enhanced by coordination between two or more separate systems or organizations. Coordination between buyers and sellers gives rise to the commodity exchange and the stock exchange. Coordination between purchasing, production and sales systems made possible the enormous improvements in efficiency and speed of delivery that have been achieved by just-in-time inventory management. Coordination of reservation, ticketing and routing systems between competing airline companies has increased the volume and reduced the cost of air travel by providing travelers with easier, more frequent connections between different airlines.

Coordination is even more powerful when it is between distinctly different types of organizations. Coordination between biotechnology and agriculture created the technology of the Green Revolution. Coordination between universities and business has aided the development and commercialization of today's computers. Coordination between computers and telecommunication systems gave birth to the Internet. The US space program that placed a man on the moon in less than ten years was the product of one of the most complex efforts at coordination ever attempted, involving cooperation between more than 400,000 people in thousands of different public and private scientific, commercial and governmental agencies.

Ultimate Determinant

The introduction and assimilation of any new activity moves through a series of stages from formal organization to institution to culture. The further it progresses in this process, the more deeply and naturally it is integrated into the life of the society. The greater the integration, the more efficiently the activity is carried out and the more productive it becomes. The final stage of this process is reached when the activity is so fully accepted that it is internalized as a value of the society and is perpetuated by the customs and beliefs of the population without the need of any external or formal means of support.

A value is something whose importance is fully understood, accepted and cherished for its own sake. Whatever an individual or a society values, it dedicates itself to nourish and protect. Values are an ultimate organizing principle that direct and control the way human energies are expressed in activity. Values are the most powerful determinants of social accomplishment. They are laden with their own inherent authority. Physical skills direct the energies of the body for productive work. Opinions direct the energies of the mind, determining how it responds to opportunities and challenges. Values direct the motive force of personality to achieve higher standards of behaviour and higher levels of accomplishment. Values are the psychological skills of society.

The efficiency of an organization is determined by its adherence to physical values such as cleanliness, orderliness, quality, regularity, and punctuality; organizational values such as discipline, standardization, systematic functioning, communication, coordination and integration; and mental or psychological values such as accuracy, honesty, respect for the individual, and harmony. Societies possess and foster these values as well. The higher the level of values to which the society is committed, the greater the society's productivity and accomplishments. Sears won and retained the confidence of middle class American consumers for nearly a century by remaining faithful to the value "satisfaction guaranteed or your money back."

The German dedication to quality has earned the highest reputation for German manufactured products around the world. The Japanese cultural commitment to harmony and consensus has powered the nation's ascent to the highest levels of economic achievement. Growing international awareness of the importance of preserving the environment is a value that is now redefining the way humanity grows crops, manufactures products, consumes energy and disposes of wastes the world over. Values are the ultimate determinant of society's development.

Government in Organization

During the past fifty years there has been a mushrooming of new types of organizations established by governments to support development at the national and international level. Export promotion councils and processing zones, specialized banking and financial institutions, stock exchanges, vocational training institutes, industrial estates and industrial development agencies, employee insurance and pension funds, producers cooperatives, state transport agencies and industrial research institutes are examples.

The role of government as creator and manager of new organizations can have a great impact on development in the measure that these organizations are integrated with and strengthen the social organization. For development to take hold and gain momentum, it is essential that any efforts by government lead to a multiplication of social organizations and social initiative by the private sector as well. The principle of organization is not limited to specialized agencies such as those listed above. In its widest sense it applies to the entire range of formal and informal mechanisms that the society employs to direct, manage and control social energies, human initiative, knowledge, information, resources and activities of all types.

Emergence of inter-governmental and private organizations at the international level has been a driving force for international economic development during this century. Global linkages between national postal and telecommunications services, global news and weather bureaus, international bank clearing houses and maritime conventions, international standards, laws and environmental conventions have elevated the organization of activities worldwide and made human society as a whole far more productive. The international community represents the final frontier for social development. Today organizational arrangements at the international level lag far behind in complexity and sophistication the organization of development at the national level. The future prosperity and accomplishments of humanity depend on building up both the formal and informal, governmental and non-governmental linkages needed to utilize the immeasurable opportunities remaining to be tapped for global prosperity.

Infrastructure

Society develops by building up higher and higher levels of organization. The establishment of each successive new layer of organization occurs as an overlay on the foundations of the society's previous achievements. We refer to these essential foundations as the infrastructure for the next stage of development. The term infrastructure is commonly used to refer to the physical infrastructure of roads, ports, navigable rivers, railways and electric power that support economic activity. Here we give extended meaning to the term by including three other levels of infrastructure – social, mental and psychological — that are necessary for further developmental achievements. The social infrastructure consists of all the laws, systems, administrative, commercial, productive and financial organizations – colleges, research institutes, banks, stock exchanges, courts, etc. — built up during previous stages of development that serve as a foundation for future progress. The mental infrastructure includes the availability of information, the level of education and awareness in society, the technical knowledge and skills of the workforce. The psychological infrastructure consists of the collective social energy, aspirations, attitudes and values that make the society open to new ideas, responsive to opportunities, willing to change, dynamic and hard working – all of which are essential characteristics for rising to higher levels of development.

Infrastructure is the structure below. It is itself a level of organization supporting as a foundation further levels of organization above it. The infrastructure of highways is a physical organization of linked roads connecting major centers of population, production, trade and consumption making possible the organization of commerce, industry and tourism. The educational infrastructure consists of a network of schools, colleges and training institutions covering different levels and specialized fields making possible the dissemination of acquired knowledge and skills together with research and experimentation. The legal infrastructure includes an interdependent fabric of laws, law-makers, enforcement agencies, judicial authorities, penal institutions and legal practitioners that serve as an essential foundation for maintenance of peace, the organization of civil society and commercial activity. The established fields of knowledge in society are similarly organized into specialized subjects, branches and levels upon which further advances of knowledge are founded. Each successive level of development requires the establishment of an essential infrastructure to support it. This conception underscores the need for multiple levels and types of infrastructure for the successful development of any new activity. The results of any development initiative will depend on the strength and quality of the underlying infrastructure. Supplying missing infrastructures can have a strong energizing effect in society.

Resources

Resources are inputs or factors for carrying out an activity effectively. Infrastructure is that which enables us to create, develop and utilize a resource more effectively. Like infrastructure, we can divide resources into four broad types. Land, water, coal, oil, minerals, power and capital are physical resources. The social resources consist of the society's capacity to manage and direct complex systems and activities. Knowledge, information, technology and the capacity to organize are mental resources. The energy, skills and capacities of people constitute the human resource.

Economics is very much concerned with the scarcity of resources. But when viewed from a wider perspective it becomes evident that while the quantity of some physical resources may be inherently limited, the notion of scarcity does not really apply to social, mental and human resources. Any of these may be limited in their immediate availability, but none are subject to inherent limits to their development. Organizational capabilities can be increased over time. The horizons of knowledge, information and technology are continuously expanding. The human resource becomes progressively more capable and productive.

As a society develops to higher levels, non-material resources play an increasingly important role as factors of production. This principle is embodied in the concept of the Information Age, an era in which access to information has become a valuable input and precious resource for improving the quality of decisions and the productivity of activities. One characteristic of information is that it is not consumed by being distributed or utilized, thus it is inexhaustible. Access to information now enables investors to move financial resources around the world instantaneously in search of higher returns. The increasing contribution of higher, non-material resources helps explain how societies have continued to expand productivity on a limited physical resource base.

Increasing the input of higher resources also makes it possible to more efficiently utilize the available material resources. Technological resources have made it possible during the past 15 years to increase the world's proven and economically accessible oil reserves by nearly 50%, while reducing the finding cost by nearly 75%. At the same time technology has reduced the materials and energy input required for a wide range of products. As Green Revolution has made the soils of India far more productive than in the past, Dutch agricultural scientists have recently demonstrated that water too can be made much more productive in agriculture. They have shown that it actually requires only 1.4 liters of water to grow a kilogram of vegetables, compared to more than 1000 liters commonly utilized by traditional cultivation practices. Henry Ford's organization of mass production dramatically reduced the requirement of human labour to assemble an automobile from 783 minutes to 93 minutes. The greater the input of higher level resources, the greater the efficiency of the activity.

These examples illustrate a fundamental principle of development. There is no such thing as a natural resource. The mind is the creator of all resources. It is the application of human intelligence and inventiveness that converts a substance into a resource. A resource emerges when the mind evaluates a material in the context of an end use. As society develops, the application of mind continuously increases the productivity of materials, finding new applications for them and more efficient ways to utilize them. The more the mind becomes open and flexible in its outlook, the greater is its power. Primitive man found that sand was a useful resource for making bricks. Early craftsmen discovered that the application of heat could convert the sand into glass. Several millenniums afterwards, we have found that the same sand can be converted into fiber optic cables and silicon chips. Sand remains the same, but its value has been immeasurably enhanced by the application of mind. Mind, the human being, is the ultimate resource that gives value to all other resources. The capacity of the human mind to acquire knowledge and devise improved technologies is for practical purposes unlimited. The concept that scarce resources impose ultimate limitations on human development needs to be reexamined from this perspective.

The Human Resource

Economics regards human labour as one of the inputs for production of goods and services and has evolved measures of productivity in terms of the labour cost per unit of output or value of national product. This is a very limited view of the contribution of human beings to social productivity that may be useful in measuring the overall efficiency and sophistication of economic systems, but reveals only a small part of their role in social development. Up to the advent of mechanization, the most prominent role of people in development was through physical labour hunting in the forests, harvesting the fields, rowing boats, laying bricks for houses and roads. But even during the earliest stages of this process, the input of physical energy was accompanied by an input of manual skill, organizing capacity and intelligent discrimination as well. Over the centuries the physical, social and mental skills of the work force developed hand in hand with the development of technology, social organization and scientific knowledge. Each advance in the methods of production, transportation, communication, and exchange required a corresponding advance in the capabilities of the work force. Even with the widespread introduction of mechanized technologies during the past 150 years, physical labour remains an essential input for all but a few fully automated production processes. However, the skill and knowledge required today for manual workers to handle materials, operate and maintain machines, conform to work rules, safety regulations and management systems, perform quality audits and coordinate activities far exceed the capacities required even for many of the most highly skilled tasks in earlier centuries. At the same time, the proportion of the work force engaged in manual labour has declined radically with the shift from agriculture-based to industrial and service economies. Attributing social development to technological advances diverts attention from the fact that tremendous increases in the depth and breadth of knowledge and technical skills possessed by scientists, engineers, designers, inventors, technicians and operators at all levels and in all fields are responsible for the development, application, diffusion and utilization of these technological advances. *Technological advances are not the accomplishments of the machine. They are the achievements of human beings.*

The remarkable advances in the development of organizations conform to the same principle. It is the continued growth in the capacity of human beings to conceive, design, plan, allocate, systematize, standardize, coordinate, and integrate actions, systems and organizations into larger, more complex and more productive arrangements that is responsible for the process of social development discussed in this paper. In this sense all development reduces itself to the development of human beings.

Looking forward, we may ask what are the limits then to social development imposed by the paramount role of people in the process. We have seen that energy, knowledge, skills, attitudes, aspirations and organizational capacities are the essential determinants of human productivity. Human energy is based on physical health. It is augmented by peace, political and social freedoms. It is released by opportunities for economic gain and personal advancement. It is elevated in its expressions by education and higher values. Humanity is healthier and better fed today than at any time in the past, yet more than a billion people still live in poverty. The physical improvement in the health and nutritional levels of the poor throughout the world will provide the physical basis for far higher levels of human productivity in the future. With the elimination of wars, the spread of democratic forms of governance and market economies, the political, social and economic conditions needed to release human energies for higher levels of accomplishment are being met today more than at any time in the past. The worldwide revolution of rising expectations is one expression. In many countries today, no more than half of the population has had the benefit of even a rudimentary primary education. No country can yet claim that even a majority of its people is truly well educated. The movement toward universal education at the primary level and advancement of more and more people to higher levels of education is still gaining momentum all over the world. With each successive decade it will add immeasurably to the quality and capabilities of the work force and the development potential of society. Increasing physical security, social freedom, economic opportunity and higher education are powerful forces for the refinement of attitudes and elevation of human aspirations. The cumulative impact of these positive influences will prepare the way for far higher levels and faster rates of social development than have been achieved or conceived of until now.

Process of Individual Development

We stated earlier that the principles of development were the same for individuals, organizations and societies. The basis for this statement should now be more evident. We have said that the process of development occurs when there is an accumulation of surplus energy, awareness of opportunities and challenges, and a strong aspiration for higher accomplishment. These conditions are as applicable to individuals and organizations as they are to societies. Individuals take initiatives to further their own accomplishments when they accumulate more energy than is needed just for their survival or maintenance of the status quo. This energy gets released when the individual becomes aware of an opportunity or is confronted by a pressing challenge. The intensity of aspiration determines the intensity of the individual's effort to exploit the opportunity or meet the challenge. We explained further the role of the pioneer and imitation in the development process. At the level of the individual, the example of other individuals is a powerful stimulus to change. Maintaining or elevating one's social status relative to peers is an unquenchable universal urge, second only perhaps in intensity to the basic urge for survival. When the society accepts a new type of activity, it takes steps to organize it and integrate it with other activities of the society, so that other members of the collective can acquire the necessary knowledge, skills and opportunity to take it up. The individual also organizes new behaviors, acquires new skills and knowledge, and integrates them within a total life style. The aspiring entrepreneur consciously designs new systems and organizes the new activities of his business to attract investors, skilled employees and customers.

The time comes when the organized activity of the society matures into an institution that can flourish even in the absence of active organizational support. So too, a time comes when the individual's new behaviour becomes a natural endowment of personality that the individual expresses naturally and effortlessly. The mature entrepreneur scrutinizes every new information and each situation looking for new opportunities, considers every new contact as a prospective investor, employee or customer, and directs all his knowledge and skill for the growth of his business.

Restatement of the Theory

Development is the upward directional movement of society from lesser to greater levels of energy, efficiency, quality, productivity, complexity, comprehension, creativity, enjoyment and accomplishment. These attributes are both the means for achieving development as well as its most characteristic expressions or results. The factor that they all have in common and which imparts to them their value is organization. Higher levels of each of these attributes are the resultant expression of higher levels of organization in society. Organization is the capacity to mobilize all the available information, knowledge, material resources, technology, infrastructure, and human abilities to meet challenges and take advantage of opportunities. *Development is the process of continuously enhancing the capacity of society to respond to opportunities and challenges by increasing its level of organization. Development is the process of creating newer organizations.*

The fabric of society consists of intricate interrelationships and interactions between different activities, systems, organizations, institutions, ideas, beliefs and values. The process of social development occurs by increasing the scope and complexity of the organization of this fabric. The movement involves a simultaneous development of the social fabric in several dimensions:

- Quantitative expansion in the size and carrying capacity of social activities, systems, organizations and institutions;
- Qualitative increase in the content, productivity and sophistication of the constituent elements of the fabric;
- Geographic or spatial extension of the organized fabric to provide more intensive coverage to larger portions of the population.
- Integration of existing and new organizational elements into an increasingly complex network of interrelationships;

A continuous process of organizational invention and innovation spurs this movement. During each phase new organizations emerge and existing organizations take on new attributes that enable them to act as spearheads of the development process. The contribution of any of these factors may for a time become so significant that we view them as essential causes in their own right. Actually they are the live evolving ends of the underlying social organization which fashions them by its excess energy and without which they cannot exist or function.

The accumulated knowledge of the society and its increasing awareness of emerging opportunities and challenges determine the overall direction given to this development process. The energy that drives the process is determined by the intensity of the collective social aspiration for higher levels of accomplishment released by this accumulated knowledge and growing awareness. These in turn are strongly influenced by the level of organization of the social collective.

Stated in other words, society becomes increasingly conscious of its inherent capabilities, the opportunities for high achievement and the means to organize itself for that achievement. The more conscious it becomes, the more its energies are released, the clearer the direction given to those energies, the more effective and efficient the organizational arrangements it fashions to support accomplishment, and the greater the magnitude and speed of social progress.

Three Stages of Social Development

The historical perspective presented thus far may create the impression that the development process is essentially a linear progression from less organized to more organized conditions generating greater benefits for society. While this is true, it is an over-simplification of what actually occurs. This complex multidimensional process of organizational development directed and fueled by social awareness and aspiration is further complicated by the gradual evolution of the society through three stages of development. By this evolution society is progressively infused by the release of greater vital energy and by the acquisition and practical application of more conscious and complete mental knowledge.

Society advances through three overlapping stages of development involving changes in the relative roles of three fundamental components of individual and collective human consciousness. We term these three components physical, vital and mental. All three components co-exist and play a role in all stages of development. The intensity of each and their relative predominance create a series of overlapping stages, rather than clearly demarcated steps. Different societies move through these stages at different times, at different rates and with variations in the relative mix of the three components. Yet despite these differences, three distinct stages can be discerned in the development of every society and in the overall development of the human community.

In the first stage there is a prevalence of the physical component. The dominant characteristic of society at this stage is a preoccupation with physical survival, protection and preservation of the status quo. There is a strong tendency toward tradition and conservatism. This is the agrarian and feudal phase where land is the primary source of wealth and the most productive resource. The primary political and social systems are based on physical, hereditary principles. Children inherit the wealth, power, occupations and social position of their parents. There is little social mobility, especially upwards. The organization of society during this stage centers around the military and land, feudal lords controlling small fiefdoms. Commerce and money play a relatively minor role. Beliefs are grounded in the past. There is little emphasis on education, experimentation or thinking outside established guidelines defined by tradition and religious authority. Skills are passed down from generation to generation by a long, slow process of apprenticeship. Guilds restrict the dissemination of techniques. The church or state controls the dissemination of knowledge. The contribution of the human resource is predominantly in the form of physical labour. Apart from a small, privileged ruling elite, the society accords little respect, rights or value to other human beings. The pace of change during this stage is quite slow, because those factors that promote rapid development are only minimally present.

The maturation of the physical stage occurs when the physical organization of society develops to the point where the increasing productivity of physical resources generates surplus produce, energy and wealth. The reorganization of agriculture in Europe following the end of Feudalism provided the basis for the rise of commerce and later industry. The vital and mental principles become more active. The generation of surplus energy and capacity in society begin to break the bonds of tradition and overflow into new fields of activity.

During the next stage, the vital factor plays an increasingly active role. The dominant characteristics of this phase are dynamism and change. The energy level in society rises. It becomes increasingly inventive, outward looking and adventurous. This was the phase in which Europe began to explore the seas, leading to the discovery of new trade routes and new lands and ushering in the age of mercantilism. *The greatest invention and discovery of this phase is the power of money.* Commerce replaces agriculture as the predominant source of wealth. Money replaces land as the most precious and productive resource. The centre of society shifts from the countryside to the cities and towns, where opportunities for trade and enterprise attract more and more people. The great urban centers grow rapidly. The rise of a merchant class wrests power from the hereditary aristocracy, at first gaining the support of ruling monarchs in exchange for economic rights and later leveraging its increasing wealth to make monarchs subordinate to parliaments. The organization of society expands rapidly during this period. New types of organizations proliferate. In order to provide an attractive environment for commerce, the rule of law and stable economic policies of the state gradually replace arbitrary decrees. Banks, shipping companies and trading houses proliferate. Religious institutions lose much of their political influence. New ways of life are accepted rather than frowned upon because they generate practical benefits. The practical comes to take precedent over the traditional. The mental influence increases markedly with the growth of experimentation, scientific discovery and new technologies. Increased travel, interaction between societies and greater flows of information engender greater tolerance and openness to new ideas and different ways of life. Expansion of commerce and rule of law increase the demand for and spread of education among the more prosperous classes.

Maturation of the vital stage through commercial and industrial expansion generates higher levels of surplus in society. Capital accumulation occurs on a large scale. An abundance of goods is produced and is available. The middle and upper classes grow in absolute and relative proportion, meaning that more people have surplus time, energy and money for consumption, education, travel and recreational pursuits. The aspiration for luxury and leisure penetrates to lower levels of society, inspiring the common man to yearn for more.

The third stage of development is one in which the mental component becomes more and more predominant. This stage has three essential characteristics that demarcate it from those that came before – a great increase in the practical application of mind to generate new inventions, in the social application of mind to generate new and higher levels of organization, and in the political application of mind to elevate the status and rights of individual human beings. The first distant origins of this phase in Europe can be traced back to the Renaissance and the Enlightenment, when ideas began to gain freedom from domination by church doctrine and traditional superstitious beliefs. *The mental component gained influence after the Reformation, which empowered the individual to seek direct relations with God.* It led eventually to the proclamation of the political ideals embodied in the American and French Revolutions and the establishment of human rights, at first in principle and much later in practice. The onset of this phase gave rise to the birth of modern science and practical experimentation. This led ultimately to the explosion of technical innovations that ushered in the Industrial Revolution, which has continued with increasing momentum for the last 150 years. Industry gradually replaced commerce as the greatest source of wealth. Technology began to challenge the position of money as the most powerful and productive resource.

Organization is a product of the mind. Therefore it is not surprising to find that the mental phase has given birth to an incredible number and variety of new forms of social innovation, equaling or perhaps even exceeding the number and variety of new technical inventions generated during this period. Huge commercial organizations have emerged, larger and more wealthy and powerful in some cases than entire countries. The world, which was criss-crossed by sailing ships in previous centuries, is now linked together and wired by a profusion of systems and structures that connect people and activities around the globe.

The physical application of mind for scientific discovery and technological invention and the social application of mind for organizational innovation have been powerful forces for social development over the past few centuries. However, the highest power of mind expresses in the field of pure ideas. It is here that mind has introduced the most far-reaching changes that are destined to transform life in the coming centuries. Ideals and ethical ideas are as old as civilization, but the practical extension of high ideas to social life has never before been accepted and attempted on such a massive scale as it is today.

The mental stage has established the principle of human rights and proclaimed the value of the individual. The 20th Century has been heralded as the century of the common man. Never before has society as a whole accorded such value and consideration for the poorest and lowliest of its citizens. The granting of universal suffrage and acceptance of the goal of universal education are unprecedented steps. Actual practices fall far short of the ideal in every society, but the direction of the social movement is clear. With every passing year new measures are introduced to extend greater physical and economic security to larger sections of the population in more countries around the world. Once this goal has been accepted by the mind of humanity, it exerts an inexorable pressure for further progress.

It is evident that the content of these three stages and the timing and circumstances of the transition from one stage to the next may vary widely between countries. However, the stamp of the physical, vital and mental components of human consciousness is remarkably similar and can be discerned even in societies that otherwise appear to have little in common. It is also evident that each country's experience is influenced by the experience of other countries that have passed before it and by those with which it is in contact or proximity at any given time. Thus, the circumstances in which universal primary education was introduced in the Netherlands after 1618 were naturally different than the circumstances faced by Japan after 1872 or in other Asian countries after 1950 when education gained momentum in these countries. The Dutch were pioneering a new concept, whereas the Japanese were spurred to imitate the example of technologically advanced US and Western Europe, and other Asian countries to imitate Japan. This is one reason why the pace of development continues to accelerate as the world accumulates greater experience and more successful models for emulation.

It should also be apparent that although we seem to suggest that each society passes from one stage to the next in mass, this is rarely, if ever, the case. The movement to the next phase invariably begins among the most advanced parts of the society, which means the urban centers, and among the most educated, wealthy and worldly classes. Thus New York, Paris, London, Moscow, Tokyo and Bombay have advanced much faster and further than isolated rural areas such as Appalachia, the Scottish Highlands, Siberia, Hokkaido and Bihar. Even today we can find the anachronism of near feudal communities existing almost side by side with the most modern industrial societies within the same nation state.

Role of Organization in the Three Stages

The evolution of society through these three stages is accomplished by the progressive development of more productive, efficient and complex social organizations. At the same time, the nature of the predominant organizations also evolves from physical to vital to mental. Each transition from one stage to another results in a tremendous increase in social productivity by several orders of magnitude. An examination of the role of organization in each of the three stages reveals the source of this phenomenal increase in the capabilities of society. *In the following section, we examine the contribution of three different levels of social organization to development – urbanization during the physical stage, money during the vital stage, and Internet as an organization of information during the mental stage.*

Development can be likened to a chemical reaction. The speed and outcome of the reaction depends on the concentration of ingredients, the temperature and pressure, and the presence of catalytic agents. These elements determine the frequency, intensity and efficiency of contact between the substrates. The greater the concentration, temperature and pressure, the faster the molecules move and the more frequently and forcefully they interact with each other. The presence of the appropriate catalyst speeds the reaction between compatible substances by serving as a medium for bringing the substrates into proximity over a larger area. *Development also depends on the speed, frequency, intensity and breadth of contacts and interactions.* Social institutions act as powerful stimuli for development by increasing the number, frequency and intensity of interactions between compatible elements.

Population Growth and Urbanization

The most discernible trend during the physical stage of development is growth of population. In the physical stage, the primary goal of society was to ensure the survival of the community in the face of war, famine, and epidemic disease. The first result of progress in agriculture, defence and urban settlements was an increase in population. In the modern age of the population explosion, growth of population is often viewed as a barrier to development rather than a measure of it. But in prior centuries, population growth has always been limited by the capacity of society to sustain larger numbers of people. Until very recently, each improvement in agricultural productivity and food supply has resulted in a significant expansion of population. Before the invention of cultivation about 10,000 years ago, the total population of the world probably did not exceed 10 million people. During the next 8000 years, the world's population increased about 30 times to reach 300 million in 1 AD. Since then it has grown another 20 fold. It reached 500 million in 1650, then doubled to cross one billion by 1800, doubled again to 2 billion by 1930, then tripled during the last six decades. The 12-fold growth of population over the past 300 years as a result of tremendous increases in food production and public health is an indication of the order of magnitude of social progress during this period.

These enormous increases in population were made possible by tremendous advances in the organization of society around urban centers. Historically, the first major organizational innovation was the transition of primitive society from hunting and gathering to cultivation and rearing of domesticated animals between the 7th and 3rd Millennium BC. The capacity to generate reliable supplies of food from the land made possible the establishment of permanent sedentary human settlements. As agricultural productivity increased the supply of food, the surpluses freed more and more people from the necessity of producing and gathering food, so they could specialize in other activities. The size and location of these early settlements was limited by the productivity of the surrounding lands. Later, improved transportation made possible by the development of the wheel, roads, boats and canals enabled food to be carried over greater distances from fields to towns.

The concentration of population in early agricultural settlements led to development of fortified towns, providing physical security from external threats. The creation of towns represents the development of a higher type of physical organization. With few exceptions, these cities were very small by modern standards, rarely exceeding 100,000 inhabitants, but more densely populated than the most crowded modern metropolises. The formation of towns required the evolution of new organizations for governance, external defence, internal security, regulation of property rights, production, trade, distribution, education and religion. Within the town, the workforce divided and specialized into military, political, administrative, agricultural, industrial and commercial categories. The concentration of larger populations increased the frequency, speed and intensity of social interactions, providing far greater need and opportunity for economic exchange than occurred in sparsely populated rural areas. It created pressure on society to continuously increase food production. It created a growing market for goods and services that encouraged social inventiveness.

The growth of these population centers in turn depended upon and was facilitated by advances in the physical organization of the settlement. Towns were organized into sectors. Roads were laid, bridges were built, markets were constructed and ports were developed. In some instances aqueducts were built to transport drinking water and sewers were dug to carry away wastes and drain rainwater. This physical infrastructure enabled towns to grow into larger urban centers, further intensifying the number, size and variety of economic interactions. Cities became centers for government, trade, manufacturing, education, recreation and cultural activities. These densely populated areas where people, capital and knowledge accumulated became powerful engines for development. Packed into close quarters, news and rumors spread swiftly. The population became far more aware of what was taking place in other places. Pioneering inventions and innovations were quickly imitated by others. *The growing frequency, efficiency, speed, complexity and intensity of human interactions through the organization of urban communities was the basis for the significant developmental achievements of the physical stage.*

The process of urbanization that began with permanent agricultural settlements progressed very slowly up through the Middle Ages. The dual imperatives of defence and sustenance remained the principle rationale for cities and fortress towns under the feudal order. Urban communities in Europe grew more rapidly in size and number with the decline of feudalism and the rise of the mercantile era from the 12th Century onwards. Commercial communities governed by merchant councils flourished throughout Europe and exerted continued pressure for increasing economic freedom and political autonomy from feudal and monarchical power, which led eventually to the emancipation of individuals as well. The growth of merchant cities was made possible by the rapid development of a higher level of commercial organization and the increasing role of money. The growth of the money economy ushered society into the vital stage and spurred the remarkable expansion of global economic activity that led up to the Industrial Revolution.

The Role of Money in Development

With the rise of large commercial urban centers, the principle instrument for development shifted from physical matter to social institution — from arable land to money. Money has been the single greatest organizational invention of the past five thousand years. The emergence of money as a preeminent social institution vividly illustrates the central role of organization in the process of social development.

The creation of money was made possible and spurred by the generation of food surpluses. One of the earliest forms of money was the receipt issued for grain deposits at government warehouses in ancient Babylon, which gradually became transferable to third parties. The capacity of early farmers to produce more food than was required for consumption by the family naturally prompted them to trade their surplus for other goods or services. As long as these exchanges were conducted by means of barter, they were severely limited both in volume and speed. Barter exchange required the double coincidence of a buyer and seller both wanting what the other possessed in surplus. It also involved a very complicated form of valuation, since every type of commodity would have a different price depending on the goods or service for which it was to be exchanged. Direct barter involving 1000 different commodities would require 500,000 rates of exchange. Barter transactions worked best within a narrow geographical area due to the physical difficulties of transporting products over long distances. The perishable nature of many products also limited barter exchanges. Producers had no incentive to produce more than they were confident of either consuming or exchanging with other consumers during the period before a product deteriorated.

The use of money spread gradually from one country to another by a process of imitation similar to the manner in which ideas, technologies and other social institutions are transmitted from one place to another and bear fruit wherever the soil is sufficiently prepared. The adoption of money in place of barter had a tremendously liberating and expansive impact on early society. As urbanization increased the number, size and speed of transactions by bringing many more people into proximity, money increased the number, size, speed, and efficiency of transactions even over long distances. The capacity to convert the fruits of one's labour into money meant that those fruits could be stored indefinitely, overcoming the limitations of time and providing an incentive for people to exert themselves much harder and longer than if what they produced must be consumed immediately. The capacity to convert physical goods into portable money overcame the limitations imposed by space. Whereas products could be transported long distances only at considerable cost and difficulty, money could be moved quickly and inexpensively, making possible trade over much larger geographic areas. Money also provided a common standard for valuation of all products and services, thereby vastly reducing the complexity of exchange rates. By eliminating the necessity of the double coincidence required for barter trade, money made it possible for a much larger number of transactions to be completed. At the same time, its ease of movement and accounting enormously increased the speed of commercial transactions. *The increasing volume and speed of transactions made possible by money combined with the increasing size and density of urban populations had an exponential impact on the development of society.*

Money had a transforming effect on society equivalent in magnitude to that brought about by the emergence of urban communities. It helped liberate society from the strict confines of the land and the retarding influences of tradition, spurring the evolution from the physical to the vital stage of social development. Before money, land was the principle productive resource and source of wealth. Those who controlled the land controlled the wealth of society. The hereditary transmission of property rights during the feudal period left little incentive for individual initiative and little room for individual advancement. During the Middle

Ages, European society actually reverted for a time to barter before money returned and gained ascendance. The return of money and the rise of commerce in European society coincided with the demise of the agrarian based feudal system. Money gradually replaced heredity not only as a source of wealth, but as a source of social power and privilege as well. The moneyed commercial classes became increasingly influential, creating the backdrop for the emergence of democratic values and forms of government a few centuries later. Money freed the individual from servitude to the soil. A person could earn money and use it to purchase whatever was required for personal sustenance and also utilize it as capital to earn a living. It impersonalized and democratized transactions, empowering the possessor with economic voting power that drastically reduced discrimination based on class and status. Money increased the individual's freedom of choice and gave greater scope for the development of individual talents and potentials.

Social organizations that spur development at one stage tend to ossify and die out later on, as hunting tribes, guilds, East India companies and colonial empires, feudal and monarchical institutions have in the past. Some institutions exhibit the capacity to evolve along with society, adapting and changing to match the character of the times. Money has exhibited this capacity to evolve with the times. Sharing the characteristics of this physical stage of development, early money was itself a physical commodity, grain, gold or silver. Only gradually did representative forms of money appear, but these too were full-bodied commodity money, convertible at any time into the commodity that they represented. During the vital stage, more symbolic forms of money such as certificates of deposit, bank notes, checks, letters of credit, bonds and other forms of negotiable securities came into prominence. The complete separation of money from its physical roots came at a much later stage of social development with the appearance of fiat money that does not have a commodity value and cannot be redeemed for a commodity.

Money as an Organization

Money plays a crucial role in development. Money is the product of organization. In earlier societies, land was the principal form of wealth. The productivity of the land was the primary resource for development and that productivity depended on the organization of society for agricultural production. The growth of commerce depended on creation of more liquid forms of wealth that could be moved and traded for precious goods. Money replaced land as the principal form of wealth. But money by itself has no inherent value and cannot produce or develop anything. Money depends for its productive power on organization. The creation and operation of a money economy depended from the beginning upon the establishment of governmental organizations that could issue new forms of money, financial organizations that would honor, store and transfer it, and commercial organizations that would accept it in exchange for goods and services.

Money not only depends on organization; it is itself an organization. Money is a commodity such as gold or an officially issued coin or paper note that is legally established as an exchangeable equivalent of other commodities and is used as a measure of their comparative values on the market. It is an abstract unit of account in terms of which the value of goods, services and obligations can be measured. The systems of exchange, valuation, issuance and conversion of one form of money into another constitute elements of that organization. The value of money depends directly on the level of this organization. The more developed it becomes, the greater the productive power of money.

Money is often regarded as a unique social institution, but actually it derives its productive power from characteristics which it shares in common with other forms of social organization. Like other organizations, the development of money has occurred on the foundation of four types of organized infrastructures. In early times, a physical infrastructure of towns, ports, and roads provided the necessary conditions to stimulate the growth of commercial transactions based on money. A social infrastructure was also necessary to support the evolution of money from a commodity into a symbol. An essential requirement was for a stable government to issue and redeem the symbol for the underlying commodity. The development of money coincided with the emergence of nation states that possessed the stability and continuity necessary to stand surety for symbolic forms of money.

In addition, the development of banking, stock exchanges, legislative, judicial and administrative infrastructures became essential supports for the growing use of money. In modern times, the role of money has been expanded enormously by the development of complex mental infrastructures consisting of an intricate web of technology, organization and information. Systems for international banking, telecommunications, and computerized financial transactions serve as essential infrastructure for the rapid movement of money around the world.

The emergence of money also required the development of a sophisticated psychological infrastructure in society. The progression from physical to symbolic forms of money involved a huge leap of faith for early physical man still struggling, against the direct evidence of his senses, with the concept that a round earth revolved around the sun. It must have required an irresistible urge for accomplishment and great spirit of adventure to forego the security of pure commodity money for pieces of paper and promises of redemption. The magnitude of that psychological leap is evidenced by the persistent preference of some Asian populations today for the certitude of gold in an age where much higher returns and greater security are offered by symbolic forms of money. The development of money required that people accept record keeping and systematic functioning as a way of life and have sufficient trust to deposit their funds with others. Money has long since passed from the stage of organization to that of an ubiquitous global, social institution that derives support from many organizations but does not depend on any for its existence.

As an organization, the power of money is based on authority. The value and productive power of money depends directly on the perceived strength of the issuing government and the authority conceded to it by the population. This authority has an economic aspect, its capacity to maintain fiscal discipline, to collect taxes, to prevent counterfeiting. It also has a wider political and social aspect. The value of money issued depends on the perceived strength and stability of the government, the military strength and stability of the country and its relationship with other nations, and its capacity to enforce rule of law among its citizens. Authority and trust are complementary forces. Ultimately the strength of a currency depends on the extent to which it gains the trust and confidence of society, which today means the global financial community. Remove this trust and confidence, as occurred during the US banking crisis of the Great Depression or during the recent financial crisis in Asia, and the entire monetary system is threatened with collapse. The ultimate foundation that gives force and effectiveness to this greatest of social institutions is not hard core physical assets but an intangible human value.

As an organization, money also derives power from the systems of which it is constituted and through which it acts. The value and productivity of money is directly proportionate to the quality of systems for minting, storage, accounting, transfer, exchange, savings, borrowing, investment, credit and information flows. It is indirectly proportionate to systems for administrative decision-making and enforcement, trade, manufacturing, R&D, transport, telecommunications, education and training. The productivity of money depends upon the velocity with which it circulates through these systems. Each system contributes directly or indirectly to determine the overall speed of circulation, which increases with each advance in social development. The establishment of a sophisticated global communications system now enables hundreds of billions of dollars to flow back and forth around the world on a daily basis in search of higher rates of return.

Organizations derive their power from the complexity of the activities to which they relate and the breadth of activities with which they are integrated. As the complexity of the interconnections between the synaptic junctions in the human brain determines the degree of intellectual capacity, the intricate interrelations forged between activities determine the degree of social development. Money has a powerful catalytic effect on development arising from its capacity to relate to, integrate with and energize virtually every other activity in society. Not only every variety of product and service, but also every variety of social activity has come to be valued in monetary terms. Late during the monarchical period, aristocratic titles became available to wealthy merchants for a price. Education, the traditional mark of the nobility, opened up to all with the money to acquire it.

Marriage, civil claims and personal injury suits, civil and criminal judgements, tithes for religious salvation, political election and appointment, copyrights, patents, knowledge, information and even artistic inspiration have been translated into monetary terms and stimulated in their own development by the development of money. Although this characteristic of complexity and integration is most apparent with regard to money, every social institution has a similar type of impact on existing social activities. Thus, the creation of a national organization of highways or a national system of education promotes national defence, agriculture, industry, trade, tourism, recreation, education, immigration, publishing, and so forth.

The ultimate determinants of the power of social organization are the values of society. The institution of money has been so deeply accepted and internalized by every society in modern times that it would appear to have assumed the status of an ultimate value in itself. The constitutional and legal framework of the nation state provides protection for all types of property rights. Monetary incentives are utilized everywhere to encourage higher levels of individual productivity and group performance. Brushing aside hereditary claims for social status, society accords the greatest respect to those individuals, organizations and nations that have amassed the most wealth. But this apparent preeminence of the money value is misleading. The remarkable creativity and productivity of money is itself based on a bedrock of other social values without which it could not produce anything of worth. The value of money depends directly on all the values that support its functioning as an organization.

These include physical values such as accuracy, orderliness, punctuality, regularity and efficiency; organizational values such as discipline, standardization, systematic functioning, communication, coordination and integration; and psychological values such as trust, integrity, harmony and creativity. Take away these intangible but priceless social accomplishments and the value of money quickly vanishes into obscure symbolism. Money is a tremendously productive social organization, but like every social organization it depends on an incorporeal human foundation for its existence.

The ultimate foundation for the value of money is not material wealth but the value of human beings. Money has grown in its power and productivity not because society has accorded it ultimate value, but because it has become an instrument and medium for fulfilling human aspirations and elevating people. The more society has come to recognize the inherent value and potential of the human being, the more productive the individual, society and money have become. Money has served as a symbol of the infinite potential for human accomplishment. As such it has released enormous energy, creativity and initiative in society. But the ultimate source of that unlimited creative energy is the individual and the society, not money.

Organizations of the Mental Stage

Knowledge is the central characteristic of the mental attribute of human consciousness which has assumed an increasingly dominant role during the last few hundreds years. Although we speak of the mental phase as being of very recent origin, it is evident that the mental component has been an active contributor to development since primitive societies developed agriculture and invented the wheel. What has changed very markedly is the relative contribution of this mental attribute, which is made visibly evident by the increasing speed of development in modern times. The knowledge that the mental component acquires and applies to further human progress has had a profound effect on all aspects of social life ranging from pure mental concepts to practical physical applications. The action of mind in four specific fields has had an especially powerful influence on the course of global development — political thought, social organization, education, science and technology.

The development of philosophical thought and values expresses in social life as changing concepts about the purpose of life, the role and nature of human beings, and the relationship between the individual and the collective. This abstract and exalted field of mental speculation appears far removed from practical considerations. Yet it has been the source of the revolutionary thoughts and values that have radically transformed the political and social structure of civilization over the past five centuries, leading to the establishment of democratic principles and forms of governance as a global standard, if not quite yet a global practice. This movement can be traced back to the revival of humanistic thought, spread of education and secular values that arose during the Renaissance. It gained momentum with the spiritual empowerment of the individual by the Reformation, the birth of modern science, the affirmation of rationalistic ideals during the Enlightenment, and the declaration of human values by the American and French Revolutions. These movements have culminated during this century in the collapse of colonial empires following World War II and the rapid spread of democratic forms of government in Latin America, Eastern Europe and Africa over the past two decades. The tremendous release of individual energy and collective dynamism that accompanied the practical acceptance of these ideals has provided the impetus for momentous social accomplishments that until recently seemed inconceivable.

Education

This transformation of the political organization of societies which has extended basic human rights at first to the middle class and eventually to the common man was mirrored by a parallel development of the social organization for education that was equally far reaching and powerful in its impact. Education is the systematic organization of the cumulative knowledge and experience of humanity and the transmission of that knowledge to the next generation in a concentrated and abridged form. It is the central instrument for making the past discoveries and experience of humanity more and more conscious and accessible for application by society to meet the opportunities and challenges of the future. If the distribution of political power to the entire population was inconceivable to the pre-revolutionary aristocracy and common people of Europe, then the concept and practice of universal education prevalent today would have been absolutely unthinkable. The Renaissance and Reformation led to a revival of interest in education that, like science and philosophy, had been eclipsed in Europe during the Middle Ages. Prior to 1600, education was confined to a small population consisting mostly of Christian scholars and the nobility. Both Luther and Calvin believed that every individual should read the Bible and urged establishment of state educational systems. In the 17th Century education spread gradually but maintained a strong religious orientation. Leading thinkers of the Enlightenment stressed the importance of intellectual knowledge to the practical advancement of society and the importance of secular education. During the next century secularism and social progress began to prevail and for the first time advanced scientific and mathematical knowledge became a part of the school and university curriculum in Europe and North America. The growing recognition of the importance of education for social progress led to the extension of elementary education to the middle classes and prompted more states to assume responsibility for establishing and maintaining national school systems.

Over the last two hundred years, education has become one of the principle organizations in modern society. Since the end of World War II, it has come to be universally recognized as a principle instrument for national development, leading to a worldwide expansion of primary and secondary education along with a multiplication of colleges, universities and professional schools. At the same time, the breadth of the educational curriculum has been expanded and significantly reoriented to cover a great many areas of applied knowledge such as specialized fields in engineering, physical and biological sciences, business management, economics and most recently computer sciences. Education has awakened the mind of humanity to its innate potentials and to the enormous untapped opportunities in its external environment. This growing awareness has released infinite energy for mental creativity, social innovation and practical invention. It has raised the aspirations and expectations of people everywhere for the fruits of progress. It has equipped individuals with the mental knowledge and skills to fashion and manage more and more powerful and complex forms of social systems, and to design, manufacture and operate more and more powerful and complex forms of technology. It has created an unprecedented openness and tolerance, which are an essential basis for global development in the coming years.

Technology

Mind applying itself to the field of thought creates new concepts and more powerful ideals. Applying itself to the field of society, it creates new and improved social organizations. Applying itself to the field of matter, it discovers the physical laws of nature and creates new technologies and inventions. The application of mind's creative powers to the field of science, technology and practical invention has had an enormous impact on social progress during the last two centuries. History reveals a slow and uneven advance in applied scientific knowledge and technology. There have been periods of great inventiveness and great discoveries in the distant past, followed by periods of stagnation. But nothing can equal in sheer numbers and significance the explosion of human invention that has occurred since the onset of the Industrial Revolution. A classic study by Lilly found that the relative rate of inventiveness rose seven-fold between 1700 and 1900 to reach a level at least ten times higher than had been achieved during earlier millennia.

A number of specific factors have contributed to this accelerating rate of inventiveness, but the essential cause has been the emergence of the mental principle as the spearhead of social development. Its energies released by politically awakening and social freedoms, its thought liberated from blind submission to tradition and refined by education, the power of mind has applied itself to transform the social and material life of humanity. Superstitious beliefs and religious dogma characteristic of the physical stage have been powerful deterrents to fresh thinking and innovation during much of human history. In the Middle Ages in Europe, inventions that seemed a little too clever or unusual were frequently condemned as satanic and their inventors persecuted. Thus, Copernicus' heliocentric theory was rejected as inconsistent with the scriptures and remained unpublished during his lifetime. Churchmen condemned Galileo's refracting telescope as an instrument of the devil. After he openly endorsed Copernicanism, he was sentenced to life imprisonment for 'vehement suspicion of heresy'. The movement of rationalist thought ushered in by the Enlightenment reduced the inhibiting influence of superstition and religious dogma and cleared the way for the emergence of the experimental sciences.

There is a common tendency to view technology as a thing apart and to explain the developmental achievements of the last

200 years exclusively or primarily in technological terms. This view is inadequate because it attempts to isolate advances in technology from the general advance of knowledge and social organization characteristic of the mental stage of development. In earlier periods, scientific investigation and technological innovation were carried out as isolated activities without the support of the social organization. Prior to the 15th Century, there were no reliable mechanisms for the recording, preservation and dissemination of inventions, so most discoveries were applied only locally and a great many were lost altogether. Individual inventors adapted and improved mechanisms for specific applications, but in most cases their innovations were never transmitted to others or standardized for widespread use. The technological developments of the Industrial Revolution would not have been possible without the organization of scientific knowledge and the establishment of scientific associations throughout Europe in the 16th and 17th Century. The publication of scientific journals aided the conservation and organization of society's technical knowledge. Until legal protection for patents was introduced at the end of the 18th Century, inventors had no way of knowing about similar inventions and no way to stake an economic right to their discoveries, except by keeping them secret. In France exclusive rights to an invention were protected by letters of patent granted only by royal authority and records were kept in a single central location inaccessible to all but a few.

Technology is knowledge of matter organized and applied through a practical organization. The widespread application of technology during and after the Industrial Revolution depended on the development of several other types of social organization. The organization of agriculture by enclosure of common lands in England generated surplus farm incomes, freed people to migrate to the towns, and fueled rapid population growth, which resulted in an increased market for manufactured goods and made mechanization feasible. The organization of urban commercial centers, transport and foreign trade created demand for larger volumes of production than could be readily produced by human labour. Poor roads in 17th Century Europe retarded industrial invention. There was little incentive to increase production so long as expansion of the market was severely hindered by poor transportation. The development of sea trade routes during the 18th Century opened a much wider market for manufactured products, stimulating a new outburst of invention. The organization of mass production according to the principles of division and specialization of labour made the adaptation of mechanized technology practical. The organization of education equipped the society with the skills necessary to design, manufacture and utilize an endless stream of more complex and sophisticated inventions. Technology developed as an integrated part of the evolving fabric of the social organization.

The tendency to attribute invention to independent individual creativity ignores the cumulative process of discovery and innovation that builds incrementally on past accomplishments as well as the vast system of social organization that actively supports, propagates and applies the discoveries and innovations of the individual over a wide territory. Individual invention depends on and is an expression of the society's unconscious preparedness and collective aspiration for higher accomplishment. At each stage it has to confront and overcome social resistance to further advancement. In medieval Europe the guilds imposed severe limits on new invention. The advance of medical technologies was very slow in Europe until new scientific associations persuaded physicians to disclose their successful remedies, which were previously kept secret. When Denis Papin demonstrated the first steam driven water pump and paddle wheel ship at the beginning of the 18th Century, German authorities fearing the spread of unemployment discouraged the application of mechanized power. When John Kay developed a flying shuttle textile loom, he was denounced and physically threatened by English weavers fearing loss of their jobs and forced to flee to France where his invention was adopted by the government. When the first Jacquard loom was installed in Lyons, French silk weavers smashed it to pieces. The mechanization of agriculture in the 1890s provoked similar fears throughout rural America. The application of biotechnology for genetic engineering and the rapid spread of computers today raise widespread anxiety. However justified or fanciful the social resistance to invention may appear at the time or in retrospect, these instances underline the obvious fact that technological advancement occurs as an integral and inseparable part of the wider process of social development described in this paper. The more receptive and supportive the social organization is to technical innovation, the more of it occurs and is applied practically.

Development and Conflict Theory

The concept of "development" cuts across many levels. It refers to macro issues (such as patterns of a nation's growth), as much as it refers to meso problems (such as river-basin plans), or to micro problems (such as local community development). All three levels — macro, meso, and micro, are interwoven. And at all levels, many different dimensions — economic, cultural, religious and gender — affect and are affected by development. This research addresses the links between the promotion of social change associated with development aid and conflict.

Development should be understood as a process, not a product. Societies are always changing. Some improve, while others fail. Development theory aims at explaining both processes. Development practice intends to provide tools that can be applied to entire societies or specific communities. Such interventions are intended to move communities or societies from a situation in which they are believed to be worse off to a situation in which they are assumed to be better off.

Current links between development and conflict theory stress the provision of aid in cases of violent conflict. Peacebuilding interventions after violent conflicts address the same concerns as development interventions. Clearly, development is at the core of post-conflict interventions, where the physical and social landscape has been damaged. In such cases, development assistance is provided. Yet development aid goes beyond development assistance. Aid refers to general support for the improvement of Third World societies, which may or may not be, in violent conflict. Perhaps because development aid does not deal directly with violence, conflict and conflict resolution have not been topics of major concern to development theorists or workers. This, however, has started to change.

The Millennium Development Goals illustrate how development is an interdisciplinary field, which implements programs in various areas and deals with innumerable variables—such as economic, social, political, gender, cultural, religious and environmental issues. The field is further complicated because these variables are highly intertwined. Therefore, the analysis of gender issues must also consider the affects of and on linked economic, religious, and cultural issues. Similar links exist with many other development topics. Such links become clear in the findings of this research.

Development and Structural Change

Societal change most often requires structural change. While this may be true in any country, it is probably more often true in the developing world. Yet most development intervention is locally targeted and short-term. It does not try to implement structural change across the entire society. This disconnect creates something of a "Catch-22" — a vicious cycle in which development leads to conflict, and the lack of conflict resolution practices interferes with further development.

Ignoring structural factors means not only overlooking dimensions that take place at the macro level, but also not paying enough attention to the micro-level effects of development and conflict in society. One shocking example was recently publicized by an opinion poll, according to which 67% of Brazilians are functionally illiterate. That means they have great difficulty in understanding very basic information. How can one promote rational processes of conflict resolution in this situation?

Such functional illiteracy is caused, in part, by the fragility of the educational system. Deteriorated schools mirror the economic crisis of developing countries as well as the lack of importance attributed to education by the society. This is largely a result of long-standing social inequities maintained by an elite that benefits from the resulting patron-client relationship. These relationships are so strong that the structural problems continue, even after some conflict resolution measures are taken, such as the empowerment of powerless groups.

Development and Conflict

The interconnection of development factors often causes further conflict escalation. For example, administrative chaos in under-financed governmental bodies often causes the transference of responsibilities from the central state to NGOs, local governments, and the private sector. The result is that such organizations assume duties that may go well beyond their capacities, which causes further conflict. For example, NGOs, local governments, and the private sector lack training in facilitation, mediation, and negotiation, as well as the theoretical knowledge of conflict resolution. So conflicts escalate, with no one knowing what to do about it.

There are few institutions in most developing societies that understand or engage in the practice of conflict resolution. But even when they do, they tend to work with inadequate win-win frameworks. In some cases, for example, negotiation through typical win-win processes is blocked because the powerful within poor communities are criminals. In Brazil, criminal elements are able to exert full control over large territories, mostly within metropolitan areas, from where they traffic in narcotics and weapons. This is one of many reasons why traditional interest-based, win-win negotiation does not work in many cases in developing countries.

In Brazil, the criminal sector has been able to recruit children as young as nine years old. The profile of the typical youth taken to reform schools is shocking. The majority are around 13 years old, yet they are fathers and breadwinners. Most often, they turned to crime because they do not have other employment options nor do they have an expectation of a better life. Due to the economic crisis of the last ten years, permanent and secure employment was largely replaced by "flexible," insecure contracts without the guarantees of the official social security system. This has particularly affected women and other vulnerable groups in society, who form the majority of those working in the informal sector.

This informality has brought further constraints to conflict resolution in developing countries. Many young people are already the second, or even the third generation of families who are mainly employed in "flexible," or "odd" jobs. They lack the culture of work, and the values attributed to it.

Social values are also often undermined by the official educational system, since information disseminated by books in public schools is embedded with prejudice and stereotypes that, for example, overvalue men in detriment of women.

Development aid tries to change such problems. These factors, among others, are the target of the Millennium Goals. However, in many instances, development interventions underestimate local politics, social realities, and belief systems. These are strong factors affecting the opportunities for conflict resolution, which nevertheless have remained overlooked by those working in the field of development theory and practice.

It is remarkable that conflict resolution theory and instruments are also not taken into account either by indigenous organizations, or by international development agencies. This is clearly evidenced by the Human Development Report 2003, published by the United Nations Development Program (UNDP). The report reflects a deep concern with armed, violent and military conflicts such as interstate or civil wars. However, it does not consider other more subtle forms of conflict, or the notion that conflict processes can preclude the achievement of development goals. An understanding of the nature and effects of international development illustrates the reason for this.

Development History

Development practice is not new. It dates back to the European colonies, when colonizers enforced a "civilized," ordered, white, male, Christian ethic. Organized, ongoing development aid followed during the post-colonial period. Development theory, however, came along much later, emerging as a stable, academic field of inquiry only after World War II, when European countries were trying to keep their former colonies at arm's length. Throughout these years, development theory and practice was strongly characterized by the transmission of moral values from industrialized countries to less-industrialized, rural countries.

The development field has always been highly influenced by economic thought, as exemplified by the fact that development has been primarily measured by increases in gross national product (GNP). According to Dennis Rondinelli, during the 1950s and 60s, development intervention assumed that "successful methods, techniques, and ways of solving problems and delivering services in the U.S. or other economically advanced countries would prove equally successful in the developing nations." Therefore, at the very start of development theory, there was a notion of direct transferability, or a "one size fits all" type of development assistance. However, delivering aid was not just a technical matter; it also involved political concerns. For example, during the Cold War, U.S. provision of aid was largely directed to those countries that were, or could come, under Soviet influence.

The 70s were marked by rapid growth of American and European multinational companies in the developing world. While these companies expanded markets and made new goods available, they also exerted predatory competition on indigenous industries. Two theoretical debates emerged in developing countries, especially in Latin America: the dependency theory and the centre-periphery theory. For dependency theorists such as Paul Baran, Andre Gunther Frank, and Fernando Henrique Cardoso, developing countries were trapped in a cycle of dependence on international capital in which there was little room to maneuver. The centre-periphery (or metropolis-satellite) theory developed by Immanuel Wallerstein, argued that movement within and between the centre and the periphery was possible. This theory introduced the concept of a world economy, and said that movement within and between the strata of this economy was regulated by market forces.

Such movement became especially difficult, however, in the 1980s. Due to the financial crisis of this decade, many developing countries could not pay their external debts, and had to adopt economic adjustment measures imposed by the International Monetary Fund (IMF) and the World Bank in order to borrow money. Such measures included cuts in public expenditure, and the development of a more efficient, transparent and accountable state. Though the World Bank recommendation was that "an effective state — not a minimal one — is central to economic and social development," in reality IMF and World Bank requirements have resulted in large cuts in states' size and functions, and little or no increase in accountability and transparency.

During the 90s, the IMF maintained its structural adjustment plan, while the World Bank gained a deeper understanding of other factors that can affect economic performance. Academics such as Nobel laureates Robert Coase (1991), Gary Becker (1992), Douglas North and Robert Fogel (1993), John C. Harsanyi, Reinhard Selten, John F. Nash Jr. (1994), and Amartya Sen (1998) were amongst several authors who focused on transaction costs, property rights, institutions, non-market behaviour and welfare economics in their development theories.

In the 90s, this renewed focus on institutions was combined with a series of world summits organized by the United Nations to discuss development. Environment and development was the theme of the 1992 Rio de Janeiro summit. In 1993, a human rights conference took place in Vienna. Cairo hosted a conference on population and development in 1994. Social development was discussed at the Copenhagen 1995 world summit. Gender issues, especially the role of women, were discussed in 1995 in Beijing. The last conference, Habitat-II, took place in Istanbul to discuss urban issues.

Current Development Theory

While much of development thinking and practice has changed, the moral and political dimensions still remain. Critics of current development theory such as Jonathan Crush and Arturo Escobar, see development as a set of rational, managerial prescriptions through which industrialized nations have largely imposed their views and models onto the beneficiaries of their aid, forcing, to some extent, a change in the identities of those who have been "benefitted." It is still common for academics and practitioners in developing countries to believe that development is a direct transference of Western values onto non-Western cultures. Organizations such as the World Bank, and USAID are believed to impose expertise and authority, silence alternative voices, promote a dependent path to development, and keep their eyes closed to the power imbalances they create.

However, development is not the only influence on a nation; local political processes also have significant effects. Additionally, the development field helps to overcome human rights abuses, protect the environment and empower women. While the debate about the pros and cons of different approaches to development still rages, the constant critiques have inspired a quest for diversity among development theories. As was noted earlier, development interventions are intended to move societies from a situation in which they are believed to be worse off, to situations in which they are assumed to be better off. Certainly, there is a great deal of contention on what determines who is "worse" and who is "better." The traditional paradigms of development theory have historically been similar to those of economics. Specifically, the field of Development Economics tries to explain differences in development conditions mostly through macroeconomic factors. A country's GDP has been, for most economists, the major parameter with which to measure development success. Recently, the contributions of the Nobel laureates of the 1990s, who stressed the political and social dimensions of development, have come under more consideration. Research on development has become multi-disciplinary, embracing policy analysis and starting to focus on the major symptom of failed development, poverty.

Such a multi disciplinary view of development opens an avenue for fresh thinking on the human dimensions of development. The argument for such a view is that development is not an end in itself, but rather a means for achieving better and more equitable living conditions for human beings. Associated with this view, the focus on sustainable development aims at integrating economic, biological, social, cultural, and political dimensions.

Today, all approaches co-exist, and in many instances there is an attempt to reconcile all views of development. There are, certainly, nuances. The two tables below show the approaches to development topics from the World Bank and from the Eldis Gateway to Development, which presents a more academic view of development. The Eldis Gateway tends to emphasize anthropological and sociological approaches, while the World Bank's literature tends to stress the economics of development.

4

Max Weber: The Fundamental Concepts of Sociology

Definitions of Sociology and Social Action

Sociology is a science which attempts the interpretive understanding of social action to arrive at a casual explanation of its course and effects. Sociology seeks to formulate type concepts and generalized uniformities of empirical processes. (History, on the other hand, is interested in the causal analysis of particular events, actions or personalities.)

Action is human behaviour to which the acting individual attaches subjective meaning. It can be overt or inward and subjective. Action is social when, by virtue of the subjective meaning attached to it by the acting individual(s), it takes account of the behaviour of others and is thereby guided. Social action may be oriented to past, present, or predicted future behaviour of others. Others may be concrete people or indefinite pluralities.

Not all action is social: if it ain't oriented to the behaviour of others, it ain't social. Also, it is not merely action participated in by a bunch of people (crowd action) or action influenced by or imitative of others.

Action can be causally determined by the behaviour of others, while still not necessarily being meaningfully determined by the action of others. If I do what you do because it's fashionable, or traditional, or leads to social distinction, its meaningful. Obviously the lines are blurred (pp 113-114), but it's important to make a conceptional distinction.

Modes of Orientation of social action:

Uniformity of social action = action which is wide-spread, frequently repeated by the same individual or simultaneously performed by many individuals and which corresponds to a subjective meaning attributable to the same actors.

Usage: probability of a uniformity in the orientation of social action, when the probability is determined by its actual practice ('it is done to conform with the pattern).

Custom: usage when the actual performance of the action rests on long familiarity. Non-conformance is sanctioned externally. Action can also be uniform if the actor acts in his self-interests. The uniformity rests insofar as behaviour is determined by purely rational actions of actors to similar ulterior expectations.

Types of Social Action, identified by mode of orientation:

- Rational orientation to a system of discrete individual ends. individuals can choose and adjudicate between both means and ends, though these considerations may be with reference to other absolute values.
- Rational orientation to an absolute value, involving conscious belief in the absolute value entirely for its own sake and independent of prospects for external success. Can choose b/t means, but only with relation to absolute, fixed end. Absolute values are always irrational.
- Affectional orientation. If this is uncontrolled reaction to some exceptional stimulus, it is not meaningful — grey areas.
- Traditional orientation. If this is strict imitation, it is not meaningful — grey areas.

Foundations of Sociology

There are 2 kinds of meaning: 1) actually existing meaning in a given concrete case of a particular actor, or average or approximate meaning attributed to a given number of actors; and 2) theoretically conceived pure types of subjective meaning attributed to hypothetical actor(s) in a given type of action (like an ideal type).

The line between meaningful action and reactive behaviour w/o subjective meaning is blurry. The basis for understanding meaning may be either rational (logical or mathematical — clear intellectual grasp of things) or emotionally empathetic or artistically appreciative (though sympathetic participation we grasp the emotional context in which the action took place).

For purposes of ideal type analysis, it's convenient to treat irrational (from the point of view of rational pursuit of a given end) action as deviation from a conceptually pure type of rational action. We compare this analytically clear type to empirical reality, and that increases our understanding of how actually action is influences by irrational factors. The more sharp and precise the ideal type (and thus the more abstract and unrealistic) the more useful it is in clarifying terminology and formulating classifications and hypotheses.

Some phenomena are devoid of subjective meaning. What is intelligible about an object is its relation to human action in its role either of means or of end, a relation which actors can be said to be aware of and to which their action has been oriented. If you can't make this relation (for example a hindering or favorable circumstance) it's not meaningful in the sense we care about.

There are 2 kinds of understanding: 1) direct observational understanding of subjective mean of a given act (eg, if i start to shout at you, you could directly observe my irrational emotional reaction by virtue of my shouting). 2) explanatory understanding: we understand motive, or, what makes an individual do a particular thing in a particular circumstance. Since we are interested in the subjective meaning of action, we must place an action in the complex of meaning in which it took place. A motive is a complex of subjective meaning which seems to the actor and/OR the observer an adequate ground for the conduct in question.

In most cases, actual action goes on in a state of inarticulate half-consciousness or actually unconsciousness of its subjective meaning. The ideal type case of meaning is where meaning is fully conscious and explicit: this rarely happens in reality.

Adequacy on the level of meaning: a subjective interpretation of a coherent course of conduct when its component parts in their mutual relation are recognized as a 'typical' complex of meaning.

Eg, according to our current norms of calculation and thinking, the correct solution to an arithmatical problem.

Casual adequacy: there's a probability it will always actually occur in the same way. Eg, statistical probability, according to verified generalization from experience, that there would be a correct or incorrect solution to the arithmatical problem. Depends on being able to determine that there's a probability a will follow b.

Subjectively understandable action exists ONLY as the behaviour of one or more individual human beings. States, for instance, are results of particular acts of individual persons. There is no such things as a collective personality that acts. These concepts of collective entities DO HAVE meanings in the minds of individual persons, and so actors orient their actions to them as if they existed or should exist.

Functional analysis is a good starting point for sociology. We need to know what kinds of action is functionally necessary for survival, and also for the maintenance of a cultural type and the corresponding modes of social action. We are interested, though, in the subjective meaning of actions to component individuals. The interesting question, then, is what motives determine and lead the individual members and participants in this situation to behave in such a way that the situation came into being in the first place.

Concept of Social Relationship

Social relationship: the behaviour of actors in so far as, in its meaningful content, the action of each takes account of the others and is oriented to the behaviour of others. Mere group membership is not sufficient. The relation of the actors may be solidary, or the opposite. Eg, a 'state' ceases to exist when there is no longer a probability that certain kinds of meaningfully oriented social action will take place. The subjective meaning need not be the same for all parties to the relationship. The relationship may be temporary or long term. Its subjective meaning may change over time.

The Concept of Legitimate Order

The validity of an order is the probability that people will orient their action to it.

Types of Legitimate Order

Legitimacy of an order can be upheld in 2 ways:

- Purely disinterested motives a) purely affectual, b) rational belief in absolute validity of an order as an expression of ultimate values, c) religious attitudes, through belief in need to follow order for salvation
- Entirely through self-interest based on ulterior motives

Convention: system of order where infraction meets with sanctions of disapproval and orders are considered binding.

Law: system of order where the above is enforced by a functionally specialized agency (e.g., the police). A system of order with external sanctions may also be guaranteed by disinterested subjective attitudes. Eg, it can be both morally wrong and illegal to murder.

Bases of Legitimacy

Legitimacy may be ascribed to an order by those subject to it in the following ways:

- Tradition, belief in legitimacy of what has always existed.
- Affectual attitudes, legitimizing the validity of what is newly revealed or is a model to imitate
- Rational belief in its absolute value
- Legality. Readiness to conform with rules which are formally correct and have been imposed by accepted procedure.

Submission to an order is almost always determined by a variety of motives.

Max Weber: Class, Status and Party

All communities are arranged in a manner that goods, tangible and intangible, symbolic and material are distributed. Such a distribution is always unequal and necessarily involves power. "Classes, status groups and parties are phenomena of the distribution of power within a community" (927). Status groups makes up the social order, classes the economic order, and parties the legal/political order. Each order affects and is affected by the other.

Power

Power is the "chance of a man or a number of men to realize their own will in a social action even against the resistance of others who are participating in the action".

Power may rest of a variety of bases, and can be of differing types. "Economically conditioned power is not identical with power... The emergence of economic power may be the consequence of power existing on other grounds. Man does not strive for power only to enrich himself economically. Power, including economic power, may be valued for its own sake. Very frequently the striving for power is conditioned by the social honor it entails. Not all power entails honor." Power is not the only basis of social honor, and social honor, or prestige, may be the basis of economic power. "Power, as well as honor, may be guaranteed by the legal order, but... [the legal order] is not their primary source. The legal order is rather an additional factor that enhances the chance to hold power or honor; but it cannot always secure them".

Class

Class is defined in terms of market situation. A class exists when a number of people have in common a specific casual component of their life chances in the following sense: this component is represented exclusively by economic interests in the possession of goods and opportunities for income under conditions of the commodity or labour markets.

When market conditions prevail (eg, capitalism), property and lack of property are the basic categories of all class situations. However, the concept of class-interest is ambiguous. Collective action based on class situations is determined by the transparency of the connections between the causes and the consequences of the class situation. If the contrast between the life chances of different class situations is merely seen as an acceptable absolute fact, no action will be taken to change the class situation. A class in and of itself does not constitute a group (Gemeinschaft). "The degree in which social action and possibly associations emerge from the mass behaviour of the members of a class is linked to general cultural conditions, especially those of an intellectual sort".

"If classes as such are not groups, class situations emerge only on the basis of social action."

Status Groups and Honor

Unlike classes, status groups do have a quality of groups. They are determined by the distribution of social honor. A specific style of life is shared by a status group, and the group itself is defined by those with whom one has social intercourse. Economic elements can be a sort of honor; however, similar class position does not necessitate similar status groups. People from different economic classes may be members of the same status group, if they share the same specific style of life.

The way in which social honor is distributed in the community is called the status order. Criteria for entry into a status group may take forms such as the sharing of kinship groups or certain levels of education. The most extreme of a status system with a high level of closure (that is, strong restriction of mobility between statuses) is a caste system. There, status distinctions are guaranteed no only by law and convention, but also by religious sanctions.

Relationships between Class and Status group; between Class situation, Status Situation, and Stratification. Status groups can sometimes be equal to class, sometimes be broader, sometimes more restrictive, and sometimes bear no relation to class (duh). In most cases, status situation is the apparent dimension of stratification: "stratification by status goes hand in hand with a monopolization of ideal and material goods or opportunities". Class situation can take precedence over status situation, however. "When the bases of the acquisition and distribution of goods are relatively stable, stratification by status is favored". Technological and economic changes threaten stratification by status, and "push class situation to the foreground.... Every slowing down of the change in economic stratification leads, in due course, to the growth or status structures and makes for a resuscitation of the important role of social honor" .

Parties

"Parties reside in the sphere of power". "Parties are... only possible within groups that have an asssociational character, that is, some rational order and a staff of persons". Parties aim for social power, the ability to influence the actions of others, and thus may exist in a social club, the state, or a cohort of graduate students at the University of Chicago.

Parties may represent class or status interests, or neither. They usually represent a mix. "The structure of parties differs in a basic way according to the kind of social action which they struggle to influence.... [T]hey differ according to whether or not the community is stratified by class or status. Above all else, they vary according to the structure of domination".

The Protestant Ethic and the Spirit of Capitalism

Though knowledge and observation of great refinement have existed elsewhere, only in the West has rationalization in science, law and culture developed to such a great degree. The modern West absolutely and completely depends for its whole existence, for the political technical, and economic conditions of its life, on a specially trained organization of individuals, so that the most important functions of everyday life have come to be in the hands of technically, commercially and above all legally trained government officials. Nowhere else does this exist to such a degree as it does in the West.

The most fateful force in modern life is capitalism. The impulse to acquisition has existed always and everywhere and has in itself nothing to do with capitalism. Capitalism is the pursuit of profit, and forever renewed profit, by means of continuous, rational, capitalistic enterprise. This enterprise must be continuous, because in a capitalistic society, anyone who did not take advantage of opportunities for profit-making would be doomed to extinction.

A capitalistic economic action rests on the expectation of profit by the utilization of opportunities for exchange, on (formally) peaceful chances for profit. Where this is rationally pursued, calculations in terms of money are made, whether by modern bookkeeping or more primitive means. Everything is done in terms of balances of money income and money expenses. Whether the calculations are accurate, or whether the calculation method is traditional or by guess-work affects only the degree of the rationality of capitalistic acquisition. Characteristics of modern Western capitalism: rational industrial organization (that is, attuned to a regular profit and not to political nor irrational speculative opportunities for profit); separation of business from the household; rational bookkeeping. Capitalistic adventurers (in search of booty, whether by war or exploitation) have existed everywhere, but only in the modern West has developed... the rational capitalistic organization of (formally) free labour.

The rationality of MWC is dependent on the calculation of technical factors, and so is dependent on the development in science of the exact and rational experiment. C'ism did not cause this development: but, the continuing development of this type science is supported by capitalistic interests in practical economic applications.

The peculiar rationalism of Western culture extends to many fields — science, mystical contemplation, military training, law and administration. Each of theses fields may be rationalized in terms of very different ultimate values and ends, and what is rational from one point of view may well be irrational from another. The development of economic rationalism is partly dependent on rational technique and law, but it also requires people to have a favorable disposition toward adopting certain types of practical rational conduct.

Religious Affiliation and Social Stratification

Catholics show a stronger propensity to remain in their crafts, and become master craftsmen, while Protestants are attracted to a larger extent to the upper ranks of skilled labour and administrative positions in factories. Protestants own a disproportionate share of capital. All other things equal, Protestants have been more likely to develop economic rationalism than Catholics. Weber seeks the explanation in 'the permanent intrinsic character of their religion,' and not only in their temporary external historico-political situations.

The Reformation meant not the elimination of the church's control over everyday life, but a substitution of a new form of control for the previous one. While the Catholic church was fairly lax, Calvinism 'would be for us the most absolutely unbearable form of ecclesiastical control of the individual which could possibly exist.' Protestantism must not be understood as joy of living or in any other sense connected with the Enlightenment. Early Protestantism (e.g., Luther, Calvin) had nothing to do with progress in an Enlightenment sense. Not all Protestant denominations had an equally strong influence on the development of members' business acumen and spirit of hard work.

The Spirit of Capitalism

The spirit of capitalism is "an historical individual: a complex of elements associated in historical reality which we united into a conceptual whole from the standpoint of their cultural significance". Ben Franklin is an example of someone who espouses a philosophy of avarice which is: the ideal of an honest man of recognized credit. It includes a duty on the part of an individual toward the increase of his capital, which is assumed as an end in itself. It is not mere business astuteness, it is an ethos; infraction of its rules is not foolishness or bad business, but forgetfulness of duty.

In this ethic, economic acquisition is no longer considered a means of subsistence: it is the ultimate purpose of a man's life. This is combined with the strict avoidance of all spontaneous enjoyment of life. People now are born into a capitalistic economy which presents itself to them as the unalterable order of things in which they must live. In so far as a person born now is involved in the system of market relationships, he must conform to capitalistic rules of action. Today's capitalism selects the subjects it needs through economic survival of the fittest.

In order to arise, the spirit of capitalism had to struggle with its 'most important opponent,' traditionalism. For instance, workers will respond to an increase in piece rates by doing less work, collecting the usual amount of money, and going home early. Men do not "by nature" wish to earn more and more money, they simply wish to live as they are accustomed to and to earn as much as is necessary for that purpose.

Another way of attempting to increase productivity is to lower wages or piece rates, so that workers must work harder and longer to earn the same amount as before. This method has its limits. It (and capitalism) requires a surplus population which can be hired cheaply in the market. Also, too large a surplus population can encourage the development of labour intensive methods, rather than more efficient methods: low wages do not equal cheap labour. And, if you pay people too little, their efficiency and attentiveness decreases.

Thus, it would be better if labour were performed as if it were an absolute end in itself. This can only be the process of a long and arduous education (for example, being raised Pietist). Capitalism "now in the saddle" can fairly easily recruit the required workers, but this was not always the case.

Capitalism can exist with a traditionalistic character. The animating spirit of the entrepreneur may be the traditional rate of profit, the traditional amount of work, the traditional manner of labour-management relations, and the essentially traditional circle of customers and manner of attracting new ones. Take the example of the putting out system.

In such a system, this leisureliness can be destroyed, without any essential change in the form of work organization (such as vertically integrated factories). The spirit of capitalism is the cause of this change. Where the spirit of capitalism appears and is able to work itself out, it produces its own capital and monetary supplies as the means to its ends, but the reverse is not true. Protestantism was not merely a stage prior to the development of a purely rationalistic philosophy, however. Rationalism shows a development which by no means follows parallel lines in the various departments of life. Since life may be rationalized from fundamentally different basic points of view and in very different directions, we must ask the origin of the irrational element which lies at the basis of this particular concrete form of rational thought: the conception of a calling.

Luther's Conception of The Calling

The idea of a calling — a life-task, a definite field in which to work — is peculiar to Protestants. Protestantism had a further new development, which was the valuation of the fulfillment of duty in worldly affairs as the highest form which the moral activity of an individual could assume. The only way of living acceptably to God was solely through the fulfillment of the obligations imposed upon the individual by his position in the world (his calling), NOT by trying to surpass worldly morality by monastic asceticism.

Remember important part of Reformation: By faith, not works, shall ye be saved. You are justified by faith, etc. So all those indulgences earned by crawling on your knees up stairways, etc. don't get you anything. For the time being (before Calvin et al. got hold of it), the idea of the calling remained traditionalistic and its only ethical result negative: worldly duties were no longer subordinated to ascetic ones; obedience to authority and acceptance of things as they were, were preached.

Religious Foundations of Worldly Asceticism

However, this idea of the calling was not sufficient for the development of the spirit of capitalism. We needed the effects of forms of ascetic Protestantism: Calvinism, Pietism, Methodism and the Baptist sects. An important thing to keep in mind is that these folks were not motivated by acquisitive lusts, but rather by salvation of the soul. Calvinists believed in predestination. God designated before the creation of the world who would be saved and who would get to rot in hell. All creation exists for the sake of God, and has meaning only as means to the glory and majesty of God. Human merit or guilt plays no part in the possession of grace, since that would make God's decrees subject to human influence. This doctrine 'must above all have one consequence... a feeling of unprecedented inner loneliness of the single individual'. The individual was forced to follow the path of his own destiny decreed for him from eternity without help from others or from the Church — complete elimination of salvation through the Church and the sacraments (which Lutheranism retained). This meant the elimination of magic from the world. [It also meant the doing away with a periodical discharge of the emotional sense of sin (confession).]

Now, the elected Christian should glorify God in life by fulfilling God's commandments to the best of his ability. This requires social achievements of the Christian because God decrees that social life shall be organized according to his commandments.

Fear and lack of knowledge of whether or not one is going to rot in hell led to a need for ordinary men to find certitudo salutis (certainty of salvation). Pastoral advice to these poor, tortured dudes contained two themes: 1) an absolute duty to consider oneself chosen and to combat all doubts as temptations of the devil, since lack of self-confidence is the result of insufficient faith, hence of imperfect grace. 2) Intense worldly activity as the most suitable means to attain that self-confidence [thus we eliminate the free rider problem]. The Calvinist sought to identify true faith by its fruits: a type of Christian conduct which served to increase the glory of God. Good works do not affect salvation, but they are indispensable as a sign of election. In practice, this means God helps those who help themselves. The Calvinist creates a conviction of his own salvation.

For Catholics, good works were not a part of a rationalized system of life — they could be performed sporadically, to atone — whereas for Calvinists they are. The God of Calvinism demanded not single good works, but a life of good works combined into a unified system. The moral conduct of the average man was subjected to a consistent method for conduct as a whole. The end of this asceticism was to be able to lead an alert, intelligent life: the most urgent task the destruction of spontaneous, impulsive enjoyment. The most important means was to bring order into the conduct of its adherents. Hence we have methodically rationalized ethical conduct.

The Calvinistic doctrine of predestination was only one of several possible motives which could have supported the methodical rationalization of life. However, it had not only a unique consistency (by virtue of being based on logical deduction, rather than religious experience) and was psychologically extraordinarily powerful.

Pietism

This sect sought to make the invisible Church of the elect visible on this earth. By means of intensified asceticism these folks hoped to enjoy the blissfulness of community with God in this life. Sometimes this latter tendency led to displays of emotion, which were antithetical to Calvinist restraint. Other than that, however, the practical effect of Pietistic principles was an even stricter ascetic control of conduct in the calling:

- Methodical development of one's own state of grace to a higher and higher degree of certainty and perfection in terms of the law was a sign of grace.
- A belief that God's Providence works through those in such a state of perfection.

Since some of these folks believed grace subject to repentance, by the creation of methods to induce repentance even the attainment of divine grace became in effect an object of rational human activity.

Methodism

Though rebirth, an emotional certainty of salvation as the immediate result of faith was an important factor, the emotional act of conversion was methodically induced. Emotion, once awakened, was directed into a rational struggle for perfection. This provided a religious basis for ascetic conduct after the doctrine of predestination had been given up by these folks.

The Baptist Sects

The church was viewed as a community of personal believers of the reborn. Salvation was achieved by personal, individual revelation; it was offered to everyone, though not everyone took it.

The injunction was to be in the world but not of it, so worldly enjoyments and unnecessary social intercourse with non-reborn folks was avoided. The Holy Spirit worked in daily life, and spoke directly to any individual who was willing to hear. This leads to an eventual elimination of all that remained of the doctrine of salvation through the Church and sacraments. This accomplished the religious rationalization of the world in its most extreme form.

Conscience is the revelation of God to the individual. The rationalization of conduct within the world, but for the sake of the world beyond, was the consequence of the concept of calling of ascetic Protestantism.

The Spirit of Capitalism

In Puritan thinking, the real moral objection to possession of wealth is to relaxation in the security of possession, the enjoyment of wealth with the consequence of idleness and the temptations of the flesh, above all distraction from the pursuit of a righteous life. It is only because possession involves this danger that it is suspect at all. Not leisure and enjoyment, but only activity serves to increase the glory of God. Waste of time is thus the first and in principle the deadliest of sins. Thus, inactive contemplation at the expense of work is right out. Labour is an approved ascetic technique, but is also considered in itself an end of life as ordained by God. Unwillingness to work is symptomatic of the lack of grace. Wealth does not exempt anyone from this.

The division of labour, which has a providential purpose in the thought of the Puritans, leads to qualitative and quantitative improvements in production, and thus serves the common good. But, in addition, specialization is encouraged by the calling, to which it provides an ethical justification; for, "outside of a calling the accomplishments of a man are only casual and irregular and he spends more time in idleness than in work." If God presents to His elect a change for profit, he must pursue it: the Christian must follow the call by taking advantage of the opportunity. The acquisition of wealth in the performance of a calling is morally permissible and enjoined.

- Asceticism turned against the spontaneous enjoyment of life. So, sport, for instance, is acceptable only if it serves a rational purpose, say, increasing physical efficiency.
- The powerful tendency toward uniformity of life, which today so immensely aids the capitalistic interest in the standardization of production, had its ideal foundation in the repudiation of all idolatry of the flesh (eg, non-ascetic, flashy or attractive clothing).

The Puritan outlook on life 'stood at the cradle of modern economic man'. This religious epoch bequeathed to its utilitarian successors "an amazingly good... conscience in the acquisition of money, so long as it took place legally". In addition, the power of religious asceticism provided owners with sober, conscientious and industrious workmen. And, it provided comforting assurance that the unequal distribution of goods in the world was ordained by God. The religious basis had died away by Ben Franklin's time. Limitation to specialized work is now a condition of any valuable work in the modern world. "The Puritan wanted to work in a calling; we are forced to do so.

For when asceticism was carried out of monastic cells into everyday life, and began to dominate worldly morality, did its part in building the tremendous cosmos of the modern economic order This order is now bound to the technical and economic conditions of machine production and today determine the lives of all the individuals who are born into this mechanism, not only those directly concerned with economic acquisition, with irresistible force."

Religious Rejections of the World and Their Directions

Individual spheres of value presented here as ideal types have a rational consistency rarely found in reality. This essay proceeds from the most rational forms reality can assume; it attempts to find out how far certain rational conclusions, which can be established theoretically, have been drawn in reality. Perhaps, also, we can find out why those rational conclusions have not been drawn.

Typology of Asceticism and Mysticism

Two contrasting abnegations of the world:

- Active asceticism that is a God-willed ACTION of the devout who are God's tools. Rationally active asceticism, in mastering the world, seeks to tame what is creatural and wicked through work in a worldly vocation (inner-worldly asceticism);
- Contemplative POSSESSION of the holy as found in mysticism. The individual is not a tool, but a vessel of the divine. Desired: other-worldly religious state; contemplative flight from the world.

Active asceticism may confine itself to controlling wickedness in the actor's own nature; in this case, it avoids any action in the orders of the world (asceticist flight from the world). In external bearing, it thereby comes close to contemplative flight. Conversely, the mystic may determine s/he need not flee from the world, and so be an inner-worldly mysticist, remaining in the orders of the world.

Abnegation of the World

Formulated abstractly, the rational aim of redemption religion has been to secure for the saved a holy state, and thereby a habitude that assures salvation. This takes the place of an acute and extraordinary, and thus a holy state which is transitorily achieved by means of orgies, asceticism, or contemplation. Most prophetic and redemptory religions have lived not only in an acute, but a permanent state of tension in relation to the world and its orders. The more the religions have been true religions of salvation, the greater has this tension been. The tension has been greater the more religion has been sublimated from ritualism and towards 'religious absolutism.' Indeed, the further the rationalization and sublimation of external and internal possession of — in the widest sense — things worldly has progressed, the stronger has the tension on the part of religion become. For the rationalization and conscious sublimation of man's relations to the various spheres of values, internal and external, as well as religious and secular, have then pressed towards making conscious the internal and lawful autonomy of the individual spheres; thereby letting them drift into those tensions which remain hidden to the original naive relation with the external world.

The more comprehensive and the more inward the aim of salvation has been, the more it has been taken for granted that the faithful should ultimately stand closer to the savior, the prophet, the priest, the brother in the faith than to natural relations and to the matrimonial community. Prophecy has created a new social community; thereby the relationships of the sib and of matrimony have been devalued.

Communities of villages, members of the sib, the guild or of partners in seafaring, hunting and warring expeditions have known two elemental principles: first, the dualism or in-group and out-group morality. For in-group morality the principled obligation to give brotherly support in distress has existed. All this followed the principle of "your want of today, may be my want of tomorrow" (this principle was not rationally weighed, but it played its part in sentiment). Accordingly, haggling in exchange and loan situations, as well as permanent debt-enslavement and similar kinds of enslavement, were confined to outgroup morality and applied only to outsiders. The religiosity of the congregation transferred the ancient economic ethic of neighborliness (I'll help you out today, since I may need you to help me out tomorrow) to the relations among brothers of the faith.

What had previously been the obligations of the noble and the wealthy became the fundamental imperatives of all ethically rationalized religion (to care for orphans and widows, to give alms).

The principle that constituted the communal relations among the salvation prophesies was the suffering common to all believers (whether or not the suffering actually existed or was a constant threat, whether it was internal or external). The more imperatives that issued from the ethic of reciprocity among neighbors were raised, the more rational the conception of salvation became, and the more it was sublimated into an ethic of absolute ends.

The Economic Sphere

The tension between brotherly religion and the world has been most obvious in the economic sphere. All the primeval magical or mystagogic ways of influencing spirits and deities have pursued special interests. The sublimated religions of salvation, however, had been increasingly tense in their relationships with rationalized economies.

A rational economy is a functional organization oriented to money-prices which originate in the interest-struggles of men in the market. Calculation is not possible without estimation in money prices and hence without market struggles. Money is the most abstract and impersonal element that exists in human life. The more the world of the capitalist economy follows its own immanent laws, the less accessible it is to any imaginable relationship with a religious ethic of brotherliness. Ultimately no genuine religion of salvation has overcome the tension between their religiosity and a rational economy.

The paradox of all rational asceticism is that rational asceticism has created the very wealth it rejected.

There have only been two consistent avenues for escaping the tension between religion and in the economic world in a principled and inward manner:

- The Puritan ethic of the vocation. Puritanism, as a religion of virtuosos, renounced the universalism of love and rationally routinized all work in this world into serving God's will and testing ones state of grace. Puritanism accepted the routinization of the economic cosmos, which, along with the whole world, it devalued as creatural and depraved. It involved a renunciation of salvation in favor of the groundless and always only particularized grace. Actually, this standpoint of unbrotherliness was no longer a genuine religion of salvation. A genuine religion of salvation can exaggerate brotherliness to the height of the mystic's acosmism of love.
- Mysticism. The mystic's benevolence does not inquire into the man to whom and for whom it sacrifices. Mysticism is not interested in his person. Mysticism is a unique escape form this world in the form of an objectless devotion to anybody, not for man's sake, but purely for devotion's sake.

The Political Sphere

The consistent brotherly ethic of salvation religions has come into an equally sharp tension with the political orders of the world. Local (community, tribe, household, etc.) gods and magic were not a problem The problem arose when these barriers of locality, tribe and polity were shattered by universalistic religions. And the problem arose in full strength only when this god was a god of 'love.' The problem of tension with the political order emerged for redemption religions out of the basic demand for brotherliness. In politics as in economics, the more rational the political order became, the sharper the problems of these tensions became. The brotherliness of a group of men bound together in war appears valueless in brotherly religions; it is seen as a mere reflection of the technically sophisticated brutality of the struggle. It's consecration appears as the glorification of fratricide.

The only two consistent solutions (first three guesses don't count...): puritanism and mysticism. Puritanism believes God's commands should be imposed on the world by the means of the world — violence, so "just war" is not a problem for Puritanism

(God is on their side). The mystics take a "radical political attitude" of "turning the other cheek" which makes them appear "necessarily vulgar and lacking in dignity in the eyes of every self-assured worldly ethic of heroism."

Organic social ethics (where religiously substructured) stands on the soil of brotherliness, but, in contrast to mystic and acosmic love, is dominated by a cosmic, rational demand for brotherliness. It point of departure is the experience of the inequality of religious charisma. The fact that the holy should be accessible to some and not all is unbearable to organic social ethics. It therefore attempts to synthesize this inequality of charismatic qualifications with secular stratification by status, into a cosmos of God-ordained services which are specialized in function. Certain tasks are given to every individual and every group according to their social and economic position as determined by fate. Without something like the Indian doctrine of Karma (which says there's a reason why you're bottom dog), every organic social ethic unavoidably represents an accommodation to the interests of the privileged strata of the world.

From the standpoint of inner-worldly asceticism, the organic ethic lacks the drive for an ethical and thorough rationalization of individual life. In such matters, it has no premium for the rational and methodical patterning of personal life in the interest of the individual's own salvation. The organic pragmatism of salvation must consider the redemptory aristocracy of inner-worldly asceticism, with its rational depersonalization of life orders, as the hardest form of lovelessness and lack of brotherliness. It must also consider the redemptory pragmatism of mysticism as a sublimated and unbrotherly indulgence of the mystic' s own charisma. Both inner-worldly asceticism and mysticism ultimately condemn the social world to absolute meaninglessness (or, at least they hold that God's aims concerning the world are utterly incomprehensible).

The rationalism of religious and organic doctrines of society cannot stand up under this idea; for it seeks to comprehend the world as an at least relatively rational cosmos in spite of all its wickedness: the world must hear at least traces of the divine plan of salvation. The organic ethic of society is an eminently conservative power hostile to revolution. Virtuoso religion is a potentially revolutionary force. Its revolutionary turn may assume two forms:

- It becomes a religious duty to realize this divine natural law. This corresponds to an obligation to crusade.
- The commands of the world do not hold for the man who is assured in his obsession with god.

Aesthetic Sphere

The development of intellectualism and the rationalism of life make art become a cosmos of more and more consciously grasped independent values which exist in their own right. Art comes to provide a salvation from the routines of everyday life, and begins to compete directly with salvation religion. [The refusal of modern man to assume responsibility for moral judgements tends to transform judgements of moral intent into judgements of taste.]

Erotic Sphere

The brotherly ethic of salvation religion is in profound tension with the greatest irrational force of life: sexual love. The more sublimated sexuality is, and the more principled and relentlessly consistent the salvation ethic of brotherhood is, the sharper is the tension between sex and religion. A principled ethic of religious brotherhood perceives that inner, earthly salvation by mature love competes in the sharpest possible way with devotion to a supra-mundane God. Inner-worldly and rational asceticism (vocational asceticism) can accept only the rationally regulated marriag·

Intellectual Sphere

The tension between religion and intellectual knowledge comes to the fore wherever rational, empirical knowledge has consistently worked through to the disenchantment of the world. Every increase of rationalism in empirical science increasing pushes religion from the rational into the irrational realm; but only today does religion become the irrational or anti-rational supra-human power.

The less magic or merely contemplative mysticism and the more pure doctrine a religion contains, the greater is its need of rational apologetics. The more religion became book-religion and doctrine, the more literary it became and the more efficacious it became in provoking rational lay-thinking, freed of priestly control. However, there is no "unbroken" religion working as a vital force which is not compelled at some point to demand the credo non quod, sed quia absurdum (some saint said this, but i can't remember which one, it means "i believe it because it is absurd". i think it was said in reference to the trinity), the sacrifice of the intellect.

Redemptory religion defends itself against the attack of the self-sufficient intellect, by raising the claim that religious knowledge moves in a different sphere.

The need for salvation, consciously cultivated as the substance of religiosity, has resulted from the endeavor of a systematic and practical rationalization of life's realities. All religions have demanded as a specific presupposition that the course of the world be somehow meaningful, at least in so far as it touches upon the interests of men (this claim arises first as the problem of unjust suffering and just compensation for the unequal distribution of individual happiness in the world). From here, the claim has tended to progress toward an ever increasing devaluation of the world. For, the more intensely rational thought has seized upon the problem of a just and retributive compensation, the less an entirely inner-worldly solution could seem possible, and the less an other-worldly solution could appear probable or even meaningful.

The intellect, like all culture values, has created an aristocracy based on the possession of rational culture and independent of all personal ethical qualities of man. The aristocracy of intellect is hence an unbrotherly aristocracy. Worldly man has regarded the possession of culture as the highest good. In addition to the burden of ethical guilt, however, something has adhered to this cultural value which was bound to depreciate it with still greater finality, namely, senselessness (if the cultural value is to be judged in terms of its own standards).

The pure inner-worldly perfection of self by a man of "culture", the ultimate value to which "culture" has seemed to be reducible is meaningless for religious thought. This meaninglessness follows for religious thought from the obvious meaninglessness of death when viewed from the inner-worldly standpoint. The cultivated man can die weary of life, but never satiated with it; for, the perfectibility of the man of culture, in principle, progresses indefinitely, as do the cultural values.

Culture appears as man's emancipation from the organically prescribed cycle of natural life. For this reason, culture's every step forward seems condemned to lead to an every more devastating senselessness. The advancement of cultural values seems to become a senseless hustle in the service of worthless, moreover self-contradictory, and mutually antagonistic ends. The advancement of cultural values appears the more meaningless the more it is made a holy task, a "calling." These specific intellectual and mystical attempts at salvation in the face of these tensions succumb in the end to the world dominion of unbrotherliness. One the one hand, their charisma is not accessible to everyone. Hence, in intent, mystical salvation means aristocracy; it is an aristocratic religiosity of redemption. And, in the midst of a culture that is rationally organized for a vocational workaday life, there is hardly any room for the cultivation of acosmic brotherliness, unless it is among the strata of the economically carefree. Under the technical and social conditions of rational culture, an imitation of the life of Buddha, Jesus or Francis seems condemned to failure for purely external reasons.

General Economic History

C'ism is present wherever the industrial provision for the needs of a human group is carried out by the method of enterprise. A rational capitalistic enterprise is one with capital accounting, according to the methods of modern bookkeeping and the striking of a balance. In a given economy, parts may be capitalistically organized, and other parts not so. An epoch is capitalistic if the provision of its wants is organized capitalistically to such a degree that the whole economic system would collapse if we take away the capitalistic form of organization.

General presuppositions for the existence of modern day capitalism (thinking along the ideal type line):

- Rational capital accounting. This involves the appropriation of all physical means of production as the property of autonomous private enterprises.

- Freedom of the market, in the sense of the absence of irrational limits on trading in the market.
- Rational technology, to permit the required calculability. This implies mechanization.
- Calculable law, the dependability of calculable adjudication and administration.
- Free (not slave or serf) labour, people legally in the position to, and economically compelled to, sell their labour on the market without restriction.
- Commercialization of economic life: general use of commercial instruments to represent share rights in enterprise and also in property ownership.

Development of Industrial Technique

Real distinguishing characteristic of the modern factory: the concentration of ownership of workplace, means of work, source of power and raw material in the hands of the entrepreneur.

Development of use of coal, and subsequent production of iron had 3 important consequences:

- Released technology and productive capabilities from the limits inherent in the qualities of organic industry (eg, horses get tired, the wind doesn't always blow, etc.)
- Mechanization of the production process thorough the steam engine liberated production from the organic limitations of human labour (it ain't just horses that get tired; and people can't lift as much, work as fast, as reliably, etc.)
- Through union with science, the production of goods was emancipated from the bonds of tradition and came under the dominance of freely roving intelligence.

Recruitment of the labour force for this new form of production was carried by means of indirect compulsion. The enclosure movement and changes in agricultural production left a bunch of people wandering around without jobs, who were forced into jobs by being threatened with the "workhouse" if they didn't take jobs in the new factories. From the beginning of the 18th c., there began to be laws to regulate employers conduct toward their employees, to ensure laborers were paid in money and not in kind. War needs and luxury consumption fed capitalism's growth. However, all those silly folks who've argued that war was the driving force are wrong. While the desire of nobility and the upperclasses for luxury goods was important, the increasing production of tapestries and carpets was a key marker of the democratization of luxury, which is the crucial direction of capitalistic production. The decisive impetus for c'ism could only come from mass market demand.

Citizenship

Outside the occident there have not been cities in the sense of a unitary community. Occidental cities originally arose through the establishment of a fraternity; it was in its beginnings first above all a defence group, an organization of those economically competent to bear arms, to equip and train themselves. These folks owned their own arms: this is key.

In places like Egypt, Asia, India and China, irrigation was a big issue, and so kings' bureaucracies developed. The king and his staff required the compulsory service of the dependent classes; they in turn were dependent on that bureaucracy. The king also held a military monopoly. In the west, self-equipment and religious brotherhoods (eg, crusaders) meant kings did not have a military monopoly, and so cities could be formed in a western sense, based on mutual defence.

Rational State

Modern capism can survive only in the modern rational state. Characteristics of the Modern Rational State:

- Expert officialdom and rational law. Key: rationalization of procedure... formal juristic thinking inherited from Roman law.
- Economic policy that is continuous and consistent and not dependent on ritualistic/traditional considerations. The first appearance of a rational economic policy was mercantilism: external economic policy consists in taking every advantage of the opponent, to strengthen the hand of the government in its external relations. Mercantilism signifies the development of the state as a political power, this development is to be done directly by increasing the

tax paying power of the population. However, mercantilism wasn't free market: the govt supported monopolies, gave colonial privileges, etc. It disappeared when free trade was established.

Evolution of Capitalistic Spirit

While several factors fed into the development of capitalism, "in the last resort the factor which produced capitalism is the rational permanent enterprise, rational accounting, rational technology and rational law, but not these alone. Necessary complementary factors were the rational spirit, the rationalization of the conduct of life in general, and a rationalistic economic ethic". In the middle ages, the position of the church on economic ethics was that it excluded "higgling" (cute word; he means haggling), overpricing and free competition and included the principle of a just price and the assurance to everyone of a chance to live.

Since Judaism made Christianity possible and gave it the character of a religion essentially free from magic, it rendered a service by removing one of the most serious obstructions to the rationalization of economic life (magic). Prophesies (rather than oracles by lot, etc.) have released the world from magic and in so doing have created the basis for our modern science and technology, and for capitalism.

Basically, then, Weber chats re: the spirit of capitalism, which you know all about from somewhere else.

As noted earlier, the breakdown of the dual economic ethics was key. A note on class conflict: "It was possible for the working class to accept its lot as long as the promise of eternal happiness could be held out to it. When this consolation fell away it was inevitable that those strains and stresses would appear in economic society which since then have been growing rapidly. This point had been reached at the end of the early period of capitalism, at the beginning of the age of iron, in the 19th century".

Basis of Legitimacy

Domination is defined as the probability that certain specific commands (or all commands) will be obeyed by a given group of people. A certain minimum of voluntary submission is necessary;

thus on the part of the submitter there is an interest (whether based on ulterior motives or genuine acceptance) in obedience.

- Not every claim protected by custom or law involves a relation of authority. For instance, if I ask Charles to pay me for the work i do as fulfillment of our contract, I am not exercising authority over him.
- The legitimacy of a system of authority may be treated sociologically only as the probability that to a relevant degree the appropriate attitudes will exist and the corresponding conduct ensue.
- Obedience means the action of the person 'obeying' follows a course such that the content of the command can be taken as the reason for his/her action.

Pure Types of Legitimate Authority

- Rational/legal grounds. belief in the legality of patterns of normative rules and the right of those elevated to authority under such rules to issue commands. Authority held by legally established impersonal order, extends to people only by virtue of offices they hold.
- Traditional grounds. established belief in the sanctity of immemorial traditions and the legitimacy of the status of those exercising authority under them. Authority held by person of the chief who occupies the traditionally sanctioned position of authority; matter of personal obligation and loyalty within the scope of tradition.
- Charismatic grounds. devotion to the specific and exceptional sanctity, heroism or exemplary character of an individual person, and of the normative pattern or order revealed by him. Leader obeyed by personal trust in him, his revelation, heroism, coolness, as far as those qualities fall within the scope of the obeyers belief in his charisma.

Rational Legal Authority

Typical person in authority occupies an office. Person who obeys authority does so only in his capacity as a member of the corporate group, and what he obeys is only the law. Fundamental Qualities:

- Continuous organization of official functions bound by rules
- Specified spheres of competence involving a) sphere of obligations as marked out by a specialized division of labour, b) provision to incumbent of necessary authority to do his sphere of thangs, c) necessary means of compulsion clearly defined and their use subject to definite conditions.
- Organization of offices follows principle of hierarchy.
- Rules which regulate conduct of an office can be either technical rules or norms. when their application is fully rational, specialized training is necessary.
- Office holder separated from ownership of means of production and administration (first of all, separation of house from workplace)
- Complete absence of appropriate of position by incumbent
- Acts, rules and decisions are formulated and recorded in writing.

BUREAUCRACY, almost the same...

- Office holders personally free and subject to authority only within the scope of their impersonal official obligations
- Hierarchy of offices
- Sphere of competence
- Free selection into office; filled by free contractual relationship; always free to resign
- Candidates appointed, not elected, on basis of technical qualifications
- Remuneration is by fixed salaries of $$
- Office is sole or primary occupation of incumbent
- Constitutes a career; system of promotion
- Official can't own means or appropriate position
- Official subject to strict and systematic discipline and control in conduct of office.

Monocratic bureaucracy is capable of attaining the highest degrees of efficiency and is the most rational means known of carrying out imperative control over people. Makes possible a high degree of calculability. Bureaucratic administration means fundamentally the exercise of control on the basis of knowledge.

General Social Consequences

- Tendency of levelling in the interest of broadest possible recruitment in terms of technical competence
- Tendency to plutocracy due to interest in greatest possible length of technical training
- Dominance of spirit of formalistic impersonality. Sine ira et studio, w/o anger or passion, and hence without affection or enthusiasm. All subject to formal equality of treatment.

Traditional Authority

Traditional authority is bound to the precedents handed down from the past and to this extent is oriented to rules. Leaders' commands legitimated in one of two ways:

- In terms of traditions which themselves directly determine the content of the command and the objects and intent of authority.
- A matter of the chief's free personal decision, in that tradition leaves him some leeway.

When resistance occurs, the accusation is that the chief is not following the tradition. The system itself is not questioned. A chief can have an administrative staff: patrimonial recruitment of staff comes from people who have a traditional tie of personal loyalty to the chief (children, slaves, clients, etc.). Extrapatrimonial recruitment comes from people in a purely personal relation of loyalty (vassals, etc.)

The staff lacks: clearly defined spheres of competence subject to impersonal rules; rational ordering of relations of superiority and inferiority; regular system of promotion and free contract; technical training as a requirement; fixed salaries in $$. Gerontocracy and Patrimonialism are forms of traditional authority w/o a personal administrative staff of the chief. G is rule by elders, and P is where there's rule by someone designated by inheritance. There is still a general idea of everyone being a member of the group, though there is by no means equal distribution of power. With the development of a purely personal administrative staff, we get patrimonialism. Members of the group are now treated as subjects. A patrimonial retainer can be supported by: maintenance at his lords table, by allowances from the chief (primarily in kind), by rights of land use in return for services, by appropriation of property income, fees, or taxes, by fiefs.

Charismatic Authority

The basis for obedience lies in the conception that it is the duty of those who have been called to a charismatic mission to recognize its quality and to act accordingly... it's a matter of personal devotion to the possessor of the quality. There is no legal wisdom oriented to judicial precedent. Charismatic authority is specifically irrational in the sense of being foreign to all rules. It repudiates the past, and is in this sense a revolutionary force.

It is hostile to everyday economic considerations. It can only tolerate irregular, unsystematic, acquisitive acts. In traditional periods, it is the greatest revolutionary force. Reason is equally revolutionary, and works from without by altering the situations of action, or it intellectualizes the individual. Charisma may involve a subjective or internal reorientation which may result in a radical alteration of the central system of attitudes, a completely new orientation towards different problems and structures of the world.

The Routinization of Charisma

In pure form, charismatic authority exists only in the process of originating. It becomes either rationalize or traditionalized, or a combo of both for the following reasons:

- Ideal and material interests of the followers in the continual reactivation of the community
- Interests of the administrative staff, disciples or followers of the char'ic leader in continuing their positions, so that their own status is stable on a day to day basis.

As soon as the position of authority is well established, and above all as soon as control over large masses of people exists, it gives way to the forces of everyday routine. There is an objective necessity of patterns of order and organization of the administrative staff in order to meet the normal, everyday needs and conditions of carrying on administration. In addition, there is a striving for security, requiring legitimation of positions of authority and social prestige and economic advantages held by the followers.

The process of routinization is thus not confined to the problem of succession, and does not stop when it is solved. The most fundamental problem is the transition from the charismatic administrative staff and its mode of administration to one that can handle everyday conditions.

Possible Types of Solution

- Search for new charismatic leader on basis of criteria that will fit him for position of authority
- Revelation thorough oracles, lots, etc... legitimacy is then dependent on technique of selection, which means a form of legalization
- By designation by leader of his successor
- Designation of successor by charismatically qualified staff, and successors recognition by the community... legitimacy can come to depend on technique of selection, again legalization
- Hereditary charisma... this may lead to either traditionalization or legalization (divine right, etc.)
- Charisma transmitted by ritual means from one bearer to another, or created in a new person... this may become charisma of office (eg, the Big Potato, the Pope himself).

Routinization also takes the form of the appropriation of powers of control and economic advantages by the disciples. Again, it can be either traditional or legal, depending on whether or not legislation of some sort is involved. This is how we get differences between, say, the clergy and the laity.

Methodology of the Social Sciences

The purpose of this new journal (where this essay appeared) is "the education of judgement about practical social problems" and "the criticism of practical social policy."

Questions to be addressed: What is the validity of the value-judgements which are uttered by the critic? In what sense, if the criterion of scientific knowledge is to be found in the 'objective' validity of its results, has he (the critic) remained within the sphere of scientific discussion? In what sense are there in general 'objectively valid truths' in those disciplines concerned with social and cultural phenomena?

The science of social institutions and culture arose for practical considerations, with the purpose of producing value-judgement as measures of state policy. Knowledge of what "is" was conflated with knowledge of what "should be"; this was because natural laws and evolutionary principles dominated the field. This journal will try to reject this conflation, since "it can never be the task of an empirical science to provide binding norms and ideals from which the directives for immediate personal activity can be derived." Value-judgements should not be eliminated, but subjected to scientific criticism. Science can help an actor choose between alternative ends by analysing the appropriateness of a means for an end, and by providing information on what a desired end will cost in terms of the loss of other values. The acting person can then choose from among the values involved according to his own conscience or personal view. Science can show him that all choosing involves the espousal of certain values.

Every science of cultural life must arrive at a rational understanding of the ideas which underlie every concrete end. Science can judge these ideas and ends ONLY according to a logical and historically defined standard of value which can be elevated to a certain "level of explicitness" beyond individual sentiment. Science can tell a person what s/he can do, not what s/he should do. Put another way, treating the ideas as a coherent system of thought, science can point out to an actor what is possible within his or her value system, and what would be contradictory to that value system.

Problems of social policy are not based on purely technical considerations of specific ends, but involve disputes about the normative standards of value which lie in the domain of general cultural values. This conflict over general cultural values does not occur solely between 'class interests' but between general views on life and the universe as well (take that, Karl). It is NOT POSSIBLE to establish and to demonstrate as scientifically valid 'a principle' for practical social science from which the norms for the solution of practical problems can be unambiguously derived. While social science needs the discussion of practical problems in terms of fundamental principles, that is, the reduction of unreflective value-judgements to the premises from which they are logically derived, the search for a "lowest common denominator" of in the form of generally valid value judgements is not empirical, impractical and entirely meaningless. We cannot establish on the basis of ethical imperatives or norms for concretely condition individual conduct, normatively desirable cultural values.

Objective science must distinguish between value judgements and empirical knowledge, and try to see factual truths. However, value-judgements of the practical interest of the scientist will always be significant in determining the focus of attention of analytical activity (my values direct me in what I think are interesting or important questions or matters to investigate — this gets called, value-relevance elsewhere: there is no harm, according to Max, in allowing your values, personal interests or social commitments to guide you in the selection of research topics; however, once you start researching, you need value-neutrality).

This journal will pursue logical analysis of the content of ideals, while not ignoring how ideals motivate value-judgements. It will present social policy, i.e., the statement of ideals, in addition to social science, i.e., the analysis of facts. In non-scientific discussions of policy, it must be made clear where the investigator stops analysing and where the evaluating and acting person begins to present his sentiments (make value judgements). Again, individual sentiments don't have to be eliminated, nor can they be, but they should be kept strictly separate from scientific analysis. "An attitude of moral indifference has not connection with scientific 'objectivity'."

As said before, every recognition of a scientific problem reflects specific motives and values on the part of the investigator. This journal, a good journal, will try to avoid developing on a character on the basis of the values of its common contributors.

A social science problem is one which throws light on the "the fundamental socio-economic problem: the scarcity of means" For us, phenomena have the following cultural significance (since we are interested in socio-economic data), "economic," "economically-relevant,". "economically-conditioned." This journal (thus, by extension, our buddy Max), considers all of these as important since material interests influence all aspects of culture w/o exception.

Our science, the science of economic cultural phenomena seeks particular causes for these phenomena, so it is also interested in historical knowledge. We want to investigate the general cultural significance of the socioeconomic structure of the human community and its historical forms of organization. Treatment of these social problems will (hopefully) result in solutions for social policy.

This limited scope (focus on the socioeconomic aspect of cultural life) is deliberately one-sided, because general social science is ambiguous without some specification of the way in which this social is to be investigated. This journal is interested, however, in the economic interp of history, not the materialist conception of history as a causal formula (take that, Karl). Karl's materialist conception is popular among laymen and dilettantes (not to mention, so I hear, hat-wearing, feminist vegetarians) who are not satisfied until they find economic causes for every freakin' thing under the sun.

The explanation of everything by economic causes alone is never exhaustive in any sense whatsoever in any sphere of cultural phenomena, not even in the economic sphere itself. We choose this one-sided approach, however, as a way to investigate cultural reality by specific technical means and using qualitatively similar categories (remember, though, material interests are found in every aspect of culture).

There is no absolutely objective scientific analysis of culture independent of special and one-sided viewpoints according to which social phenomena are selected, analysed, and organized for expository purposes. These view points are necessary in order to engage in an empirical science of concrete reality which seeks to understand the cultural significance of individual events in their contemporary manifestations and the causes of their being historical so and not otherwise. The infinite multiplicity of life means that we can select only a segment of it for scientific investigation.

Ideal Type: Formulated by exaggerating one side of reality, or selecting multiple aspects of reality and synthesizing them into a unified analytical construct. The analysis of reality is concerned, for Max, "with the configuration into which (hypothetical!) 'factors' are arranged to form a cultural phenomena which is historically significant to us". The ideal type is derived inductively from the real world. You compare the type with empirical reality to see how it differs. Then, you look for the causes of the deviations.

Methodology of the Social Sciences

Value-judgements are practical evaluations of the unsatisfactory or satisfactory character of phenomena subject to our influence. In teaching, a lecture should be different from a speech, and teachers should not impose their ideas on their students simply because students are prevented from leaving and from protesting. There is no specialized qualification for personal prophesy, and for that reason it is not entitled to freedom from external control. Students should gain from teachers today: 1) the ability to fulfill a given task in a workmanlike fashion; 2) the ability to recognize facts, even those which may be personally uncomfortable, and to distinguish them from his/her own evaluations; 3) learn to subordinate himself to his task and repress the impulse to exhibit his personal tastes or other sentiments unnecessarily.

The unresolvable question—unresolvable because it is ultimately a question of evaluation—as to whether one may, must, or should champion certain practical values in teaching, should not be confused with the purely logical discussion of the relationship of value-judgements to empirical disciplines such as sociology. The distinction between empirical statements of fact and value-judgments is difficult. However, all recognizable value judgements should be made rigorously explicit to both the researcher him/herself and his/her audience.

Weber does not believe in value free sociology, he believes in striving for value-neutral sociology The specific function of science is to ask questions about the things which convention makes self-evident. Understanding" explanations do justice to a person who really or evidently thinks differently. They are scientifically valuable 1) for the purposes of a causal analysis which seeks to establish the motives of human actions and 2) for the communication of really divergent evaluations when one is in discussion with a person who really or apparently has different evaluations from one's self. The shallowness of our routinized daily existence in the most significant sense of the word consist in the fact that the persons who are caught up in it do not become aware, and above all do not wish to become aware, of the motley of irreconcilably antagonistic values that they hold... value-spheres cross and interpenetrate.

The discussion of value-judgements can have only the following functions:

- The elaboration and explication of ultimate, internally consistent value-axioms, from which the divergent attitudes are derived. People are often in error, not only about their opponents' evaluations, but also their own. The procedure for this analysis begins with concrete particular evaluations and analyzes their meanings and then moves to the more general level of irreducible evaluations. It is not empirical and it produces no new knowledge of facts. It's validity flows from its logic.
- Deduction of implications for those accepting certain value-judgements which follow from certain irreducible value axioms when these axioms alone are used to evaluate certain situations of fact. This deduction depends partly on logic, and partly on empirical observation for the most complete casuistic analyses of all such empirical situations subject to practical evaluation.
- Determination of the factual consequences which the realization of a given practical evaluation must have: 1) in the event of being bound to certain indispensable means, 2) in the event of the inevitability of certain, not directly desired repercussions (these empirical observations may lead us to determine the end cannot be achieved, or that in its achievement there may be other, undesired consequences which make our end too dangerous to

pursue. We may be made to reconsider our ends, means and repercussions, so that they become a new problem for us, or we may discover new axioms which we had not previously taken into consideration).

Problems in social science are selected by value-relevance — relevance for values of the researcher/problem-selector. The task of a value-neutral science, once the problem of interest is chosen, is the reduction of, say, a communist standpoint to its most rational and internally consistent form, and the empirical investigation the pre-conditions for its existence and its practical consequences. This analyses, though, can never tell us whether or not we should be communists; no science can. Strictly empirical analysis can provide a solution to a problem only where it is a question of a means adequate to the realization of an absolutely unambiguous end.

When the normatively valid is the object of empirical investigation, its normative validity is disregarded. Its existence and not its validity is what concerns the investigator.

Politics as a Vocation

Politics is a strong and slow boring of hard boards.

First, a general chat on states.

Politics is any kind of leadership in action (Class, Status, Party: remember, social clubs and grad school cohorts can have parties, just as states can). For this lecture, we will understand politics as the leadership or influencing the leadership of a political association, today (1918) a state.

The decisive means of politics is violence. A state is defined by the specific means peculiar to it, the use of physical force. The state is a human community that successfully claims the monopoly of the legitimate use of physical force within a given territory. Politics, then, means striving to share power or striving to influence the distribution of power, either among states or among groups within a state. The state is a relation of men dominating men by means of legitimate violence (you already know the three ways it can get legitimated, so I'm not telling you). Leaders may arise on those three foundations as well.

How do the politically dominant powers maintain that dominance? Organized domination calls for continuous administration, requires that human conduct be conditioned to obedience to the power-bearers. It requires control over the material goods necessary for the use of physical violence. Thus, it requires control of the personal executive staff and the material implements of administration. All states may be classified by whether the staff of men themselves owns the administrative means, or whether they are separated from it (necesse. for bureaucracy).

Now to chatting about politics as a vocation. There are two ways to make politics your vocation: you can live for it or off it. It you live for it, you make it your life in an internal sense, either because you enjoy power or because you serve some cause. If you live off it, you strive to make it your permanent source of income (cf Dan Rostenkowski). All party struggles are struggles for the patronage of office, as well as struggles for objective goals. Setbacks in participating in offices are felt more severely by parties than is action against their objective goals.

The development of politics into an organization which demanded training in the struggle for power, and int eh methods of this struggle as developed by modern party policies, determined the separation of public functionaries into two categories: administrative officials and political officials.

Political officials can be transferred any time at will, and can be dismissed or at least temporarily withdrawn. Cabinet ministers often are much less in control of their areas than divisional heads, who are long-term, administrative appointees; a minister is simply the representative of a given political power constellation.

The genuine official, even a political official, conducts his business sine ira et studio (at least formally, as long as the vital interests of the ruling order are not in question). To be passionate, on the other hand, is the element of the politician and above all of the political leader.

"Since the time of the constitutional state, and definitely since democracy has been established, the demagogue has been the typical political leader". The current state of affairs is a "dictatorship resting on the exploitation of mass emotionality". Next to the qualities of will, the force of demagogic speech has been above all decisive in the choice of strong leaders. "What kind of man must one be if he is to be allowed to put his hand on the wheel of history?". He must have passion, a feeling of responsibility, and a sense of proportion. Passion in the sense of matter-of-factness, of passionate devotion to a cause, to the god or demon who is its overlord. Responsibility to the cause must be the guiding star of action. For this, a sense of proportion is needed Warm passion and a cool sense of proportion must be forged together in one and the same soul.

The politician must combat vanity, in order to be matter-of-factly devoted to his cause and preserve some distance, not least from himself. Lack of objectivity and irresponsibility are the two deadly sins of politics; vanity, the need to personally stand in the foreground, temps the politician to commit these sins. The final result of political action regularly stands in completely inadequate and often paradoxical relation to its original meaning (oh, cheery old Weber).

Because of this fact, the serving of a cause must not be absent if action is to have inner strength. Exactly which cause looks like a matter of belief. Some kind of faith must exist in a politician, "otherwise it is absolutely true that the curse of the creature's worthlessness overshadows even the externally strongest political successes".

Then is a discussion of two ethics, the ethic of ultimate ends and the ethic of responsibility. They are fundamentally different and irreconcilably opposed. The ethic of ultimate ends, formulated in religious terms, is: "The Christian does rightly and leaves the results with the Lord." If an action of good intention leads to bad results, then, in the actor's eyes, not he, but the world, or the stupidity of other men, or God's will who made them thus, is responsible for the evil.

The ethic of responsibility, on the other hand, requires one to give an account of the foreseeable results of one's action. The man who believes in an ethic of responsibility takes into account precisely the average deficiencies of people. He does not feel in a position to burden others with the results of his own actions so far as he was able to foresee them; he will say, these results are ascribed to my action. On the other hand, the ultimate ends dude feels a "responsibility" only to keep his intentions good. In many cases, the attainment of good ends is bound up with the price of using morally dubious or dangerous means, and must face the possibility of evil ramifications.

From no ethics in the world can it be concluded when and to what extent a good ends justifies ethically dangerous means and ramifications. The ethics of absolutism goes to pieces on the problem of justification of means by ends.

Everything that is striven for through political action operating with violent means and following an ethic of responsibility endangers the salvation of the soul. If, however, on chases after the ultimate good in a war of beliefs, following a pure ethic of absolute ends, then the goals may be damaged and discredited for generations because responsibility for consequences is lacking. A man following an ethic of responsibility will arise at a place where he must say, Here I stand; I can do no other. Here, the ethic of ultimate ends and the ethic of responsibility are supplements, which only in unison constitute a genuine man, a man who can have the calling for politics.

The Social Psychology of the World Religions

The world religions, to Max, are Confucianism, Hinduism, Buddhism, Christianity and Islam, and they are chosen because they have a large number of followers, and for no other reason. He will also consider Judaism, since it is an important precursor to Christianity and Islam and because of its significance for the development of the economic ethic of the West. The term 'economic ethic' points to the practical impulses for action which are founded in the psychological and pragmatic contexts of religion. The religious determination of life conduct is only one of the determinants of the economic ethic. The religiously determined way of life is itself profoundly influenced by economic and political factors.

Those strata which are decisive in stamping the characteristic features of an economic ethic may change in the course of history;

nevertheless, as a rule one may determine the strata whose styles of life have been at least predominately decisive for certain religions. For example, Confucianism was the status ethic of prebendaries, men with literary educations who were characterized by a secular rationalism.

Christianity began its course as a doctrine of itinerant artisan journeymen. It is not the case for Weber that "the ruling ideas of any epoch are the ideas of the ruling classes," however. And, however incisive the social influences, economically and politically determined, may have been upon a religious ethic in a particular case, it receives its stamp primarily from religious sources, and most predominantly from the content of its annunciation and promise.

One of the foci of religious ethics has been the evaluation of suffering. By treating suffering as a symptom of secret guilt and of a crime in the sight of G/god/s, religion has psychologically met a very important need. The fortunate is seldom satisfied with the fact of being fortunate. Beyond this, he needs to know that he has a right to his good fortune. Good fortune wants to be legitimate fortune. Religion provides the theodicy of good fortune for those who are fortunate.

Salvation religions are religions of suffering. Under the pressure of typical and ever-recurrent distress, the religiosity of a 'redeemer' evolved. This religiosity presupposed the myth of a savior, hence (at least relatively) a rational view of the world. In Judaism, the term messiah was originally attached to the saviours from political distress, as transmitted by the hero sagas.

In Judaism, and in this clear-cut fashion only in it and under very particular other conditions, the suffering of a people's community, rather than the suffering of an individual, became the object of hope for religious salvation. The usual rule was that the savior bore an individual and universal character at the same time that he was ready to guarantee salvation to the individual and to any individual who would turn to him.

The tribal and local gods, gods of the city and the empire, have taken care only of the interests that concern the collectivity as a whole. In the community cult, the community as such turned to its god. The individual, however, turned to the sorcerer and magician for help with his personal evils. Hereditary dynasties of mystagogues or trained personnel under a head determined in accordance with certain rules developed. Collective religious arrangements for individual suffering per se, and for salvation from it, originated in this fashion.

The typical service of magicians and priests becomes the determination of the factors to be blamed for suffering; that is, the confession of sins. Where religious development was decisively influenced by prophecy, sin was no longer merely a magical offense: it was a sign of disbelief in the prophet and his commandments. While prophets have not generally been descendants of depressed classes, it has generally been the depressed classes who need a redeemer. Thus, most prophetically announced religious of redemption have been located in the less-favored social strata. For these, such religiosity has been either a substitute for, or a rational supplement to, magic.

The need for an ethical interpretation of suffering and of the meaning of the distribution of fortunes among men increased with the growing rationality of conceptions of the world. There have been three rationally satisfactory answers to questions about the basis of the incongruity between destiny and merit: Karma, dualism (from Zoroastrianism) and the predestination decree of the deus abscondidus (the absconded god; kind of a cool phrase). These solutions are rationally closed, and are found in pure form only as exceptions.

Ecstatic states (orgies, quietistic edification, contemplative mortification, etc) have been sought first of all, for the sake of the emotional value they offered the devout. Rationalized religions have sublimated the orgy into the sacrament. Every hierocratic and official authority of a church fights against virtuoso religion and its autonomous development. The church is the holder of institutionalized grace, and seeks to organize the religiosity of the masses.

The kind of empirical state of bliss or experience of rebirth that is sought after as the supreme value by a religion has varied according to the character of the stratum that was foremost in adopting it. The conception of the idea of redemption is very old, if one understands by it a liberation from sickness, hunger, etc., ultimately from suffering and death. However, redemption attained a specific significance only where it expressed a systematic and rationalized image of the world and represented a stand in the face of the world.

Not ideas, but material and ideal interests, directly govern men's conduct. Yet very frequently the world images that have been created by ideas have, like switchmen, determined the tracks along which action has been pushed by the dynamic of interest. From what and for what one wished to be redeemed, and let us not forget, could be redeemed, depended upon one's image of the world.

Behind every religion lies a stand toward something in the actual world which is experienced as specifically senseless. Thus, the demand has been implied: the world order, in its totality, could, and should somehow be a meaningful cosmos.

The various great ways of leading a rational and methodical life have been characterized by irrational presuppositions, which have been accepted simply as given and incorporated into life. What these presuppositions have been is historically and socially determined, to a very large extent, through the peculiarity of those strata that have been the carriers of the ways of life during its formative and decisive period. The interest situation of these strata, as determined socially and psychologically, has made for their peculiarity.

Where prophecy has provided a religious basis, this basis could be one of two fundamental types of prophesy: exemplary and emissary. Exemplary prophesy points the way to salvation by exemplary living (usually contemplative and apathetic-ecstatic ways of life). Emissary prophesy addresses its demands to the world in the name of a god. These demands are ethical, and often of an active acetic character.

The civic strata, conditioned by the nature of their life, which is greatly detached from economic bonds to nature, tend toward a practical rationalism in conduct. Their whole existence has been based on technological or economic calculations and upon the mastery of nature and man. These strata tend toward religions of active asceticism. Wherever the direction of the whole way of life has been methodically rationalized, it has been profoundly determined by the ultimate values toward which this rationalism has been directed.

All kinds of practical ethics that are systematically and unambiguously oriented toward fixed goals of salvation are rational, partly in the same sense as formal method is rational, and partly in the sense that they distinguish between valid norms and what is empirically given.

All ruling powers need legitimacy, which comes in three kinds... In the main, it has been the work of jurists to give birth to modern Western states, as well as modern Western churches. Jurists work in the realm of formal rationalization, they follow procedures, etc. With the triumph of formalistic (rather than substantive) juristic rationalism, the legal type of domination appeared in the West.

5

Theory of Social Development

Introduction

For the scholar, development is a particular activity of society seen in certain periods. For the social being it is an ever-present, non-stop activity whose intensity varies with periods and circumstances. This is true of survival, growth, development and evolution. These are all the same activity at root with varying degrees of energy, intensity, organisation, result and aims. That is why we say that these four phenomena exist in each of them. Evolution can be termed as fast moving sûrvival and survival is evolution at its slowest pace.

Development begins as a physical activity. The energy released by the physical is always the lowest and the conscious awareness of the being is also at the lowest in the physical and highest in the mind. The true centre of energy is vital. It is the vital that energizes the body as well as the mind. Still, the physical work releases the energy in low volumes. Mind, by lending its comprehension to the vital, is capable of energising it several-fold. As the development experience started with the physical and essentially remains in that plane, development is necessarily slow and unconscious.

Man, having started his life in the body and not in the mind, experiences work and life. Body is not conscious and is subconscious. It learns by doing. Learning succeeds doing. This is also so because existence and survival compel man to act and to do. He has to eat, drink and sleep. His act of eating over the centuries makes him learn how to gather food more efficiently. The compelling need of thirst sets him in quest of water. He cannot wait to learn about food and drink. Long practical experience leads to knowledge of the process. That is true till now. The cities man has built, the religion he soared to, the science he has discovered and all he has achieved today are achievements in experience, not experiences that issued out of knowledge.

A few thousand years of man's existence which is studded with rich experiences have not led him to know the knowledge-basis of those experiences. Medical theory is of recent origin. No theory of history is yet born. Science is striving its best to found itself on a theory. As for social development, we do not have any indications of thinkers trying to evolve a theory. Hundreds of theories have been discovered and have gained social acceptance, but they are of partial phenomena, rather a particular phenomenon. There seems to be no theory or even an attempt at it.

As man starts his experiences in the physical plane and moves to the vital and mental planes later, a theory can emerge only when his activities reach the mental plane. They have not yet reached that elevated, exalted plane. What has happened is the physical plane is getting saturated with physical experiences. Saturation leads to maturity and maturity will lead to moving to the higher planes. A theory can only emerge when the experiences reach the mental plane.

The world's developmental experience has not only saturated the physical plane in several countries but also has saturated the vital plane. As both planes are nearing saturation, the mind can act. Perhaps only when the whole of humanity is essentially covered by physical experience will the mind sail into action.

As the experiences of the physical and vital planes are exhausted, saturated and the planes are mature with experience, it is time to evolve a theory. Also, in the past man has never attempted development as a conscious effort. The hundreds of developmental failures are an indication that no conscious attempt has been resorted to. This again is an indication that the time has come for conceptualisation. What the body is forced to do, it experiences as movement. The vital chooses to do what the body feels compelled to do. The vital experiences in energy what the body experiences in matter. At the next stage the same is experienced by the mind as comprehension.

Theory is the mind in its comprehension codifying what the body experiences in physical substance-matter. The twentieth century seems to be the watershed between developmental experience and a theory of development. Two or three events of importance stand out. One is the backlash of expanding development in the form of pollution which indicates that in some fashion the development effort cannot go further. For humanity to accept development as a full time vocation, it must have assured peace. War, as known by this century, has been abolished for all intents and purposes. The nervous energy of mankind engaged in the tension of the cold war has now been released. Assured peace and the stalling of the further spread of development augur well for the emergence of a theory.

At least from two highly placed persons the idea was mooted. One was chief of the UNDP advisory board and the other the UN chief. The latter described the evolution of a theory of development as an intellectual challenge of this century. People placed at the helm of world affairs looking for a theoretical framework for the guidance of their main activities is certainly a symptom that the mind of humanity may be ready for that conceptualisation.

Great national events have shaken the world decade after decade. Several of them were successfully tackled and a catastrophe averted, but several others had their sway. The Great Depression, the two World Wars, the Green Revolution, emergence of Japan, the demise of empires, and the spread of education were there. Wherever tragedies were averted, they were not done so consciously. Without exception all human victories of the Green Revolution type have been unconscious.

Theoretical knowledge validates past practical experience. If that validation is logically perfect, theoretically it enables one to project the theory into the future for purposes of prediction. Logically perfect theories, like that of Marx, may lead to practical disaster. But when a logical theory has the advantage of being tested against past experience, it is validated in theory and practice, thus enabling it to be a future instrument of development. In this way theory can accelerate future development. It is the process of an unconscious equipment becoming a conscious instrument. The unconscious element in our equipment leaves several chinks in our armour, making us vulnerable to the environment and future forces, physical and non-physical. Becoming conscious means the body is guided by the mind or mind uses the power of the body. Naturally it becomes more powerful by the mind sharing the power of the body, and speedier by the body using the speed of the vital and mind. Nations, corporations, and organisations can plan with a knowledge they do not have now. That planning cannot go astray because it is comprehensive. Without being conscious one cannot be comprehensive.

Economists the world over talk of development as the development of wealth, infrastructure, comforts, conveniences, technology, and resources possessed. They see land, oil, natural resources, buildings, roads, airport, education etc. as development. But these are the results of development, not development. Again, community development, national extension service, hybrid seeds, fertilizers, and liberalisation are spoken of as development. These are strategies, programmes and projects. They are the means to development but not development itself. A social energy helps develop. A certain will of the society releases that energy. Sometimes that energy is directed to become a social force. That direction is given by the social attitude and social goals. An organisation in the society converts that force into social power. The available social skills convert that social power into the social results mentioned above. The process by which the social energy is converted into social results is a social process. It is this process that is called development.

Development is a process and not a programme or a policy. Will, energy, direction, force, organisation, power, and skill all go to accomplish development. All together they make up the development organisation which incidentally includes a part known as organisation too. It is this that serves as the lynch pin for development. In a sense this developmental organisation is the backbone or social structure that enables the process of development to complete itself.

Over long centuries society developed the million fingers of this central organisation by an unconscious process of slow trial and error. Without any knowledge of the goal or process, it seeks to be consciously organised at a centre. The organisation itself does not seem to be aware of its whole existence or its centre or the relationship of the centre to its terminal fingers. Only the ends are visible to man, and perhaps also to the self-awareness of the organisation only the ends are revealed, not the whole.

The Growth of Organisation

That organisation is composed of systems and subsystems which are truly the skills of the organisation. For its functioning it needs what are called infrastructures that enable the organisation to achieve its goals. Infrastructures exist as physical components, vital attitudes crystalising into institutions, and mental beliefs that guide the mass of men as rules, laws, customs and usages. As the society grows it sheds lower skills and acquires higher skills. By skills of the society we mean the organisation and its systems. As in the path of every progress, achievements of the past, however glorious, have a way of becoming obstacles for future progress. Neither the shining monarchies of the past, nor the wisdom of Socrates, nor even the findings of Newton can hold forever with the same aura. Developmental effort proceeding unconsciously has the painful necessity of breaking down the obstacles to make the transition complete. Conscious development, guided by a theory has the option of transforming the past obstacles into future opportunities.

Infrastructure—Levels of Infrastructure

Infrastructure is the support for the main structure of development in physical, social, mental, and psychological forms. It is a part, sometimes subordinate, sometimes that which makes the structure meaningful. It is known as infrastructure as it underlies the main structure. This being a widely known term, we would like to accept it as it is and define it as it is meant among the scholars of development. To go into the origin of the word and make it theoretically precise is not possible, because occasionally the sum total of infrastructures act as the cumulative structure without any structure being there, as in education. The field of education is filled with the physical buildings of schools and colleges, the vital component of students and teachers, the mental part of the school organisation, the syllabus, the lessons, etc. and the psychological values of discipline, pursuit of knowledge, and dedication to learning. All these are physical, vital, mental, and psychological infrastructures of education which when removed leave no structure by itself. We may consider the UGC, the department of education, and the university as the structure at the core and the rest as infrastructure. It may be a matter of convenience, not a principle that can be defined precisely.

Our subject is development of society or social development. It may be proper to define society as the structure and everything which supports society as the infrastructure. By extension we can say the departments of society like economics, education, defence, administration etc. are the structures that hold society together while dozens of infrastructures support the main structures. The imprecision arises from the insufficiency of the language as well as a lack of clear demarcations in the process of development. For the present let us settle for what is available and define it well enough to serve our purpose of presenting our principles in a coherent fashion. The field of education provides enough examples of what we mean by infrastructure. If it is to be made comprehensive, an example from each of the fields of commerce, defence, administration, social existence, finance, and corporate life should be given.

Infrastructure is needed to make the activity possible. Without a building for the school, or students or teachers there will be no education. Education of children being the activity and children being the vital infrastructure of education, an overlapping of thought occurs adding to the obstacle of creating precise definitions. Education is the process of knowledge transmitted to the children by the teachers. Teachers and children are part of the vital infrastructure. Infrastructure makes the activity possible, is essential for the activity to be completed and is often part of the activity. To think of transport without roads, warfare without communication, administration without rules, schools without a syllabus or timetable is not possible.

The infrastructure is spread out horizontally or arranged in vertical grades or ordered to appear in succession or made to act in unison with another infrastructure or two. They underlie the structure or cumulatively act as the structure. Horizontal, vertical, sequential, and clustered placements of infrastructure are possible.

Infrastructure takes the field to a wider area in space, helps extend the activity in time, relates each activity with the other, renders the results possible, delivers the results to the beneficiary, makes the effectivity of the activity greater, and helps expand the field in inherent value.

Four Levels of Infrastructure Explained

We need to distinguish the infrastructure from the component or input. Even here the same confusion sometimes arises since the infrastructure is the component or input itself. Society has four levels of existence and therefore the infrastructure of its development process also lies on four levels. So also any work exists on the same four levels. Society, work, development and man who develops the society exist at four levels and that is the rationale of infrastructures coming in four levels.

As communities, ideas, and activities relate among themselves often generating unforeseen good, infrastructures too relate among themselves. This is a fertile field of creative development. Libraries are mostly unused in Indian universities. Even in an advanced nation like USA, only 50% of the knowledge generated in the laboratories reaches the field. The interrelation is useful, productive, dynamic, and creative.

Individuals, events, organisations and existence have the same structural composition. The structures rise from below or descend from above. Man, understanding an activity and creating it from his own thought, starts in the mind and provides the vital energy and physical base. In that case the structures of the mental thought create the energy structures of attitudes that rest on the physical basis of work. A new work, new to humanity, starts at the physical level, energises with enthusiasm and finally is capped with an understanding. In either case the structures contain mental ideas, vital attitudes and physical skills. Whether organised or unorganised, individual or collective, the structure is composed of these three components.

It is true infrastructures make the activity possible. Often they are the vehicles of spreading the activity. In commerce, it is the retailers who help complete the cycle of distribution and it is through the retailers the product spreads far and wide. It is not so in the school that serves a similar function. It is obvious that the physical infrastructure cannot be so energetic as the vital infrastructure. Changes in the higher levels of infrastructure can have greater impact on the process and the result. A school having new buildings will offer greater facilities but will not affect the results of the school. A change for the better in the discipline and dedication of the pupils and teachers will certainly have a commendable effect on the results. In the 50's population was apathetic but the same population is now dynamic. The changed attitude of the population is an important cause for India's great dynamic progress now. In the 50's ports were built, road transport and education were emphasised and a host of other things very desirable in themselves were done, but the country was not astir because they were improvements in the physical infrastructure, while what is witnessed now is a change in the mental and vital infrastructure.

The importance of the infrastructure depends on the importance of the plane in which it is. It is necessary to draw the distinction between an infrastructure, a system, a component and an input. Land is infrastructure whereas fertiliser is an input; the bunds and boundaries are components of land; the method of cultivation is a system. As we said earlier, there are occasions where a system can function as an infrastructure. A system is an arrangement of work for better execution, serving as a miniature organisation and thus is self-contained. We have the system of distribution in sales, the system of gathering a stock of food grains to build up a buffer stock. The godowns that hold the food grains are the physical infrastructure; the retailers and wholesalers belong to the vital infrastructure. The system is an arrangement based on an idea different from the godowns or the distributors.

At each level the results have determinants. The physical level's efficiency is determined by the funds available. The determinant of the vital level is the discipline the society has in general. Education and information determine the efficacy of the mental infrastructure. The cultural heights of the society determine the psychological infrastructures.

Funds determining the size and quality of the buildings is a known fact. Punctuality in the West is an article of faith whereas with us punctuality is a known concept, but not so well known as a practised concept. Whether it is sports or a national function or election or school, the general level of social adherence to punctuality is a determinant of their efficiency. The final results of a Planning Commission or Panchayat administration are determined by the educational attainments of that society. Development is a whole of which infrastructures are a part. Their interdependence is inherent. As is the infrastructure, so is the development. As the part decides the whole, the whole decides the part. A very efficient, high level tourist hotel serving as an infrastructure of tourism in a backward country whose general development is low cannot flourish. The country's stage of development determines the success of the hotel.

There are times when a part outshines the whole, especially when new-fangled methods are introduced. The introduction of computers in offices now puts the existence of the entire office in the shade. People forget that, after all, computers are only office machines.

The distinction between essential and non-essential components based on their determining value of the final result applies to this also.

Infrastructures are only parts, but occasionally by their inherent value or their value to the final outcome they become as important as the whole or outshine the whole. A cultural event in a conference by its inherent value behaves like that. Modern machines in a factory have the character of making the people forget the company and mistake the new machines for the whole of the company. Especially in the days when machines were invented, the character of those machines carried this stamp. Ford's assembly line became very important and dominated the entire industry for a decade and we all easily forgot that it is one part by itself of a great whole.

Measurement of Infrastructure

Measuring is numerical understanding. All progress has as its foundation energy and understanding. Work done by energy and understanding leads to progress, because progress is change for the better. If we examine the point of history at which measurement arose, it will reveal itself as a point of progress.

Measurement is there in a variety of fields, maybe in every field. Primarily, it is a measure of numbers. Areas, volumes and weights are also measured. Quality also lends itself to measurement. Often the quality of a thing can be reduced to a number and measured like the body temperature and blood pressure. Measurement presupposes a scale of measurement and often a device for the purpose. At bottom, measurement is a kind of organisation. Therefore, it is an instrument of conception and further, an instrument of progress.

Measurement starts with length, area, weight, quantity, size, extent, duration, number, amount and extends to all conceivable things. The science of statistics has these measurements as one of its bases. Imagine if today such measurements are no longer there or are not possible, all scientific studies and work based on them will come to a halt. Roads are measured in length and graded in quality. Population is a head count and permits its own classification. Money goes with number and number is the domain proper for money. Literacy too has its levels and numbers at each level. Natural resources like coal, oil, metals, water, forest wealth and a host of other things lend themselves to measurement of deposits or quantity when converted into refined end products, and even the period over which they will be available before coming to a point of exhaustion. The length of rivers has been measured over the ages. The quantity of flow over the differing seasons, its depth and breadth are measured too. Measurement has become a science by itself. The amount of oxygen consumed by a brain cell as well as the amount of time required for a rocket to go to the moon and return are within the reach of measurement. Alongside, measuring devices refining their previous capacity have made themselves available in the hundreds and thousands. In an age of computer, measurement rules high.

Numerical representation of time, space, volume, quantity, quality, design, and property is one of the first steps in fully grasping the entire process of development finally. The Indian development effort so far has not lent itself to such a measurement. The country's development can take further great strides if that one thing is accomplished. In a country like India where personal progress does not mainly issue out of the individual's effort, his own income is an insufficient index of his development. As the government exerts itself more in the domain of public welfare which results in individual betterment, existing statistics cannot and do not fully reflect the true state of affairs. Fresh thought must go into it and fresh scales must evolve before the development effort can have a measurable basis, if not a scientific foundation. This is true all over the world in a variety of ways. The per capita income does serve as a good measurement of the individual's economic status. This was precisely so till the components of individual progress were such that they could be measured in terms of their monetary value.

Human attitudes, and much more so, human opinions are greater determinants of one's development than human resources measurable in terms of money. Further lie values. They do not have so much relevance now as we conceive of development only as material objects and their availability. It is not an easy task. But a far better measuring scale can be evolved than is available at present in the world, if development is defined in all the terms that it comprises of and every component that goes into it is listed without fail. Fifty years ago one's development of landed property and its income entirely depended on one's own resources which meant that until he came to that point of qualifying, he could not move. And it was a crucial point in one's life. Today the lending policy of public institutions goes out of its way to bring the whole population into its net of support. It does make an enormous difference when we set about measuring one's development. Measurement is a science by itself.

A part of any system is the registers. We know cases where systems were introduced at the top level and work at the bottom remained where it was. The introduction of systems requires several graded steps of implementation, of which maintenance of registers is an essential part. After the large-scale introduction of computers, we witness dozens of cases of computer systems inoperative for want of data being put in. No system can yield its expected results if the registers are not filled in regularly.

Drucker's forecast fell on deaf ears except for two clients whose marked progress made everyone open their eyes. Numbers, measurements, relating them to numbers in other areas, projecting them according to a pattern have now come to stay as a part of planning. Life has several departments. Its departments are powerfully related to one another. Some relationships are on the surface for all to see as the amount of liquor consumed and crimes committed. Many are not there on the surface, such as the level of employable skills that are determined by education. It took a World Bank study to discover that in agriculture even primary education has a good indirect effect. How can we see that there exists a relationship between consumption of sugar and the spread of media. When each of these fields is reduced to numbers, someone can examine if numbers in two columns bear any relationship at all and when they do whether it is sustained.

Development in any field can be seen fully reflected in numbers. It can also be seen that numbers — quantifying — have made further development in these fields possible. The field of medical science is one instance. A man's health is measured in terms of temperature, blood pressure, level of hemoglobin and a dozen other classifications, all in numbers.

In the absence of measurement, we have to use grades like small, medium, or big in describing the audience of a speaker. 20, 200, and 25,000 if described as small, medium and big will fit very well, but will not be explanatory to the listener, since 2000 and 25,000 come under the category of big as against 20 and 200. Measurement makes precise what is otherwise vague.

Measurements are numerical, unidimensional, multidimensional and can extend to areas, volumes, duration, and extension. Anything can be measured if appropriate conceptions are developed and are reduced to figurative representation. Measurement is a means where quantity reveals quality just as quality changes as quantity differs. Whether in learning or earning, as the quantity rises, the quality of the person does change.

Measurement has a maximum use value which often leads to a very precise understanding of the situation. As the normal sugar level is 130, when we measure a person's sugar level as 462, it sends a precise message to the doctor of how the treatment should be given. At its lowest, measurement shows a trend, a direction, if not more. Absolute measurement reveals the quantitative extent of a part. It can be seen relatively as the measurement of the whole since the part, often, is a determinant of the whole.

The percentage of literacy or graduates in a population can indirectly determine the wealth of the country and can even say whether it is a dictatorship or democracy. To make a part a symbol of the whole is a very effective way of measurement and issues from a comprehensive knowledge.

To measure the part by the whole is not always possible. When it is possible, the knowledge always becomes integral.

Distinction between Institution and Organisation

Learning is a process that begins with the mind and ends in the body travelling through the vital. It is always the mind that learns, at best the mind in each part of the body. There is a mental part in the vital and a mental part in the physical. The process of learning goes through several stages. We can locate at least three stages of it. The three stages can be described as skill, capacity and talent. Any activity is first learnt as a skill. When the skill fully matures, it becomes capacity. In fact, the learning of several skills leaves a residual essence in man which becomes capacity and shows behind an individual skill as capacity. Skill reinforced by capacity becomes a talent in the area of that skill.

Organisation is the skill of a society while Institution is the capacity of the same collectivity. Rising still further, when a society reaches the level of talent with respect to that organisation, the Institution matures into the tradition of that society. We call it culture. This happens when the social acceptance is total. An organisation has to be maintained by external human agencies. They could even be social agencies. As systems are called the skills of organisation, organisation is the skill of a society. An institution is self-existent, as no one operates it. It functions by itself. That is why it is said "institutionalise values" so that values will be self-operative.

An organisation such as an office functions through systems and individuals appointed by a central authority and it is run by rules. We cannot think of an office without an officer, staff, rules, etc. But we know that festivals and religious functions like Krishna Jayanthi are not organised by anyone. People celebrate these festivals themselves. Surely when Krishna Jayanthi was instituted, there was an organisation monitoring it. It is no longer so. Customs and usages have taken over. Individuals honour those customs. There is no central authority here. The central authority is replaced by the social tradition. The weight of people's belief constitutes the social tradition.

As values are spiritual or psychological skills, we may say an institution is the system of social tradition run by the weight of beliefs. An organisation is more physical and material whereas an institution is more invisible, intangible, and psychological.

Social habits start physically and mature into psychological responses. Arranged marriages giving place to love marriages is an instance. Religious worship in its early days began as an organised activity of the community. Later the individual followed it without the society having to monitor it. An organisation exists by the work of men; an institution exists by the beliefs of the society. At the time of organising a human settlement — a village, cleaning the streets was organised by the village and enforced. As time passed, every household took upon themselves the job of cleaning the streets before their houses.

It is not as if organisations and institutions are two different sets of entities. They go together, organisation forming the foundation and institutions existing at their top. Organisational charts are the heart of an organisation. No such chart can be drawn for institutions. An administration can introduce an organisation, not an institution. We can think of the government starting a school in a town. Can we imagine someone introducing good manners or punctuality?

The best example of an institution is society while government is an organisation. As organisations mature into institutions, institutions can give birth to organisation at the next higher level. The world does not give thought to this potentiality or phenomenon. Society which is an institution gave birth to government which is an organisation. The government through its existence has given rise to a host of social behaviours as in traffic rules, tax payment, law abiding habits, etc. The existence of the police department generates good behaviour in the population. Religion is an institution. How many organisations like the church it has generated. The capacity of each institution to generate organisations at the next higher level is a potential power of development.

Work is organised; values are institutionalised. When organisations lose life or energy, they become rigid. Institutions in similar situations do not become rigid but their traditions get more entrenched.

Errors Relating to Infrastructure

Excavations in mines create deep holes and they continue to remain as holes. If life must resume there, these holes will make it impossible. People who served in the active services retain to the end the discipline the army has given them. Habits once acquired die hard. We often hear "Once a soldier, a soldier forever." This is true not only of positive endowments, but also of errors. Errors relating to infrastructure have a way of coming to stay forever. They turn into obstacles and remain as obstacles. Any instrument of civilisation, government, society, family or individual which was once created as a help, turns in the next phase into an obstacle. This the history of change and progress. The procedures the government of India created originally as instruments of progress and change settled down in history as red tape. They have have prevented retired IAS officers, chief engineers, and sitting governors from receiving their pensions before three or four years! The most classic example is the Englishman coming from cold UK to hot South India who found the necessity to be dressed in a shirt, suit, necktie and hat. This was a dress necessary at a temperature of 10° F and not at 104° F. He could not bring himself to think that he could work as an officer without wearing those woollen clothes.

Under ideal conditions, all instruments of progress must undergo the appropriate changes when the basic society that created the instruments of progress is changing. Neither life nor society functions like that. In practice, instruments once created perpetuate themselves. The greenbench is a classical example. The sacred thread of the Brahmin, the tuft and all the household rituals created once to meet the requirements of the day survived the passing centuries and changing customs. It is said the dog that sleeps on a mat goes round three times before he lies down. This is a habit the dog acquired in the forest to clear the sleeping space, but it still lingers.

The human being exists in his body, by his nervous emotions and in his mind. Organisations have their counterparts. The rules laid down by the mind are different from the emotional enthusiasm with which the members work. The registers they keep are the physical part while the rules are their mental creations. Of these three things, the physical part of the organisation resists change the most, the mental rules the least. The organisations that were collecting fees in the shape of currency will not readily accept if the currency notes are replaced by cheques. It demands a change in their physical habit and the office will refuse to accept the new form of cash. Even when the physical forms part of the mental rule, it will have a way of being rigid.

In Pondicherry in the French judicial system, cases were presented by the lawyers in written form, not in the spoken form as in the British system. The French system almost made the courts silent dispensing with 95% of the spoken part of the case. After the merger, the Union Territory took to the British system. The most efficient lawyers in the previous system found themselves inefficient under the new system which eased them out. After all, we may say, what is the difficulty for the lawyer who previously wrote down the case in speaking it out to the judge? The physical habit refuses to change, even as auditors stuck to their adding habits after the arrival of the calculator.

Our idea of progress is vertical growth; but life admits of horizontal expansion that needs no psychological effort. The physical being incapable of psychological effort prefers not to change. Cooks who were used to firewood ovens shunned the gas ones when the change was coming about. At the turn of the century when the Indian took to wearing the shirt in place of his towel, he could not part with the towel and added it on to the shirt. Even over the coat he put on his towel. He could not part with it. Neither the British crown nor the Indian Rashtrapathi switched over to the motorcade from the cavalcade. It goes in the name of tradition. Truly it is not tradition that resists, but the physical habit. It is an error in the infrastructure in one form or another. The itinerary of the Prime Minister is not under his control but under the officer in charge of bandobust. When Nehru defied this protocol to go to Conjeevaram instead of Madras, the Collector stopped him on his way and requested him to go back which Nehru, true to his mettle, refused to do!

For social progress to be real, the old order should yield place to the new. That which yields place does not disappear but changes into an obstacle. The new cola was refused by the customers. Presently religious fundamentalists all over the world are a standing example of this principle. Democracy grew out of monarchy where the king was worshipped as the divine representative. His word was law, his wish was authority. Democracy outgrew monarchy, eschewed the theory of divine right. That is social evolution. The leader was elected. Having elected the leader, those who had elected him treated him as the uncrowned king. Instead of asking him to represent their wishes, they echoed his will, worshipped him, adored him, obeyed him as if he were king. The errors of the earlier system they had revolted against were made into tradition and revered.

The Negro was the slave. He was granted freedom a hundred years ago. His freedom remained on the statute book. He retained the slavish mentality in one form or another. Instead of slaving for the master, he became the slave of his lower propensities such as laziness and dissipation. A few centuries have not given him any commendable progress.

In the earlier decades the farmer was fond of dumping his fields with cow dung and garbage. Later concentrated fertiliser replaced cow dung. Today he continues to retain the tendency of dumping the fields with fertiliser. The land soon becomes uncultivable.

The Vedas were esoteric doctrines. No one knew their meaning. People were asked to memorise the text. The Brahmin hails from the tradition. Now he does not read the Vedas but reads astrophysics and organic chemistry. He needs to understand them, but continues to memorise them. Radhakrishnan memorised his own speeches. V.S. Srinivasa Sastri memorised the dictionary! Memorisation remains, and remains an obstacle. It prevented Radhakrishnan from thinking. He could not bloom into a thinker because he could not outgrow the tendency to memorise whatever he read. India ushered in development banking. The purpose was to create assets in the clients who were without assets. Banking is a field of money lending. They asked the clients for security. Programmes that are development-oriented are being implemented by an attitude that is security-oriented.

When life was physical, disputes were settled by physical fights in a duel or street brawl. Rationality evolved discussion and created Parliament as its crowning body. The street brawl lingers in the Parliament. IMF is the apex body of development banks. Its founding principle is to help create the ability to earn money. It is trying to implement that policy by money value which has become an anachronism. USSR which banned the Communist party and abolished state tyranny is now implementing democracy as dictatorship. A small businessman who prospered by thrift and secrecy is unable to part with them even after becoming the chairman of a Public Limited Company. Late arrival, a habit developed when one travelled in his own cart, is carried into air travel. Flights are missed as a result.

Feudal habits are retained in modern business ruining them. The greatest obstacles to development today are the errors that related to infrastructures in earlier times.

Levels of Comprehension, Enjoyment, Values, Attitudes and Motives

In a situation that is witnessed by several people, comprehension of different people varies according to their apperceptive mass which serves as their mental background. The situation itself has several dimensions and that too influences the comprehension of the individuals. The words comprehension and understanding are used as synonyms. Still understanding is to get at the core of a thing as our mind sees it, while comprehension is to know the thing as fully as possible.

When Visweswarayya passed away at the age of 104, a poor, starving man exclaimed, "He had enough to eat." That is the view of the empty stomach. As he was a brahmachari or a grass widower, many understood his long life from that point of view.

In a situation when something is lost, the first response of a guilty person is that he should prove his innocence. He understands from his point of view. Comprehension is a mental identification with an external fact or situation or a concept. The fact, situation or concept may be in his own mind. As all knowledge is knowledge by identity in one form or another, comprehension is one such identification.

What makes for comprehension is mental energy; when organised, that energy takes the forms of understanding, idea, thought, opinion, preference, construction or habit. Fresh organisation of mental energy results in understanding. That understanding becomes an idea when it is closer to knowledge and a thought when it is closer to fact. Energy that is organised around a thought or fact becomes a thought whereas when organised around the essence of a thought. it becomes an idea. That is why we say, "I think I should move to that house. The idea is I should live within my means." Moving to a house is a thought. Living in a house whose rent is affordable is an idea.

Senses feed the comprehension. Also mind feeds itself with its own ideas as facts. Senses are the instruments of ego and its creation. Ego feels the mind with the facts gathered by senses. Thoughts that are the results really originate in the emotions, ultimately in the body. Those who try to control thoughts feel it imperative to still the bodily movements. Brain is the apex of the body or the rarefied part of the body. Therefore the higher thoughts originate from the brain. Body is external to the mind. In the stillness of mind, a yogi who tries to silence his thoughts sees in the subtle plane that thoughts enter the mind from outside. They enter from outside through the body and its senses.

Three main characteristics of comprehension are organisation, clarity and strength. The volume of mental energy and its intensity determines the strength; the previous thought structure that receives the incoming energy determines its organisation. Thought turns into idea and finally into knowledge and light. Clarity expresses this process.

Mind seeks light but receives only facts. It tries to convert facts into light by first converting them into thought and idea. Fact is external and gross. Thought is a mental fact. Thought losing its grossness and turning into its own essence is idea. As the fabric of thoughts is composed of facts, the fabric of ideas is composed of thoughts, rather their essence. The soul in the mind holds the light; mind itself possesses knowledge. Thought is held by memory. Idea is in the domain of imagination.

Body, vital, mind, and spirit are parts of the embodied being. Each of these planes is capable of its own accomplishment. Mind accomplishes when it comprehends; the vital's accomplishment is enjoyment. Body accomplishes in the act. The instrument of mind for its accomplishment is thought; for the vital it is the nervous sensation. Body does it through physical sensation. Mind, vital and physical each have comprehension, enjoyment and accomplishment as their sub-parts. Thinking leads to comprehension, interest to enjoyment, sensation to accomplishment. Mature mental interest generates mental enjoyment when saturated. Similarly saturated mental sensation creates mental accomplishment that is comprehension.

Comprehension at the point of saturation centres itself in the physical mind. It begins as decision and finishes as determination. All parts of the being subdivide themselves as consciousness above and substance below. Mental consciousness is centred in the thinking part of the mind while brain, the expression of substance, keeps decision to itself. The substance of the vital is nerves, of the physical is the body.

It is noteworthy that the emotion is in the middle between thought and action. Emotion expresses as energy. Thought to crystallise into action or action to elevate itself into thought needs to pass through the medium of energy in the emotion. Action evolves energy of emotion and culminates as thought when mind organises it in its own plane as comprehension. Action of the body leads to energy of the emotion and ends in comprehension of the mind. When comprehension of the mind is generated originally as comprehension, it has in it all the essence of power to accomplish in the body when saturated. As the mind is a superior plane, comprehension of the mind and the work it aims at will be more powerful than the action of the body.

Primitive men worked with the body and their mental parts understood it. Over the centuries man evolved, and the body's comprehension rose to the mind as mental knowledge. Man today, while starting at this mental knowledge, can accomplish a thousand times more than the primitive man. Hence development from above is far more swift than evolution from below.

As the same term is used in ascent and descent, care must be bestowed in distinguishing one from the other as the results are far different. Comprehension, enjoyment, accomplishment are a two way process, one evolutionary and the other developmental. Each subdivides into all three, thus complicating an already complex process. Rightly understood, the complexity remains dissolving complications. The more complex it is, the richer it becomes.

To know the complication as simply complexity is knowledge. To be able to see the complexity as it weaves itself into a whole is power of accomplishment.

Levels of Enjoyment

Before energy is released there is no movement. Energy moves. Insufficient energy does not accomplish, nor does it work. Enough energy works. Energy in saturation can lead to enjoyment if there is no disharmony. Matter does not enjoy the saturated harmonious joy of Energy, Sri Aurobindo says. An act is energy turning substance into result through its organisation known as skill. Result or accomplishment has two other attributes, namely, comprehension and enjoyment. Accomplishment at any level will have built into it these two other aspects. Hence enjoyment is emotional comprehension maturing in an act.

Therefore enjoyment can be a measure or index of accomplishment. Comprehension too can be a measure of accomplishment. Accomplishment can be a measure of enjoyment as well as comprehension. Accomplishment belongs to the physical, rather the substance, enjoyment to the vital, comprehension to the mental and each can be a measure or index of the other. This is so because all the three co-exist on all the planes.

We have subdivided MAN into nine parts. Enjoyment belongs to all the nine levels. Mind enjoys comprehension, comprehending the emotion of the situation or event. Poetry is mind's emotional comprehension of life's intensities as realities. In the scale of human values, the poet is placed higher than the philosopher but lower than the yogi. When the conceptual knowledge of the philosopher enriches the sentiments of man whose knowledge of life realities extends to universal scale, the Poet is born.

Enjoyment belongs to the planes of quantity as well as quality. The rule is, quantity meets the needs, while quality enriches and therefore issues enjoyment. But when the quantity increases, enjoyment issues as if the quality has changed. Man earning money or acquiring power would seek to rise to knowledge to enjoy. But when man's wealth increases or power net widens, he begins to enjoy. Enjoyment is integral, not partial. Partial conditions do not generate enjoyment. Because it is integral, it cannot hurt a part. All parts or each part falls into its place harmoniously. The question of one hurting the other does not arise. Though enjoyment belongs to all nine levels, its proper seat is the emotional vital, level No.5. We understand enjoyment is possible in expanding. True. But there can be enjoyment in giving or taking, or for that matter in any act. It does not depend on the activity but the intensity and harmony of energies in the act.

At No. 9, especially at the level of substance, there is no movement. It enjoys non-moving stability. No. 1's idea becomes a pure concept when it detaches itself from the decision of the physical mind and the sentiment of the vital mind. Each level enjoys going to the next higher level. Ascent is the primary movement that lays the foundation. Descent is the secondary movement that completes. Ascent can be likened to the discovery in the lab; descent to the commercialisation of the product. The latter is a further movement of evolution and therefore every element there will be richer. Enjoyment in the descent is richer than in the ascent. There is an expansiveness, intensity and harmony that make for enjoyment. The Ananda splits into three aspects of Love, Beauty and Joy. Ananda received by the nerves is Joy, by the mind is Beauty, by the soul is Love.

Joy is a sensation even as being is a status and consciousness is knowledge. An individual, family, organisation or nation can be culturally evaluated by the quality of its enjoyment. Austerity is enjoyment by denial. Tyranny is the enjoyment of negative intensity. Progress issues out of either experiencing enjoyment or denying it. The wider the field enjoyment reaches, the greater is its quality.

Levels of Values

Comprehension, enjoyment, values, attitudes and motives are attributes of Accomplishment. Accomplishment itself is an attribute of Accomplishment in the sense that comprehension of the physical is accomplishment. Accomplishment at the physical level is a partial accomplishment of Man's total accomplishment even as comprehension is the mental accomplishment and enjoyment is vital accomplishment. For purposes of distinction, we may call the physical faculty achievement so that it may be distinguished from the total Accomplishment.

The theme of this chapter is — Man, the full man, accomplishes. His parts of being have partial accomplishment. Each uses a different faculty. The physical uses achievement, vital enjoyment, mental comprehension and the spiritual values. The total accomplishment carries all these as parts and there is an interplay or interaction. A strategy that can be extracted from these is when one learns to do a thing from a higher plane, his effectivity is greater. To solve problems this knowledge can be very effectively used as an ACT is constituted as mechanically or methodically as a machine.

It is common experience that as society advances people espouse higher values and employ higher skills and enjoy at a higher level. In any given society, the lower strata and the higher strata differ only in the fact that they chose different values. Social organisations and institutions are born when higher comprehension arises in the society. Their effectivity depends upon the extent to which the population honours values.

One basic work value is punctuality. The West has developed it and follows it as an article of faith. Their civilisation has risen high. In India neither work nor punctuality is developed. Life is low. Now that India has borrowed the Western ways at random at many levels, introduction of punctuality can raise the level of accomplishment very high. To introduce such a value or to be benefitted by such a value, a comprehensive knowledge of all these attributes and their interrelations needs to be known. This chapter is an attempt to deal with that subject. So also for systems. Cultural values can play a similar beneficial role in the West. Introduction of punctuality without such a knowledge of all other similar attributes will be difficult, and if one succeeds it will be painful. When achieved, it will yield the practical result with a dry human personality as the product. The best way to introduce punctuality is to start with the society. It requires social planning. Punctuality as a discipline must be introduced at the level of family, small establishments, schools, etc. and be encouraged. Without accomplishment on the agenda, introduction of a value will again be dry or mechanical. Higher production in the fields and factories introduced as an aim will give the context of encouragement so that the value of punctuality is more fully accomplished.

In a school where the result is 40%, if a target is to be fixed, it must take into account the potentials of pupils, teachers, the school and the community that serves it. Normally it will be realistic to aim at 50% from 40%. Bt when all the potentials are studied and the aim of full exploitation of the potentials is set, and for that purpose one work value or operational value like punctuality is seriously followed, the result will be more than 90% because at any time society taps only 5% of its potentials in an unorganised fashion. The present effort is an attempt at partial organisation. During such an effort, a host of opportunities and problems will arise. The ideas of this chapter will then be of maximum use.

Punctuality is understood in a school as punctual opening at the given hour. Then it becomes a one-time method, not a value. The school should be opened, closed, and the periods begun punctually. The lessons, the homework, the examinations, the valuation of papers etc. must be punctual in their operation. It is an overall endeavour which releases more energy of the community. Energy so released must be organised into skills at all levels. Otherwise it will be dissipated and the momentum lost. The handwriting is to be improved, manners are to be upgraded, cleanliness is to be raised, orderliness introduced as long as the energy is available.

In a practical experiment like that, each one of these 25 ideas will find ample scope for use. These ideas will help not to overdo a certain discipline or neglect a potential. The accomplishment taken at the level of the whole school will yield a very desirable result. When the unit of accomplishment is narrowed to class and then to the individual, not only results will be phenomenal but also we will know how to draw upon the potentials, to convert them into different stages of accomplishment. Incidentally, all the errors of the development policies of the nation can be seen at the level of school in full evidence. A school cannot embark on introducing punctuality without the individual class being motivated to achieve more, the handwriting of pupils improved, the silence of the teaching hour honoured. Teachers who bring in the social attitudes that backward caste pupils cannot perform well are a bar to the school's progress. They simply cannot be told to shed that attitude. In a minor way similar attitudes in the teachers that one cannot pass an exam at an advanced age can be countered by organising self-improvement schemes for teachers. The results of such a scheme will remove the emotional foundation for the disbelief about backward castes.

In stray cases where pupils are truthful, honest, etc. they can be shown how the energy of these values can be drawn into academic results. As the energy is true, the incentive real, the strategy has a 100% chance of becoming successful. Cleanliness and orderliness coupled with punctuality can be linked with academic results, individual as well as class. This will create a very healthy atmosphere of competition and is likely to have a chain reaction.

Opinion can be a bar or help. Recognising this, one can take up in a school dozens of opinions, e.g., geometry cannot be taught, only memorisation will help; punctuality is not possible in this town; no standards can ever be achieved in a school like ours. Gathering all these opinions, one can study them and show generally where they are invalid and why. The occasion can be taken to create new right opinions. One can witness a minor miracle that these changed opinions change a school at the 141st rank in the district to the 3rd or even the 1st rank.

Development is a science. Planning will enhance the result not by a percentage but will raise the level of performance. To introduce planning one has to know the process of development thoroughly. This chapter on values contributes its mite to that whole effort. Within its own realm, each idea here will turn into a very powerful strategy inconceivable in their isolation.

Levels of Attitudes

Accomplishment is a final physical result in concrete material terms that is usable, such as food cooked, book printed, house built, a game played, an idea understood, etc. Into this goes physical work, vital energy and mental comprehension. They are the primary elements of the basic planes of life. They shape into secondary tools when energy gets organised into skills, comprehension into opinion, energy gets directed by likes. These instruments have a way of further improving themselves into various fashions of the same intensity or higher organisation and greater intensity. Comprehension is the basic endowment of mind. It shapes into opinion, preference, construction, habit, thought, idea. Energy when organised, we know, takes the further forms of skill, capacity, ability, and talent.

Also energy of one plane is acted upon by another plane. Energy is organised into skill by knowledge in the physical plane. In the vital plane when the energy is acted upon by the knowledge of the mental plane, Attitude is born. Likes, dislikes, are energy directed by vital attraction primarily, though an element of the mind may often enter into its composition. Attraction, charm, affection are energies of higher intensity flowing towards another object by virtue of its vital strength, not so much directed by a mental idea. Whereas the vital energies, when endorsed and given a direction by a mental idea, channel into a given direction. And that direction is known as attitude.

In individual or social development accomplishment is a landmark to which we strive and it serves as a tool of measurement of our level of development. Considering it in both ways as a result and a measuring tool, we have to consider the various ingredients that go into its making. In a basic sense an accomplishment, being a miniature of human existence, contains all the endowments man has. In another sense, an accomplishment is traced back to its origin as a process and we study it as a result brought about by the ingredients at play in the previous stage of that succession of processes.

We have now taken up, in this section, consideration of the result as brought about by its component attitude. We define attitude as the combination of mental idea and vital energy. Our theme is attitude is a determinant of result. We further say the result can be upgraded or monitored by choosing the appropriate attitude.

As we go down the line from mind to the body, we see the phenomenon of emotion of each plane shaping the knowledge of that plane and further, the knowledge of a higher plane impinging on the emotion of the lower plane. Thus, opinion arises in the mental plane, attitude in the vital and motives in the physical. Mind gives the direction, energy the force and the body the organisation. Direction from the mind, force from the vital help the physical accomplish through its organisation. Mind expresses through opinion, vital through attitudes and the physical through motives. Opinion has no energy whereas attitude is full of energy. Motive has the organisation that can shape the energy into result. In the mental plane itself mental emotion converts the mental knowledge into mental opinion. Mental organisation converts that opinion into mental decision of the mental consciousness which becomes mental determination at the level of mental substance, the brain.

We are now considering only the external results as our topic is social development. We are not discussing the inner results which belong to the domain of psychology. So our context is external, social, the situation outside man, in his circumstance or environment. That environment is like a pyramid with horizontal layers of different variety and vertical layers of different intensity. As man is a unique product down to his fingertips, where the finger print stands out as unique, so the social situations in this pyramid of myriad expressions are composed of millions of individual events each of which is unique, not to speak of the equally innumerable inner stands man can take. His response to each of the outer situations gives rise to an attitude. If the outer situations are described as facts, each fact is capable of creating an attitude in man. There are as many attitudes as there are social situations or social facts.

Attitudes are the final outcome of external social situations. Therefore attitudes can be used as instruments of accomplishment. Each of the nine levels if split into three further levels of mental, vital, physical, will create 27 separate planes. Subdividing them into consciousness and substance they become 54. As a conscious movement is internal and the unconscious man is externally moved, by dividing these 54 levels into conscious and unconscious or internal and external, we land on 108 levels totally. This can be extended ad infinitum by selfish x unselfish, right x wrong, high x low, bright x darkness, if we choose. Each of these levels can have an attitude of its own.

Attitude is of the vital and therefore properly belong to 4,5, & 6 only. But, in theory emotion is there in all 108 levels even as knowledge and physicality are. We may confine our discussions to 4, 5 & 6.

In the unconscious process the external circumstances give us the attitude. In the conscious growth one acquires an attitude and determines the result. Attitudes, conscious or unconscious, decide the available energy to produce the result. It is obvious that one's opinion determines the scope of one's opportunity, action and accomplishment. In that sense, opinion, attitudes, skills are limiting factors when the available energy is abundant, while they are positive, helpful instruments where the available energy is not abundant. An opinion of a higher order compels the man to raise his otherwise sagging energies for action. In a person of overwhelmingly abundant actionable energy, a smaller narrow opinion is inhibiting.

In the light of the fact that knowledge has no energy and energy has no direction, we can say opinions and knowledge are factors that bring into our ken opportunities. Attitudes are the springs that unleash the energies and energise the opportunities and organisation (skill) is the instrument that brings about the result. In this view, right attitude helps opportunity take shape and appropriate skill converts the possibilities into actualities.

To draw a complete list of attitudes or their main representations and examine their capacity to determine accomplishment will cover the full scope of social development. All that is said here will apply to opinion in a lesser way and motive in a fuller way. Motive is a deep-seated centre of determination. Attitude directs energies. Motives direct accomplishment. Opinions give direction to knowledge. The physical by its constitution is a kind of the 'whole' man which is really his embodied being. The motive of the being which includes all the four parts is the real MOTIVE, but for purposes of a narrow field of social development, the attitude of the physical can be called the motive which determines the ultimate accomplishment.

Levels of Motives

Nature is Energy in motion. Of all the animate objects she has created, Man is the supreme being. Already he has a mind, a vital and a physical. Energy moving through these planes creates. Also it creates instruments in each of these planes. In the mind the moving energy creates ideas, in the vital it creates relationships, and in the body results are achieved. Further, the Energy creates an instrument in mind to create ideas and that instrument is opinion. Similarly, the instruments of attitudes and motives are created in the vital and physical.

Being a new subject, not having a developed terminology as yet, confusions may arise as to what is comprehension and sensation. For the present, let us use a terminology that is clear to us. Mind is the plane, comprehension is the faculty, opinion is the instrument. So also let us assume attitude and motives are the instruments of vital and physical.

In this section our purpose is to consider motive as an instrument. Further, to consider motive as an instrument of development is our aim. As we proceed from mind to body we move from conscious to subconscious. Hence motive is subconscious. As it is subconscious, it is carried by the physical cells from the parent to child. No man is endowed with the capacity to know his motive as, by definition, it is subconscious. He has to resort to subtle symptoms to decipher it. The whole process of civilisation is a process of becoming more conscious of our subconscious knowledge and achievement. The greatest achievements of civilisation came about when the collective had acquired a motive.

Motive properly belongs to the being, but in view of the fact that the physical, in one sense, is as comprehensive as being, we use the term motive for the physical urge. When one is subconscious he does not move by thought that is conscious but by an inner urge like hunger. So, motive is an internal force and for that reason very powerful. Mind gives direction, vital energises but the physical achieves a result by its organisation. All motives have an inbuilt organisation in them. The effectivity of the physical comes from its organisation. For the very same reason, the physical does not understand till it is able to do a thing because its understanding is organisation. Also the moment the physical understands, it cannot wait for action because organisation has an inherent dynamism. A motor either runs or not. It cannot be started and NOT run. When the organisation is energised by the electric current, it comes alive, it runs. We can as well say, the motor 'understands' when it runs.

The hierarchy of opinion, attitude, motive is interlinked and each determines the other. In their formative stage, they are determined by others. After they are formed, they determine the others. Normally each of them is formed on its own. In such a situation conflict ensues. Each aspect is inclusive of the other and in that measure they are harmonious. An attitude includes an opinion. Motive includes attitudes, i.e. opinion too, indirectly. At the level of Being, the motive is most harmonious. Still, individual exclusive formation is possible which generates disharmony and conflict. One who has his own motive on his side is sure of success.

As motives are subconscious, the collective motive rarely conflicts with the individual motive. An individual motive can clash with another individual's. Such clashes are most powerful. Motives continue to grow in successive generations. When the cycle is complete, it changes, often into its very opposite. A generous man's children and grandchildren are more and more generous and at one point, the next generation becomes miserly.

Motives exist in grades. They grow horizontally and vertically. The level of motives is fixed by the level of personality. The same person can have different motives of different intensities. By extension, we can speak of mental, vital motives. An urge becomes a motive when it is irresistible or consciously effective. That is the deepest psychological force of man.

Beyond the realm of social development lies the domain of psychological growth and spiritual evolution. The world is split into mystic Asia and material Europe. No one has indicated why it is so. Beyond saying it is God's will, it is difficult to assign reasons. As the highest mountain is in Asia, one may tend to think its symbolism is a clue. Mountains are, HE said, the earth's aspiration for heaven. Whatever the truth there, the fact remains that Asia and Europe have taken on themselves opposite goals. The goals have been made possible by the motives of the populations. Material goal being the motive, it was possible for Europe to achieve it, because it was within reach. Spiritual goal being lofty, it defies achievement. Hence Asia's spiritual motive, while it is alive underneath, is covered by a life that has failed to achieve material plenty.

The argument for social development in Asia is that it will surely succeed in an overwhelming measure as its deeper base is alive and strong. Only that it should awaken to its own needs.

In the individuals in whom the spiritual motive is well formed, personal development of prosperity will take on wings if they choose to exercise themselves in that direction. For that, they should appreciate the primacy of Spirit over matter.

Model of Nine Levels of Growth

Level 1

When the spirit embodied itself, it assumed a body which later developed a vital and then a mind. It may be logical that the spirit should first assume a mind and acquire the body finally. It is not so in practice. From the other end, it is logical that Mother Earth while creating would create the body first. Without going further deep into the spiritual truths of it, let us spread out our enquiry with a view to serving the theory of social development. Social development as a possible idea arose when mind knew that it could make the body work better under its hegemony. Therefore, instead of starting the study at level 9, I start at One.

Man's physical, vital, mental planes are further subdivided into mental, vital, physical in each plane, thus creating nine levels of functioning.

Number One is pure mind, the pure thinker, the seat of the philosopher. Though it evolved out of the 8 previous levels, in its own perfection it stands aloof, not related to any other centre effectively. Number 2 and Number 3 are in touch with number 5 and 7 and in that measure will be influenced by them. One too is similarly in touch with 4 & 7 and is influenced as such. But One has an aloofness at the end of the cycle of evolution even as 9 has an aloofness at the beginning. Nine lives all by itself outside the reach of the rest of the centres that are yet to be developed. We cannot say the same thing about One since it issued out of the progress the other 8 levels made. Still its character of evolving out of the previous bases enables it to stand really aloof uninfluenced by any other previous levels.

Concepts are formed in One which is the seat of the philosopher. Thought at 3 is facts or is factual, i.e. related to a fact, not self-existent. At 2 they are coloured by the emotion and acquire the garb of a sentiment. Thought shedding its factual nature and weaning itself from the sentiment becomes pure thought. Pure thought seeks to be logical and rational. Thought acquires rationality when it is organised according to logic. Thus, thought acquires a structure of organised base. Its capacity to be organised leads to its growth. Systems of thought develop. Man endowed with that capacity is a thinker. Evolving from 9 he becomes a thinker traveling through the stages of work, vitality, and scholarship. Work generates energy and energy, ideas based on facts and events. One endowed with those details is the scholar. The scholar matures into thinker or philosopher. An original thinker is one whose raw materials are not work or energy or event acts. Using thoughts as his own raw material, he builds systems of thought to become an original thinker. If his thinking creates something new to the world of ideas, he becomes a creative thinker. The mind that is capable of generating ideas not based on experience in the world but based on other original ideas is a creative mind.

One, apart from being a thinker, serves as a seat of ego where ego can strike its roots deep. Ego is called the coordinating intelligence. HE also calls it reason. Sri Aurobindo equates ego and reason. Reason organises ideas around a centre. That centre is usurped by ego. One is a centre of thought, not force. But through thought, ego tries to reach the depths of one's being to draw upon its power. Ego reaching that depth through the physical will be tenacious by virtue of its physicality, but will not have the power of penetration given by the organised idea. Nor does the vital yield powers of that dimension.

Sri Aurobindo says ideas arise from the body. It is known that there are ideas of the mind, ideas of the heart and ideas of the body. When the movements of the body are energised, they seek direction for their action. That direction is the knowledge of the body. Having originated there, it reaches the mind after certain refinements. The origin of ideas is body, rather, the movements of the body.

Social development is conceived of by One and is executed by the remaining parts. The process of the social development and the process of the individual's development from 9 to 1 and further from 1 to 9 are the same. Hence One is capable of conceiving social development as an idea.

Being mind, One does not have energy or power but has only light. The only power of mind is the power of organising the ideas into a decision for action or a determination to execute. One has no power over the rest (2 to 9) except in the measure they are willing to obey.

Intrinsically One has the power to dominate all the rest as it is drawn from them, but that power accrues only when the clarity, organisation and strength of One reaches the very depth of 9. The Mind can dominate Matter if the Mind comes into its own. Presently it is Matter that dominates Mind as the Light in the Mind is not fully emerged.

Level 2

The vital in the mind is called Two, represented by feeling and sentiment in consciousness above and substance below. Sensations begin in the body, move to vital and emotion, and in the end reach mind. They are known as physical sensation, vital sensation, emotional sensation and mental sensation. Burning, itching, thirst, hunger are physical; anger, attraction, urge, impulse are vital; affection, kindness, sympathy are emotional; curiosity, memory, imagination are of the mind. The emotional sensation is fortified or organised as a thought enters it when it becomes a feeling. Sentiment is a stronger version of it when the feeling of consciousness is accepted by the mental substance. Sensitivities arise from the sentiments.

Mind is a plane of understanding, observation, comprehension, decision, imagination, conception, sympathy. Thought, emotion and action interact in each of the 3 planes of mind, vital and physical. In each plane, the action is different. In law and order problems, the action of the authorities varies from bursting tear gas shells, to firing. They move over the scale of cane charge, lathi charge, opening fire, calling in reserve police and finally the army. Each level of deterrence is meted out by a different level of officer. The same action, gaining in intensity, demands a higher officer to execute. Thought acts differently in the physical from the mind. So also emotions act in the mind very differently from the plane of body. But it retains the character of emotion in all the planes.

Viewed in this context, Sentiment and Feeling give us more views to consider. Movement of energy is both ways, from 1 to 2 and from 3 to 2. The decision of 3 is decisive as long as sympathy does not enter into its fabric. The strength of decision is watered down by the touch of emotion. Here the strength arises from its being crude. The clarity of concept loses its precision when it admits into its fold feeling or sentiment. Moving downwards from 1, sentiment is a weakening agent, weakening of a thought. Moving upwards, sentiment weakens the crudity of a decision. Sentiment is sandwiched between the refined thought and crude decision.

Action emotionalised refines the sensational thought into pure idea, re-organising it around the mental sense instead of sensational thought. Conceptual clarity is diluted by feeling to be ready to act in the medium of life. Here it loses its refined organisation for pure thinking in favour of crude organisation necessary for action.

Action issuing out of the decision of 3 will not have the benefit of ethics of feeling and will be limited to the emotions of the vital energy which belongs to society. Social emotions to be upgraded into ethical ideals need the office of feeling and sentiment.

The process of refined ideas becoming feeling is accomplished by the emotional energy in the mental plane. Its further development to decision in the descent is achieved by the energy of feeling turning into energy of action. We witness in all the planes horizontally the movements of energy of comprehension towards energy of action via energy of emotion. Vertically too, from the body to mind and vice versa, this movement retains the same character.

Personality of man is stationed or centred only at one point. To understand a man, one has to understand all his actions from this point of reference. As the 9 or 108 levels concentrate for purposes of existence of an individual and collect at one point of his most integrated centre to make it his personality, we need to discard the general discussion in favour of a given situation. This helps us evaluate his action and enables us to advise him on self-improvement.

General consideration of an individual or an individual evaluation of a general situation opens the possibilities of discussion on all sides which is the strategy by which confusion is organised.

Passion, ambition, devotion, dedication, sensibility, sensitivity, ideal, etc. emerge into clearer foci by this classification. Two is the seat of poet as 1 is the seat of philosopher. 3 is the arsenal of the organiser. Language serves each of them differently. It supplies matter of fact phrases to the organiser, metaphor to the poet and well-defined, precise words devoid of sentiments to the scholar. Emphasizing their own version of language, the philosopher can degenerate into the doctrinaire professor, the poet into an idealist and the organiser can raise his actions to the level that demands worship or obedience.

As the descent is more powerful than the plodding ascent, we should carefully sift them out before any serious consideration.

Level 3

The mind that is seated in the brain and known to be the physical mind is 3 in our scale. This is the centre of intellectuality, decision and determination. What is decision in consciousness becomes determination in the substance. The physical substance sensitised is nerves. Its capacity to think evolves to the level of brain in the head. The physical moves and is not capable of anything other than the movement except the physical sensation. The physical movements organised by 7 become skill of a primary level. The moving physicality releases energy and generates the plane of vitality. The vital sensation going to the mind turns into thought to come back to the body to direct and dominate it. Four is the mind of the vital which gives 3 the sensational facts. Three receives the facts but not the sensation. Sensational facts when separated from the senses become pure facts. Facts are coordinated by 3 to generate thoughts. Such thoughts are organised into a system to become a decision for action. What acts in 3 is not senses but the mental sense which is the essence of senses.

This can be more fully appreciated when we consider what happens in the formation of concepts and ideas. Here it is not the mental sense that acts but the faculty of discrimination. Sense is removed from the fact so that it becomes a pure fact. Pure facts are uninfluenced even by the mental sense and lend themselves to form an idea or concept.

My friend helps me to learn the work is a sensational fact which is a rider to the work of learning. The non-sensational fact is, I am learning the work. Learning the work is a fact for the mental senses. Shorn of the mental sense, it becomes PURE when we see an unskilled part becomes skilled by the higher organised energy relating to the unorganised faculty. This is a concept, an idea. Basically, physical moves; it creates movement and thereby generates energy. The physical movements are organised by 7 as primary skill of organised physical movements. The vital organises energy to act forcefully in a given direction. Mind organises sensational facts into decision and pure facts into ideas.

Number 3 is the organiser and every little thing achieved by civilisation so far is achieved only by 3. Three is in direct relation with 6 & 9 that are physical too. Juxtaposed between 4 and 2, naturally it is in touch with them.

The physical mind, 3, is in direct relation to 7, the mind of the physical. Three is practical and receives only empirical facts. For this reason it can never fail. For the very same reason it cannot be creative because creativity requires imagination and must function in non-physical contexts.

No. 4 is the mind of the vital which thinks guided by the intensity of the energy and its effectivity. Psychologically it is selfish. Non-psychologically it is the thought of the energy, rather high energy. Therefore it is non-moral, cunning, shrewd, often unfailing. Morals issue out of ethics and belong to the plane of mind, not the mind of the vital. 3 receives the feed of 4 but sheds its sensation before it processes it. Shedding the sensation, 3 is enabled to decide on an issue while sensations will weaken the decision. At a further stage, the decision that is weakened by the sensation of 4, will be strengthened by the higher sensation of 2.

As 9 is the physical existence or awareness, 3 is mental existence or mental awareness. But 3 as it is not yet touched by 2 remains unemotional. Great administrators belong to 3. HE says Ford has pragmatic intelligence whose home is 3. Those in whom 3 is well developed will be successful executives.

No. 3's objectivity is less when sentiment of No. 2 colours it, but if the sentiment is one that is intense with the decision of 3, the decision is fortified. Thought is the product of sensation in the physical part of the mind. The function of brain produces thought, one faculty of mind, contrary to the belief that mind is the result of the functioning of brain.

3 is the seat of action because it moves 7 which is the primary actor.

Level 4

The vital plane matures when it evolves the mental element in it. It is what HE calls vital mind and we have assigned 4 to it in our scale. Any plane begins with the physical, develops the vital and ends by developing mind. That is true of the mental plane too.

The development of any plane is in two dimensions. One is from physical to mental. The other is substance to consciousness. In the vital plane at 6 a beginning is made. So 6 is physical vital substance. The mere body evolving life energy evolves it as substance of life. From there horizontally 6 develops towards 4, vertically the substance develops into consciousness. Here it is the vital consciousness. The hard, inert substance releasing vital energy becomes slowly conscious of its own vitality. That is the vital consciousness. From 9 to 1 at each level substance in its upward movement towards 1 evolves consciousness, while in the downward movement consciousness develops into matter or substance. This happens at all levels. As water expands 1700 times in becoming vapour, the upward movement is expansive in volume, while the downward movement shrinks and becomes hard. The vital power issues from this expanding volume.

If we do not consider the organisation of mind, the most efficient part of man is 4. The organisation raises the level of efficiency. As the man who has moved to 3 is not yet fully effective, No. 4 often excels him even as the graduate's earning is less than the uneducated shopkeeper. The superiority of 3 is not in question at all but till 3 comes into its own, 4 can always steal a march over him. Also, 3 being mental and rational, it is not so subtle as 4 which is entirely vital and subtle. Therefore 4 has always a penetrative insight into the weaknesses of 3 till it is fully organised. Hence the apparent superiority of 4.

3 is hampered by several aspects till it is perfectly organised when it is invulnerable. First of all, 3 is physical while 4 is mental. Therefore subtlety is greater at 4. Having come into the mental plane, 3 becomes ethical or moral while 4 is totally free of that inhibition. 4 seeks after victory at all costs while 3 is more concerned with its organisation and rightness. Victory, as anything else, pursued for its own sake, irrespective of other considerations, will certainly be more powerful and effective than result pursued under certain conditions such as ethics and systems.

Democracy made non-military civil leaders the head of a nation putting the general under them. Till then the military leader was the ruler. They were of 4. The enormous courage of 5 makes them leaders who go to victory. When that courage turns into thought, it is extremely resourceful. Sri Aurobindo says Shivaji is a vibhuti but he had no compunction to kill his opponent in a fraternal embrace, a heinous crime for a moral man. Shivaji had no moral compunctions as he was seated in No. 4. The philosopher of 1 and the organiser of 3 are objects of ridicule for men of 4. For him, philosophy is insubstantial and the organiser is too slow and too dull-witted.

As No. 7 and No. 1 are minds too, No. 4 is in direct relationship with them. No. 7 is subconscious and No. 1 is fully conscious. The thoroughness of 7 cannot be there in 4 even as the clarity of 1 is missing. Without being thorough or clear, 4 is dynamic, fast, reaches its goal unfailingly, unfettered by ideals, ethics, sentiments.

Foresters, rustic community leaders, smugglers, mafia chieftains are of 4. They are shrewd, penetrating, disciplined and therefore unfailing. There is only one punishment among them for lack of loyalty, viz. death. Obedience and adherence are total for this reason. In the individual who lacks courage, 4 gives superstition. His superstition arises not from outside but from his own fears and intense imagination. The intensity that creates insight in the strong creates intense fears in the weak.

4 is the seat of social security acting as social conscience. It is 4 that sets the fashions, lays down social norms, norms of public conduct, approved manners. In the ascent it processes the emotions of 5 into emotional thought. In the descent it receives the decision and determination of 3 and infuses emotional commitment to them. In times of social degeneration, the strength of 4 determines the length of social, psychological survival. In times of social upward movement, society moves up only to the extent 4 approves. Shrewdness, insight, penetration, alertness, resourcefulness are its endowments.

Strong 4 in the head of the family will make the family a victim of tyranny, but the family will become a success though enveloped in fear and suffused by tension.

4 is the monitor of motives in consciousness and substance.

Level 5

The vital of the vital plane is pure vital even as 1 is pure mind and 9 is pure physical. In our scale it is assigned to 5. This is the seat of the warrior, the artist and all those whose emotion rises to the peak before being touched even by the mental of the vital plane 4. The movement from below is accompanied by the phenomenon of enormous expansion of energy at the first level of physical to the vital. As energy is subtle emerging from the dense material plane, its volume expands vastly issuing power of the greatest magnitude. 5 is the peak along that path as it combines the conversion of the physical plane into the vital plane as well as No.6 into No. 5, again a conversion of the physical in the vital plane into pure vital. Next it goes to 4 when the energy becomes sensational knowledge. This conversion entails a loss of power of the vital but generates the efficacy of thought. Thought in 4 is not of the mental plane where its characteristic is ethic, logic and rationality. But it has the knowing character of thought. Knowledge unencumbered by ethical restraint, necessity of logical conversion or rational structure both of which involve considerable energy, is mercilessly powerful. Possessors of this faculty are ruthless tyrants unfailingly successful in their operations as long as their acts are in the realms outside ethics.

2, 5, and 8 are the vital parts of the various planes. Similar parts of different planes are in touch with each other. The higher inspires the lower, the lower supports the functioning of the higher. Faculties and capacities collect in each part, but will not yield results till they are saturated. When a similar part of a lower plane begins to function, the unsaturated capacities of the higher part come to its rescue. What happens in 3 cannot but influence 7 and 4 as they are similar. It is true every part influences every other part, but the mutual influence of similar parts is greater. These influences are naturally positive and negative, positive from above and negative from below. 3 is physical but mind, while 4 and 7 are mental parts. 1 directly influences 4 and 7 but 3 will influence 4 and 7 if the particular work connects them both. Such relations are a topic by themselves wide enough. 3 is mainly the organiser that organises thoughts into decision. An activity of either 4 or 7 containing an element of organisation of decision will put it in touch with 3. Suppose 8 has received a shock of fear from a fall, the great surge of courage taking place in 5 will be hampered by the resurrecting memory of 8 as it is in direct touch with it. Apart from that, as in other parts, 5 is in direct relation by sequence with 4 and 6.

In our scheme of consciousness and substance for each part we have assigned sensation and sensitivity to 5. The role of the vital is to influence the physical by bringing the mental power to bear on it. The vital organises the energies into sensations which, when reaching the mind, create thought. The body always is a docile servant to mind more than to the vital.

The five senses respond to events with their sensational energies and get coordinated as SENSATION. Mind has its own sense, better called as mental sense, which is other than the vital sensation. Mind's sense emerges when the mind separates the reports to itself from its sensational part. Power really belongs to the physical, energy to the vital, clarity to the mind. But energy too enjoys power of energy even as ideas have the mental power. Still, when the sensation seeps down to the vital substance it turns into sensitivity which has far more power than sensation. Its power comes from the fact that it goes to the substance of the vital. Really the substance in any plane is the physical of that plane. So, truly power at last comes from the physical. Five is the pure hero, the great artist, the lover who kills himself, the patriot who sacrifices everything for his country. As 5 is untouched by mind, it has the capacity to be oblivious of the environment, consequences, commitments and will go to the target straight like an arrow.

Man was in tune with nature when 5 was the height of his evolution. At that time his faculties were pugnacity, gregariousness, survival, self-preservation, abandon of self-forgetful joy, etc.

Music is the form of sound, painting is the form of colour and lines, courage is the form of force. Hence their natural seat is 5.

Negatively 5 is the seat of fear, obsession, phobia, force of superstition. Sensation of 5 energises the natural physiological functions with energy such as running in fear.

Great warriors like Shivaji, Alexander are of 5. Napoleon does not belong to 5 as he is pre-eminently the law giver, the organiser, but 5 was his most effective faculty while on the battlefield with bullets whizzing past him.

Level 6

Six is the physical part of the vital plane and is seated in the central nervous system, even as 3 is seated in the brain. The physical parts of the planes have a physical organ as the seat, 3 in brain, 6 in the nerves, 9 in the body. At 6, the human personality emerge into the vital plane which means the physical movements generate vital energies. Therefore the greatest energies are witnessed at this stage. In civilisation, this is marked by the urban commercial life from rural agricultural life. Individually the blue collar worker taking to education is at 6. Any single activity can find itself at 6, for that matter at any level, irrespective of the fact that the individual is far advanced at 1 or 2 or primitive at 9 or 8. He will find himself meeting the characteristics of 6 with respect to any one activity if it is there. An advanced thinker not used to crafts can find himself at 6 if he ever takes to it.

A dud for some reason may be evolved and find himself at 6 in shooting. As faculties and parts of man have an independent existence in exceptional cases, this state of affairs is always possible. While 6 is the point where the being enters the vital plane, 5 is the point where a further expansion of 6 into 5 — physical into vital in the vital plane — is added. This is the reason for finding people of greatest vital power at 5. It is true growth in one part or growth of a faculty is generally accompanied by growth of other parts or faculties. But that growth is only in potential, not in actualities.

It is natural that 6 is in touch with 3 and 9 as they are physical parts and with 5 and 7 which are adjacent parts. The developments of 3 indirectly influence the growth of 6, while the strength or weakness of 9 lend their support to 6 and its existence. The topic of the adjacent parts and similar parts and their influence on each part is a wide one into which I do not go here. March of civilisation finds its journey in man from 9 to 1 and from 1 to 9. Ideas, opinions, sensitivities, preferences etc. often get lodged in any part. Such opinions, etc. of the 6 cannot be removed by mental effort as there is nothing of mind in 6. Fundamentalists belong to 6. If they are to be educated, it must be vital education, not mental education. The vital is educated by sensations such as fear, attraction, not argument or explanation or reasoning. The physical cannot be educated even by sensation. It can be educated by doing a thing by itself, i.e. by direct experience only, not by other means, since it has no mind to listen to explanations nor sense centres to respond to sensations. The scientists of the world and even other social scientists have espoused the ideal of empiricism in spite of having a faculty to think and comprehend. To make a dent in their beliefs, one has to achieve in fact contrary to their beliefs. Even then, they may accept that particular achievement but in all their other fields, they will be physical with pride. The history of democracy is a standing proof of this phenomenon. After the monarch is disposed, the leader of the democracy is treated as the monarch and that attitude seeps down to the very bottom. That is the tenacity of the physical phenomenon.

During periods of calamities, man moves down to a low point. No longer the mind holds its own nor the vital. He moves down to 6 and acts only from there or from 7.

Emotion and devotion belong to consciousness and substance of 6. Devotion properly belongs to 5 but its strength and intensity reach their height only at 6.

Emotion at 4 can be coloured by some knowledge, but at 6 the scope for any tinge of knowledge is nil. Kannapan could dig out his eyes because he was a 6. Jean Valjean's emotional sense of duty to his sister rises from his being at 6. The life of a galley slave, the criminal mind, his fine emotions to Cossette all arise similarly. 6 can slave. It has no moral, ethical sense and finds it natural to be a criminal or to be a saint. To a 6, there is no difference between sainthood or a criminal life. It is simply a way of life.

6 is the point at which vital and physical sensations meet and emerge into each other in the ascent and descent. 6 is open to raw physical influence as 9 is, because it is of that type. All the power of 3 in organisation does not touch 6 because it has no idea of what it is.

Level 7

In our classification of Man into physical, vital and mental, though we have nine levels, in reality the levels are innumerable and never-ending. In each small act of ours like swallowing a mouthful of food or taking the most important decision of life, there exist strands of mental, physical, and vital intertwined. Only a general idea is attempted here, not a very minute analysis.

From such a view, 7 is the mental part of the physical which puts the physical and vital movements into an organisation that can be identified as skill. To our perception, these skills are subconscious as we are not aware of them. A subconscious skill is one that one cannot be aware of however much he tries, such as the functioning of blood circulation; but the skills acquired by 7 can be seen when we turn our attention towards them. Only they are not in our conscious perception, not so much because it cannot be known as that we do not care to take note of them. Such a subconscious skill resides in 9. When 9 is split into three parts, its mental part is subconscious which controls our involuntary organs.

Bone, flesh, nerves, tissues, ligaments, cartilage are all of different composition. Their composition varies according to their strength. Brain falls under a special category. Brain is the flesh that thinks. By thinking the flesh becomes soft, perhaps softest in the body. It is mellowed by thought. The thinking faculty of Man is carried on not only in the brain but is extended to the seat of reflexes in the spine and ends up in the cells which have a mind of their own, called by Mother "cellular mind."

For our purposes, 7 is the seat of the primary mental activity which mentalises the movements of 9 and the energies of 8. It is in touch with 4 and 1 as they too are of mind, but refuses to respond to the emotion of 4 or the ideas of 1 since it has no faculty of that description. It is just below 3, offering a constant support as foundation. Here too, the organisation, decision and determination of 3 when descending on it leaves it untouched and unmoved. As its own organisation is rudimentary, the highly complex organisation of 3 leaves it baffled. As elsewhere, 7 serves as the foundation to 3, rather offers foundational support.

The mental part turns the energies of sensation into ideas and organises them so that the idea will go back to the body to dominate it. In 7 the energies it receives are energies of physical sensation. So, the maximum possibility here is its conversion into physical ideas. Physically an idea about movement is the process of skill formation. Individual skills inside each elementary act are many. Walking, talking, drinking, driving a nail are such activities. Into any of these rudimentary acts go dozens of physical movements. For instance, in walking hundreds of muscles should learn to coordinate themselves so that the feet are firm on the ground. Walking is a willed movement. A will, a volition should arise. It is a mental movement. The body should enter locomotion if the feet are to move in steps. Blood circulation, breathing, etc. should conform to the requirements of greater energy demanded by walking. Eyes should commission themselves into seeing at a distance for clearance. A simple act of walking, before it evolved into its final shape, fashioned hundreds of individual skills as described above and then submitted them to coordination. All these are organised by 7. The organisation is there, skill formation is also there, but it is the physical skill and organisation of physical skills fashioned out of physical movements. There is no trace of thought or mind here except it is the mind of the body.

Sri Aurobindo speaks of a physical organisation that governs the world. Its organisation, the organisation of 7 and of 3 as well as the organisation of ideas into concepts at 1 have in common AN ORGANISATION. That is a physical organisation at 7 and mental organisation at 1. Sri Aurobindo speaks of discovering a higher organisation than this physical organisation to cure the disorders of Life and Mind.

Skill and capacity are its attributes in consciousness and substance. Skill converts energy by organisation into a usable tool. The essence of the effort is the process of skill formation. A great many skills forming at one level or at one point let their essences collect at that point as capacity. Skill is the process of the individual act yielding results. Capacity is the strength of their essence collected in the substance as foundation. Such a capacity can be drawn into one single skill to fortify it. That makes any skill a talent. The faculty that turns capacity to a skill for it to become a talent is ability.

The principles of formation of skills, capacity, talent, ability, etc. are the same at all levels of personality, be it physical or spiritual. The values at each point that serve as a medium are different in different planes. Coordination as in a gear plate is a physical value while fidelity to facts is a mental value at 3 where it is arriving at a decision.

Level 8

8 is the vital of the physical plane. This is the earliest of points where vitality enters human personality. Also this is the first point that is untouched by mentality. Though it is vitality, its vitality will not bear any sign of energy man knows of vitality but will be of the character of the physical, even as the mental effort of the neo-literate is education for him.

Energy and Force find their seats here in consciousness and substance. The only liveliness, freshness that can be witnessed here is the 'enormous' amount of physical energy into which the merest existence of 9 converts itself here. Movements generating energy are seen here for the first time as a phenomenon.

7 is a poor mentality and is feebly influenced by the great cunning of 4 and the brilliant ideas of 1. On a parallel, 8 is thus related to 5 and 2. Men at 8 can rise to poetry moved by the physical intensity of the occasion. At the thanksgiving function at Mother Estates, an old man moved by the emotions of the function, burst into a song that spontaneously welled up in him on the theme of the forest changing into cultivable lands. Thoughts of no description touch 8 even though primary emotion can blossom into poetry here.

Men of this type will give themselves to superstition and will not be able to question its validity. Loyalty to master, family, property, crew are too sophisticated for them. He who feels is the master, what serves is property, those who are around are kith and kin. Crew is one who happens to be around. Their emotions are still at the level of energy lacking definition of any description. Ideas of no description find an echo in them, not even mercenary gains appeal to their non-existent thoughts. Survival is right and it is their ethic. Organisation is not a concept they can identify, much less follow. Even systems do not evoke their recognition. They will find themselves identified with the plants they plant and the animals they tend. Their own families are for them extended plant and animal life. They love their soil as part of themselves and aspire to be buried where they were born.

Skills of no description can be acquired at this level, even tree climbing. As 7 is not yet born, acquiring any skill, however primary, is out of the question. Sleep is unconscious, dreams are subconscious for them. Skill in another, emotions exhibited pass them without their noticing them, as they do not have faculties to respond to them. The only endowment he has is the primary physical energy that prevents him from being condemned as a human bulk.

8 is in direct touch with 7 and 9 and in indirect touch with 2 and 5. The lives of the warrior or the poet will have in their previous generations men of 8. It receives from 5 and 2. It will be parallel to what the cream receives but will characterise the bottom.

Vitality here is still energy and no sensation. Any sensation here will be physical sensation. What does not create a physical sensation, a man in 8 will not be able to respond to. Loudspeaker, drum beating, blowing the trumpet, etc. are for men of 8. Aldous Huxley says the African drum beating and the Indian chanting will help one lose his intellectuality. "Intellectuals of the world unite, you have nothing to lose but your brains" is his description of chanting and drum beating. Chanting silences the mind, drum beating brings mind to its original physical sensations, one from above and the other from below devastatingly affecting the intellectual prowess of the brain.

Level 9

Level Nine is the pristine, pure physical, even as No. 1 is pure Mind. This is the evolutionary point at which the animal emerges into manhood. What is the bottom most point of manhood is the peak for the animal.

At this point the species has emerged into humanity but has not acquired any capacity as yet that truly belongs to man. It is just there awake. That waking state enables it to move, thus making movement possible. It is not just movement as in the stone or plant, a movement that generates outside. The animal too moves, moves by its vitality. This movement is human movement, movement of the humanised matter. In that sense, it is the greatest achievement of Nature, the evolution of Man. Its parallel now will be the appearance of the Supramental Being on earth. His own movement will not be by thought or will. It would be a self-willed movement uninitiated by thought or unexecuted by human will.

At Nine, movement and sleep are the statuses of consciousness and substance. While on the surface and awake it moves. Withdrawn into itself, the substance is in its response like a newborn baby in the womb of the mother, maybe a newly formed baby. Supramentalisation for the purpose of physical transformation takes place here at the plane of consciousness, for the purpose of the birth of Supramental being in the plane of substance.

Nine has the whole man fully in it, but in unevolved potential, not unformed potential. Nine is not in the least touched by mentality or vitality. The physical parts of No. 3 and No. 6 are in direct touch with Nine, while it can be in direct touch only with No. 8. Nine thus is the point in man which generates vitality, the vital energies and vital sensations. For that purpose it is the first focus. The freshness of physical matter yet untainted by consciously acquired habits of even physical sensation belongs to Nine.

IN the descent, the influence of all parts from levels 1 to 8 penetrates downwards and reaches Nine too. It is really mentalised only at level 3 where even the flesh becomes sophisticated into the grey matter of the brain.

In the evolutionary scheme of things, when a species emerges, its form is fixed. It does not change later. Its maximum intelligence is given to its members at the very emergence of the species. Nine holds in full potential the maximum intelligence to which man has ever reached and its first exhibition was in the primitive man's fashioning his tools out of stone.

Except at Nine, man is conditioned by sensations of the physical and vital and thought of the mind. For purposes of further evolution, man has to decondition his parts of all the acquired habits even as 9 is fresh without those conditionings.

Supramentalisation and transformation require that unconditioned purity of the being in all parts down to this level 9. Mother's vision of a seal had that character. SHE describes how that animal was pure, innocent, untouched by the possible perversions of the human mentality that is crooked. Buddhists, whose beliefs and training do not permit them to organise the ego have this character.

When talking to them, you feel like talking to one untouched by any influence of this world of ours. Their flesh is soft to touch, carrying the softeness of unspoiled purity. The nearest version of this seen in life is the artless, guileless person incapable of shrewdness or insight. Should it be strong, it will represent the highest culture man can ever attain by purity that is strong. In such a condition, increase of purity leads to increase of strength. Maybe there, strength and purity are synonyms.

To know man in his nine parts is to know him fully. To trace his growth from level 9 to level 1 and back again from 1 to 9 is a knowledge which can hold in it in sum the entire history of man on earth.

Conclusion

We know of the mental evolution by which man evolved, but we do not consider that society has a mental evolution too. In theory, not only man and society but every act, event, organisation, institution, form of life does undergo the different stages of evolution of which the mental evolution is the culmination. This is the hour when the process of Social Development has reached its point of mental evolution. Social Development which has been going on so far under the direction of vital energy and physical experience has now come under the direction of mental comprehension. What man has been doing so far without thinking must hereafter be done by conscious thought. Social Development is entering the conscious phase from its unconscious past. In that sense it is a historical moment or even an evolutionary juncture. Only Ghali has voiced the need for a theory of social development. Among the foremost of economists, the need is not perceived. In their view it is beyond the ken of human thinking. This confirms the old experience that the present establishment in any field serves more as an unthinking obstacle than a perceptive pioneer. It is striking that the recognition should come from outside the academics. What Indira Gandhi was so anxious to know of, all the senior administrators under her considered as of no significance. Social Development, thus, belongs to the political field rather than the field of economics or the practising economists.

A field lends itself to theory when the experience there saturates the different branches of it. During the past few centuries society was at great pains to conquer nature, discover ways to surmount the obstacles to peaceful living, devising instruments that make living convenient and comfortable. In that endeavour he has largely succeeded and that success has spread over a quarter of the globe. It can be considered that the developmental effort has reached a point of saturation. Mental theorising is possible only when the previous planes of vital and physical are saturated with experience.

A theory, especially one that is comprehensive, will not only embrace all areas of the subject, but will be capable of explaining every phenomenon in the field. If that is so, our theory must satisfactorily explain every stage of development society has so far passed through and every project that succeeded. In fact, a theory must be able to explain every failure so far. In that case, it will be a tool in the hands of every government, particularly governments of the developing world, for national planning. That may be considered the greatest contribution of the theory. But that will be the least valuable service the theory will be able to render.

Its highest service will be elsewhere. When an unorganised field gets organised, its power and effectivity do not rise five or ten-fold, but more than a hundred-fold is a repeated social experience as witnessed in the birth of the state, the creation of banks, the advent of money, commerce, trade routes, warfare and so on. Its minor versions are the improvements in technology such as we meet with in computer. The spread is phenomenal. Before getting organised, the mind must come to grips with the underlying process of a successful activity carried on without the precise mental comprehension directing it. A theory does it. Theorising is to understand mentally what we have been doing successfully all these years without knowing how or why. At this point the unconscious activity becomes conscious. This is a process that converts the finite resources into infinite usefulness, the fixed value of the parts and tools into unlimited value.

Mankind which has been developing so far facing constraints of all types of resources will suddenly realise its resources are infinite and the environment and circumstances that decided its course till now are determined by it. The knowledge of this theory will give man a mental freedom over the life circumstances that have presided over him so far, unparalleled in human history. He would discover that the only constraint he faces is the constraint of his comprehension.

This theory will give the world a view that every event has an infinite creative potential in it. It is very perceptive of Harlan to have seen it. It is a world view and a view of the infinite.

When framed, this theory must mentalise the process that has so far been physical. Presently there are developmental policies, strategies, programmes, approaches, etc. and there is a fertile confusion that mistakes the one for the other. The theory will codify each of them, grade them, put them all in their places and above all bring them all under one unifying umbrella of theory. Thereafter, no confusion is possible. As they fall into their allotted places, each can function with a greater vigour it was not capable of so far. The mere presence of this theory will render the policies, strategies, and programmes more effective. No doubt it will serve as a powerful tool in the hands of planners all over the world.

The field of economics has collected enough superstitions and they are all now ruling the roost. Inflation, unemployment, budget deficit, recession are the main ghosts that haunt the field. Once a theory has come into its own, it has to spell out its views on them. These superstitious positions have to describe themselves in the light of the theory which is being increasingly accepted by the world. The one result will be all these illusions will die their natural death and quickly too.

As this theory will put development on a scientific basis, scientific thinking of every other subject will rise. There is a hope of economics becoming a subject in its own right and that influence may spread to physics and botany. Presently subjects are there on the strength of the information available in the field. Some of them are governed by laws that are partial, but no subject is organised as a department of study in its own right under an outline that can be styled complete or full.

One other direct result will be that the theory will put the crime of the West and poverty of the South in their own perspective. Now that material resources are discovered in abundance and social potentials in greater abundance, poverty and crime stand no chance of survival.

Money now enjoys a prime place in the effort of development. It is in short supply in several quarters and over supply in other places. Both hurt. In areas of short supply, the theory will enable the societies to create real money ten-fold by the newfound knowledge. In areas of over supply, innovative uses of money not for generation of more money, but for the generation of higher social good can be found in great number. As the theory will be in existence by then, no one will be able to raise superstitious opinions to counter them. Humanity, which is now in a few thousand ethnic pockets dreaming of their own uniqueness and generating local tensions will then be able to conceive of the fact that aspirations all over the globe are the same. Such an attitude will form,the basis of one world. The theory will be able to show war in its implications in the past as well as future. Now that there is no cold war, war's effect can be more fully understood across the world and help to abolish wars of all descriptions.

Infrastructures will emerge into their right significance and therefore their power can multiply. More can be done with less in the future with the knowledge of infrastructures.

Social development is only a broader version of individual development, only that the application is in a wider field. The individual of every plane can emerge with this knowledge. The political individual arose by the institution of democracy. Guaranteed employment can create economic individuality. Freedom from subservience to society creates the psychological individual. Theoretical comprehension of society is the basis for the birth of the mental individual.

This theory brings in a mental freedom to all aspects of society, especially its forces of development. That freedom enhances the effectivity of the existing tools and enables us to fashion new tools such as the indicators.

Man is presently confronted with thousands of obstacles to his development or his efforts to develop the society. Every institution that served the cause of development so far will turn into an obstacle hereafter. The government administration is the primary-one. At least in India the social forces such as village unity which were initially a help have now turned into a hindrance. People joined together to defeat the very purpose of any scheme. Opinions, social customs, deep-seated beliefs, institutions social as well as organisational will rear their heads as insurmountable obstacles when the society wants to forge ahead.

6

A Historical Sketch of Sociological Theory

Classical sociological theories are theories of great scope and ambition that either were created in Europe between the early 1800s and the early 1900s or have their roots in the culture of that period. The work of such classical sociological theorists as Auguste Comte, Karl Marx, Herbert Spencer, Emile Durkheim, Max Weber, Georg Simmel, and Vilfredo Pareto was important in its time and played a central role in the subsequent development of sociology. Additionally, the ideas of these theorists continue to be relevant to sociological theory today, because contemporary sociologists read them. They have become classics because they have a wide range of application and deal with centrally important social issues.

This chapter supplies the context within which the works of the theorists presented in detail in later chapters can be understood. It also offers a sense of the historical forces that gave shape to sociological theory and their later impact. While it is difficult to say with precision when sociological theory began, we begin to find thinkers who can clearly be identified as sociologists by the early 1800s.

Development of Sociological Theory

The social conditions of the nineteenth and early twentieth centuries were of the utmost significance to the development of sociology. The chaos and social disorder that resulted from the series of political revolutions ushered in by the French Revolution in 1789 disturbed many early social theorists. While they recognized that a return to the old order was impossible, they sought to find new sources of order in societies that had been traumatized by dramatic political changes.

The Industrial Revolution was a set of developments that transformed Western societies from largely agricultural to overwhelmingly industrial systems. Peasants left agricultural work for industrial occupations in factories. Within this new system, a few profited greatly while the majority worked long hours for low wages. A reaction against the industrial system and capitalism led to the labour movement and other radical movements dedicated to overthrowing the capitalist system. As a result of the Industrial Revolution, large numbers of people moved to urban settings. The expansion of cities produced a long list of urban problems that attracted the attention of early sociologists.

Socialism emerged as an alternative vision of a worker's paradise in which wealth was equitably distributed. Karl Marx was highly critical of capitalist society in his writings and engaged in political activities to help engineer its fall. Other early theorists recognized the problems of capitalist society but sought change through reform because they feared socialism more than they feared capitalism.

Feminists were especially active during the French and American Revolutions, during the abolitionist movements and political rights mobilizations of the mid-nineteenth century, and especially during the Progressive Era in the United States. But feminist concerns filtered into early sociology only on the margins. In spite of their marginal status, early women sociologists like Harriet Martineau and Marianne Weber wrote a significant body of theory that is being rediscovered today. All of these changes had a profound effect on religiosity. Many sociologists came from religious backgrounds and sought to understand the place of religion and morality in modern society.

Throughout this period, the technological products of science were permeating every sector of life, and science was acquiring enormous prestige. An ongoing debate developed between sociologists who sought to model their discipline after the hard sciences and those who thought the distinctive characteristics of social life made a scientific sociology problematic and unwise.

Rise of Sociological Theory

The Enlightenment was a period of intellectual development and change in philosophical thought beginning in the eighteenth century. Enlightenment thinkers sought to combine reason with empirical research on the model of Newtonian science. They tried to produce highly systematic bodies of thought that made rational sense and that could be derived from real-world observation. Convinced that the world could be comprehended and controlled using reason and research, they believed traditional social values and institutions to be irrational and inhibitive of human development. Their ideas conflicted with traditional religious bodies like the Catholic Church, the political regimes of Europe's absolutist monarchies, and the social system of feudalism. They placed their faith instead in the power of the individual's capacity to reason. Early sociology also maintained a faith in empiricism and rational inquiry.

A conservative reaction to the Enlightenment, characterized by a strong anti-modern sentiment, also influenced early theorists. The conservative reaction led thinkers to emphasize that society had an existence of its own, in contrast to the individualism of the Enlightenment. Additionally, they had a cautious approach to social change and a tendency to see modern developments like industrialization, urbanization, and bureaucratization as having disorganizing effects.

Development of French Sociology

Claude Henri Saint-Simon (1760-1825) was a positivist who believed that the study of social phenomena should employ the same scientific techniques as the natural sciences. But he also saw the need for socialist reforms, especially centralized planning of the economic system. Auguste Comte (1798-1857) coined the term "sociology." Like Saint-Simon, he believed the study of social phenomena should employ scientific techniques. But Comte was disturbed by the chaos of French society and was critical of the Enlightenment and the French Revolution. Comte developed an evolutionary theory of social change in his law of the three stages. He argued that social disorder was caused by ideas left over from the idea systems of earlier stages. Only when a scientific footing for the governing of society was established would the social upheavals of his time cease. Comte also stressed the systematic character of society and accorded great importance to the role of consensus. These beliefs made Comte a forerunner of positivism and reformism in classical sociological theory.

Emile Durkheim (1858-1917) legitimized sociology in France and became a dominant force in the development of the discipline worldwide. Although he was politically liberal, he took a more conservative position intellectually, arguing that the social disorders produced by striking social changes could be reduced through social reform. Durkheim argued that sociology was the study of structures that are external to, and coercive over, the individual; for example, legal codes and shared moral beliefs, which he called social facts. In *Suicide* he made his case for the importance of sociology by demonstrating that social facts could cause individual behaviour. He argued that societies were held together by a strongly held collective morality called the collective conscience. Because of the complexity of modern societies, the collective conscience had become weaker, resulting in a variety of social pathologies. In his later work, Dukheim turned to the religion of primitive societies to demonstrate the importance of the collective consciousness.

Development of German Sociology

German sociology is rooted in the philosopher G.F.W. Hegel's (1770-1831) idea of the dialectic. Like Comte in France, Hegel offered an evolutionary theory of society. The dialectic is a view that the world is made up not of static structures but of processes, relationships, conflicts, and contradictions. He emphasized the importance of changes in consciousness for producing dialectical change. Dialectical thinking is a dynamic way of thinking about the world.

Karl Marx (1818-1883) followed Ludwig Feuerbach (1804-1872) in criticizing Hegel for favouring abstract ideas over real people. Marx adopted a materialist orientation that focused on real material entities like wealth and the state. He argued that the problems of modern society could be traced to real material sources like the structures of capitalism. Yet he maintained Hegel's emphasis on the dialectic, forging a position called dialectical materialism that held that material processes, relationships, conflicts, and contradictions are responsible for social problems and social change.

Marx's materialism led him to posit a labour theory of value, in which he argued that the capitalist's profits were based on the exploitation of the laborer. Under the influence of British political economists, Marx grew to deplore the exploitation of workers and the horrors of the capitalist system. Unlike the political economists, his view was that such problems were the products of an endemic conflict that could be addressed only through radical change. While Marx did not consider himself to be a sociologist, his influence has been strong in Europe. Until recently, American sociologists dismissed Marx as an ideologist.

The theories of Max Weber (1864-1920) can be seen as the fruit of a long debate with the ghost of Marx. While Weber was not familiar with Marx's writings, he viewed the Marxists of his day as economic determinists who offered single-cause theories of social life. Rather than seeing ideas as simple reflections of economic factors, Weber saw them as autonomous forces capable of profoundly affecting the economic world. Weber can also be understood as trying to round out Marx's theoretical perspective; rather than denying the effect of material structures, he was simply pointing out the importance of ideas as well.

Whereas Marx offered a theory of capitalism, Weber's work was fundamentally a theory of the process of rationalization. Rationalization is the process whereby universally applied rules, regulations, and laws come to dominate more and more sectors of society on the model of a bureaucracy.

Weber argued that in the Western world rational-legal systems of authority squeezed out traditional authority systems, rooted in beliefs, and charismatic authority, systems based on the extraordinary qualities of a leader.

His historical studies of religion are dedicated to showing why rational-legal forms took hold in the West but not elsewhere. Weber's reformist views and academic style were better received than Marx's radicalism in sociology. Sociologists also appreciated Weber's well-rounded approach to the social world.

Georg Simmel (1858-1918) was Weber's contemporary and co-founder of the German Sociological Society. While Marx and Weber were pre-occupied with large-scale issues, Simmel was best known for his work on smaller-scale issues, especially individual action and interaction. He became famous for his thinking on forms of interaction (i.e., conflict) and types of interacts (i.e., the stranger). Simmel saw that understanding interaction among people was one of the major tasks of sociology. His short essays on interesting topics made his work accessible to American sociologists. His most famous long work, *The Philosophy of Money*, was concerned with the emergence of a money economy in the modern world. This work observed that large-scale social structures like the money economy can become separate from individuals and come to dominate them.

Origins of British Sociology

British sociology was shaped in the nineteenth century by three conflicting sources: political economy, ameliorism, and social evolution. British sociologists saw the market economy as a positive force, a source of order, harmony, and integration in society. The task of the sociologist was not to criticize society but to gather data on the laws by which it operated. The goal was to provide the government with the facts it needed to understand the way the system worked and direct its workings wisely. By the mid-nineteenth century this belief manifested itself in the tendency to aggregate individually reported statistical data to form a collective portrait of British society. Statistical data soon pointed British sociologists toward some of the failings of a market economy, notably poverty, but left them without adequate theories of society to explain them.

Ameliorism is the desire to solve social problems by reforming individuals. Because the British sociologists could not trace the source of problems such as poverty to the society as a whole, then the source had to lie within individuals themselves.

A number of British thinkers were attracted to the evolutionary theories of Auguste Comte. Most prominent among these was Herbert Spencer (1820-1903), who believed that society was growing progressively better and therefore should be left alone.

He adopted the view that social institutions adapted progressively and positively to their social environments. He also accepted the Darwinian view that natural selection occurred in the social world. Among Spencer's more outrageous ideas was the argument that unfit societies should be permitted to die off, allowing for the adaptive upgrading of the world as a whole. Clearly, such ideas did not sit well with the reformism of the ameliorists.

Other Developments

Vilfredo Pareto (1848-1923) thought that human instincts were such a strong force that Marx's hope to achieve dramatic social changes with an economic revolution was impossible. Pareto offered an elite theory of social change that held that a small elite inevitably dominates society on the basis of enlightened self-interest. Change occurs when one group of elites begins to degenerate and is replaced by another. Pareto's lasting contribution to sociology has been a vision of society as a system in equilibrium, a whole consisting of balanced independent parts.

After his death, Marx's disciples became more rigid in their belief that he had uncovered the economic laws that ruled the capitalist world. Seeing the demise of capitalism as inevitable, political action seemed unnecessary. By the 1920's, however, Hegelian Marxists refused to reduce Marxism to a scientific theory that ignored individual thought and action. Seeking to integrate Hegel's interest in consciousness with the materialist interest in economic structures, the Hegelian Marxists emphasized the importance of individual action in bringing about a social revolution and reemphasized the relationship between thought and action.

Classical Sociological Theory

Classical sociological theories are important not only historically, but also because they are living documents with contemporary relevance to both modern theorists and today's social world. The work of classical thinkers continues to inspire modern sociologists in a variety of ways. Many contemporary thinkers seek to reinterpret the classics to apply them to the contemporary scene.

Three-component Theory of Stratification

The three-component theory of stratification, more widely known as Weberian Stratification or Three Class System, was developed by German sociologist Max Weber with class, status and party as distinct ideal types. Weber developed a multidimensional approach to Social stratification that reflects the interplay among wealth, prestige, and power.. "Weber argued that power can take a variety of forms. A person's power can be shown in the social order through their status, in the economic order through their class, and in the political order through their party.

Thus, class, status and party are each aspects of the distribution of power within a community." (Hurst, 202) Class, Status and party have a great deal of effect not only within their individual areas but also have a great deal of influence over the other areas as well.

- Wealth: includes property such as buildings, lands, farms, houses, factories and as well as other assets-Economic situation
- Prestige: the respect with which a person or status position is regarded by others-Status Situation
- Power: the ability of people or groups to achieve their goals despite opposition from others.-Parties

There are two basic dimensions of power: The possession of power and the exercising of power.

Possession of Power

According to Weber, the ability to possess power derives from the individual's ability to control various "social resources."

"The mode of distribution gives to the propertied a monopoly on the possibility of transferring property from the sphere of use as "wealth" to the sphere of "capital," that is, it gives them the entrepreneurial function and all chances to share directly or indirectly in returns on capital." (lemert, 116) These resources can be anything and everything and might include things like land, capital, social respect, physical strength, intellectual knowledge, etc.

Exercising of Power

The ability to exercise power takes a number of different forms, but all involve the idea that it means the ability to get your own way with others, regardless of their ability to resist you."For example, if we think about an individual's chances of realizing their own will against someone else, it is reasonable to believe that the person's social prestige, class position, and membership in a political group will have an effect on these chances." In terms of understanding the relationship between power and social stratification, Weber theorized the various ways in which societies are organized in hierarchical systems of domination and subordination using the several major concepts.

Class Power

"Class, at its core, is an economic concept; it is the position of individuals in the market that determines their class position. And it is how one is situated in the marketplace that directly affects one's life chances." This was theorized by Weber on the basis of "unequal access to material resources." For example, if someone possesses something that you want or need then this makes him potentially more powerful than you. He is in a dominant position and you are in a subordinate position because he controls access to a desired social resource. A classic illustration here is the relationship between an employer and employee.

Social Power (Status)

"The existence of status groups most often shows itself in the form of (1) endogamy or the restricted pattern of social intercourse, (2) sharing of food and other benefits within groups, (3) status conventions or traditions, and (4) monopolistic acquisition of certain economic opportunities or the avoidance of certain kinds of acquisitions. If you respect someone or view him as your social superior, then he will potentially be able to exercise power over you (since you will respond positively to his instructions/ commands). In this respect, social status is a social resource simply because he may have it while you may not.. "Not all power, however entails social honor: The Typical American Boss, as well as the typical big speculator, deliberately relinquishes social honor. Quite generally, "mere economic" power, and especially "naked" money power, is by no means a recognized basis or social honor."

Political Power (Party)

"Parties are associations that aim at securing "power within an organization [or the state] for its leaders in order to attain ideal or material advantages for its active members." This form of power can be related to the way in which the State is organized in modern social systems (involving the ability to make laws, for example). If you can influence this process of law creation then you will be in a potentially powerful position. Thus, by your ability to influence a decision-making process you possess power, even though you may not directly exercise that power personally. Political parties are the organizational means to possess power through the mechanism of the State and they include not just formally organized parties, but any group that is organized to influence the way in which power is exercised legitimately through the machinery of the State. "Since parties aim at such goals as getting their programs developed or accepted and getting positions of influence within organizations, it is clear that they operate only within a rational order within which these goals are possible to attain and only when there is a struggle for power"

Social Action

Social action is in direct relation to "Political or Party Power" in combination with the class situation. The influence of laws is based on the social action of members of the classes. "The direction of interests may vary according to whether or not social action of a larger or smaller portion of those commonly affected by the class situation, or even an association among them, e.g., a trade union, has grown out of the class situation, from which the individual may expect promising results for himself." "The degree in which "social action" and possibly associations emerge from the mass behaviour of the members of a class is linked to general cultural conditions, especially to those of an intellectual sort. It is also liked to the extent of the contrasts that have already evolved." We can also see this in another quote "Class-conscious action is most likely if, first, "the connection between the causes and consequences of the 'class situation'" are transparent, or clear. If individuals can plainly see that there is a connection between the structure of the economic system and what happens to them in terms of life chances, class action is more likely" The greater the numbers within these class positions will increase the chance that they will rise up in action.

Mobility

The greater the numbers within these class positions will increase the chance that they will rise up in action.

"it is noncontroversial that the class situation in which each individual finds himself represents a limitation on his scope, tends to keep him within the class. It acts as an obstacle to any rise into a higher class, and as a pair of water wings with respect to the classes below...Class type, relations with class fellows, power over outward resources adapted to the class situation, and so on." In the capitalist society movement between classes is a possibility. Hence the use of the term "The American Dream" to show the ability of people to ascend to a higher class through hard work and ingenuity. "Class composition is forever changing, to the point where there may be a completely new set of families." He saw four classes-the propertied class, non-propertied class, petit bourgeoisie and the manual labourer class.

7

Emile Durkheim: The Science of Society as Moral Order

Rules of Sociological Method

Sociology as the Study of Social Facts

Definition: a social fact is (1) any way of acting, fixed or not, (2) capable of exerting an external constraint over the individual; (3) it is general and exists independent of its individual manifestations.

Note the characteristics of a social fact: 1) Social facts are ways of being, including (ideal) representations and (material) actions;2) They have a coercive power over the individual; they are accompanied by sanctions, and thereby control the individual; this is actually how we can identify social facts, and this is because:3) They are external to the individual; they are social; society is their substratum;they cannot be reduced to its individual manifestations, which are both part social and part psychological (socio-psychological); therefore, they are not collective (shared by everyone); society is a reality sui generis.

The Study of Social Facts:

Durkheim first discusses social philosophies. These are unscientific because they substitute social reality for a certain conception of that reality. From this perspective, Durkheim discards Comte's and Spencer's evolutionary schemas, since they represent their ideas of society rather than present the facts of social life. What we need, is a clear-cut, unambiguous, and scientifically developed concept of the social. For instance, sociology should study not an idea of ethical rules but the ethical rules themselves.Consequently, Durkheim concludes that social phenomena are things and that they should be treated as such. Social facts, then, are seen to be things that exist outside of the will of people. Therefore, sociology needs to be established as a rigorous discipline, with the following principles:

Auxiliary Rule 1: Discard all preconceptions: This calls for a value-free approach to the study of social facts. Whatever moral, political, or religious concerns the sociologist may have, he cannot allow them into his investigations. Ethical considerations an the like are themselves object for sociological inquiry.

Auxiliary Rule 2: Define the subject matter in terms of the common external characteristics of a group of phenomena, and include all phenomena that correspond to this definition: This rule calls for a clearly defined subject matter in terms of its inherent characteristics. This ensures that the topics of sociological investigation do not depend on the sociologist but on the social facts. Durkheim makes the interesting comment that this rule is often not observed because many concepts in sociology, e.g. the family or law, are also common-sense notions. Another violation of this rule is that not all relevant phenomena are included in a study; a selection is made, often in terms of assuming that what holds for our society, is valid universally. One should therefore start with the observable consequences of the phenomenon under investigation to define it, that is, same effects indicate one phenomenon (e.g. crime is classified by punishment).

Auxiliary Rule 3: Social facts are studied objectively when they are isolated from their individual manifestations: This follows from the basic rule, and from the fact that objectivity is enhanced by the increasing stability of a subject matter. Hence, study social facts independent of their individual manifestations since the latter are too variable.

Social Facts and Physical Things

In the preface to the 2nd edition of Rules, Durkheim discusses some misunderstandings of his method. First, he says that social things are things like physical things but this does not mean that they are physical things. Social facts are things in the sense that they stand outside an idea, that they can only be known by observation, and that thus they must be studied as nature is studied by physicists. Second, society is, of course, made up out of individuals, but this does not mean that we should study individual consciousness, because the resulting synthesis of individuals coming together is a reality sui generis. The collective representations lead a life of their own, they exhibit their own psyche, and they reveal, as one and only one of their characteristics, the fact that they are constraining or coercive.

Distinction of the Normal from the Pathological

Science cannot decide what is good or evil for us, because it would be ideological, yet, on the other hand, science must justify itself. Durkheim sees the solution to this problem in the fact that science should ask and investigate what is actually, in a given society, good or desirable. Science is not evil or good but it can study evil and good. Here, Durkheim proceeds to do just that.

Social facts are pathological when they disrupt the normal operations of social functions in a certain society. This, of course, can vary from society to society. Note Durkheim's functionalist argument that the most widespread social forms are, in the long run and in the aggregate, the ones that survive (normality is therefore more common). Therefore, social facts can be pathological at some time in development (but not in the long run) because, and only when, they were at one time normal.

Therefore, the following rules apply to distinguishing normal from pathological.

- A social fact is normal for a specific social type, at some specific time in its social evolution, when it occurs in the average society of that species; this can be verified by:
- Demonstrating that the general character of a phenomenon is related to the general conditions of collective life; and this is necessary:
- When the social type under investigation has not yet completely evolved. An example is the demonstration of the normality of crime. Crime is normal because it is observed, in some form or another, in all societies. It is not a demonstration of the wicked nature of man, but, on the

contrary, a factor that shows the necessary integrative element in society.

Morphology, Explanation and Comparison

Above we indicated that Durkheim distinguishes different societies from one another (e.g. what is normal in one society is not necessarily normal in another). How does he make this distinction? This is the task of social morphology. Durkheim proposes to first identify the basic, crucial characteristics of societies, which can be identified in a study of the simplest of societies (this is why he undertook the study of Australian religions). This indicates the relevance of ethnographies for sociology. Therefore, he proposes to study the horde, i.e. a social formation which cannot be split up into any smaller social parts; the horde consist of individuals. Different hordes linked together form a clan. From here on, societies can be classified into social types, e.g. a simple replication of hordes or clans, a replication of these replications, and so on.

Sociological Explanation

The identification of social types, on the basis of the purpose that certain basic social facts fulfill, is insufficient to demonstrate where these facts came from. Therefore, look for the historical causes that have certain social facts as effects (very important: this shows that Durkheim was not a mere functionalist; two things are needed: identification of facts based on functions, and historical study of causes!!). Therefore, to explain a fact, study its cause and its function separately. Obviously, following from the basic rule, these functions and causes are, by definition, social and cannot be retrieved in the individual psyche, although he admits that human nature plays a part in social facts (as a kind of disturbing factor, but never as a cause). The rules to find function and cause are: the cause of a social fact lies in antecedent social facts, and the function of a social fact lies in the end it fulfils. In other words, social processes should be explained in terms of society itself (e.g. social volume and density).

This also leads Durkheim to suggest that sociology can explain what is, by finding out what has been, but not to predict what will be (against Marx and the evolutionists). Moreover, it indicates the special relevance of history to sociology. Sociology must be historical but this should be conceived as a study of the objective causes of social facts (based on principles of morphology), i.e. as a psychology of the social (since society is a character of its own). Sociology cannot be a search for individuals' inner states of mind, because introspection is only valid for individual psychology, not for sociology. Therefore too, the method of political economy to study goods in terms of the value they have for the participants in the economic process is invalid.

Sociological Proof by Comparison

Since there can be no experiment in sociology, causes of social facts are investigated by the comparative method, i.e. comparing the cases where two social facts are simultaneously absent or present, so we can discover the variations displayed in these combinations which provides evidence that one fact (cause) leads to another fact (effect). This method is guided by the rule that one cause leads to one effect (any one effect must be caused by one cause).

Note that this rule, as Durkheim admits, does not really prove causes, but that it can minimally disprove causes. Indeed, if someone states that A causes B, but we find a case where there is B but not A, then the thesis is disproved. Since social life is so complex, it can always be that we have omitted a relevant variable. A parallelism of a sufficient number of cases, however, adds value to our inferences on causal links. Then we can deduce a thesis and test it inductively. This could lead us to establish laws. What is indispensable for sociology, then, is to explain social facts by tracing its entire development throughout all social species (i.e. across time and space). In sum, sociology must make up classifications, then sociology must be historical to identify causes and effects, and finally, in being historical, sociology must be objective.

Psychology and Philosophy

It is not true, Durkheim argues, that he wants to destroy psychology and philosophy. First, sociology begins with society to see how it affects human nature, the human psyche (sociology of social facts leads to solid psychology). Second, metaphysical questions will always exist, yet sociology will force them to be asked in different form, so sociology informs philosophical inquiry. In addition, sociology can study philosophies as social facts, so sociology is also n extension of philosophy.

Suicide as a Sociological Object

First, Durkheim rules out that suicide varies with psychopathic states. It cannot be that people have only one specific type of mental illness that would lead them to commit suicide. People cannot be temporarily insane because they lack a motive to commit suicide. There is no correlation between insanity (as measured, for instance, by the number of people in an asylum) and the suicide rate. Finally, there is no correlation between alcoholism and suicide.

Second, Durkheim disproves that suicide varies with normal psychological states, such as race or heredity, since there is considerable variation in suicide rate within races.

Third, Durkheim argues that there is no relation between suicide and climate or seasonal temperature, but he finds that the intensity of life seems to have an effect (a social cause).

Finally, imitation, the mechanic reproduction of somebody else's act, does not correlate with the suicide rate, since, for instance, there are no concentrated zones of suicides.

Social Causes and Social Types

The previous investigation on non-social factors of suicide, by elimination, shows that suicide must depend on social causes. Such a sociological explanation could start from types of suicide and then look for their causes. However, this is not possible because of lack of data. Therefore, we look for causes of suicide-rates, on the premise that one cause leads to one effect. How to look for these causes? The legal establishment gives immediate motives of suicides, but this only explains individual suicides, and not the more general states that lay behind them.

Egoistic Suicide

Thesis 1: Suicide varies inversely with the degree of integration in religious society : Religion affects suicide: there is less suicide in Catholic countries, and more suicide in Protestant countries. Also, within any single nation this effect holds good. Jews generally commit even less suicide than Catholics. Note that both the Catholic and Protestant religions prohibit suicide. The essential difference, however, between Catholicism and Protestantism is that Protestantism permits free inquiry to a much greater extent, while Catholicism is organized by a hierarchical system of authority. Protestantism's free inquiry is itself the effect of a lack of traditional beliefs and practices, in short, it is a less strongly integrated church. For Jews, the great solidarity, the need to live in greater union, protects them from suicide.

This explanation is confirmed: 1) of all protestant countries, England has a lower suicide-rate, because the Anglican church is more strongly organized; 2) free inquiry stimulates a desire for learning, and, indeed, the more the craving for knowledge develops, the more does suicide (this also explains why women commit less suicide; and for Jews the thesis does not hold because their strive for knowledge has a different origin, namely to be better armed for struggle in their unfavourable position). Note that knowledge in itself is not a source for evil, and religion in general has a prophylactic effect upon suicide. But the (lack of) intense collective life along with it explains their effect upon suicide.

Thesis 2: Suicide varies inversely with the degree of integration in domestic society : Marriage reduces the danger of suicide. Other data show that:-too early marriages have an aggravating influence on suicide, especially for men;-married persons of both sexes commit less suicide than unmarried persons;-the sex committing less suicide in marriage varies from society to society;-widowhood leads to higher suicide-rates.

The privileged position of married persons, with regard to suicide, is not dependent on matrimonial selection (e.g. because men and women are recruited to marriage in the same way, but married women commit more suicide). Now, is it the conjugal group (husband and wife) or the family group (married with children!) that produces this effect. Data on families without children show that conjugality only plays a moderate role. The fact that widowers have children makes the crisis through which they pass more intense, and therefore their suicide-rate is higher.

Differences in suicide during widowhood between the sexes are explained by the suicidal tendency of the sexes in the state of marriage (where men benefit more from marriage, they also suffer more from widowhood, but are also better able to endure it). The effect of the family group is further shown by the fact that higher family density (more children) correlates with lower suicide-rates, because families with more children are more powerfully integrated.

Thesis 3: Suicide varies inversely with the degree of integration in political society : Political societies also effect suicide-rates: revolutions, wars, and other political crises lead to a reduction of the number of suicides, because (and only when) such crises can move the masses, arousing collective sentiments and national faith, and integrate society, at least temporarily, towards a single end.

Suicide Varies with the Degree of Social Integration

Something in religion, the family, and political life must be common to explain their effect on suicide: they are all strongly integrated groups. Social integration refers to the degree of bonding or attachment of individuals to society. If groups are weakly integrated, the individual is less dependent on them, they are in a state of egoism: egoistic suicide springs from excessive individualism. An entire range of ideas, feelings and practices of civilized adults are built and expanded because of the demands of the social environment; they are social demands with a social purpose. But, as individuals, we must cling to them, and we can only do so to the extent to which we are integrated within society itself. (Women live more outside of community existence, this explains the relatively lower suicide-rates of widows as compared to widowers).

Altruistic Suicide

Thesis: Insufficient individuation leads to suicide; every form of suicide is the exaggerated form of a virtue; the extremes are pathological : In the lower, primitive societies, old men, women at their husband's death, and servants at the death of their chief kill themselves because it is their duty, it is compelled, because these individuals are completely absorbed in the group, they are very highly integrated. In this case, the ego is not its own property, this is a state of altruism.

Altruistic suicide may be obligatory (the previous examples), optional, i.e. not formally required, or considered a praiseworthy sacrifice (as in some, pantheistic religions). In all these cases, the individual strips himself of his personal being, in order to be engulfed in something considered the true essence, a mental representation which springs not from the individual, but from society. In modern society, altruistic suicide can be observed in the army, not because of bachelorhood, since the soldier is not isolated at all, and also not from alcoholism, or not from disgust with the service. Actually, those that are most inclined to a military career and best suited to the needs of the army, are the ones with highest suicide-rates (note that throughout these chapters, Durkheim refutes explanations different from his owns, and he does so by controlling variables when looking at statistical data). The general loss of discipline in the army in recent years is accompanied by a general decline in the suicide-rate, again, this proves the thesis of altruism.

Anomic Suicide

Thesis: Suicide varies with the degree of social regulation

Acute anomic suicide: Economic crises increase suicide-rates, not because then life is more difficult, since even fortunate crises have this effect, but because they are disturbances of the collective order. This can be explained by the fact that man, unlike animals, has needs that are in principle infinite. If there would be no limits set to these needs, this would lead to perpetual unhappiness, and since man cannot limit the desires himself, a force outside of him must do it, an authority he respects, and this is society. Society is the moral disciplinary body whose authority must not only depend on force but also accepted as just. Now, when society is disturbed by crises, it is momentarily incapable of exercising this moral influence; society is then in a state of anomie, and this produces anomic suicide.

Chronic anomic suicide: Anomie is a regular factor in the world of trade and industry. Economic progress exists in freeing relations from all kinds of regulation, the complete liberation of desires. Anomic suicide shares with egoistic suicide that both represent an insufficient presence of society in the individual, but egoism refers to a lack of integration (the attachment of individuals to society), anomie refers to a lack of regulation (the control of basic human passions).

Explanation: The suicide of widowhood is a result of domestic anomie, and divorce shows this even more. Particularly, divorce, especially where it is legally regulated, leads to higher suicide-rates among husbands. This is explained by the nature of marriage (conjugal society). For men, marriage offers a useful regulation of sexual desires and other passions, and divorce is a sudden weakening of this regulation. For women, this is different: women are more instinctive creatures and mentally less developed, so that any regulation (marriage) for them is a constraint without great advantages, and divorce frees them from this constraint. Anomic suicide because of divorce is thus wholly to be attributed to men.

Individual Forms of the Different Types of Suicide

Now a morphological classification, on the basis of the aethiological one, can make sense, taking into account that only suicide as a collective phenomenon can be explained. Egoistic suicide refers to those types that result from highly developed individualism, from seeking the absolute only in him/herself, because society is not sufficiently integrated. The decision to commit suicide under these circumstances can be sad or cheerful. Altruistic suicide is the opposite, an active suicide, with perfect calmness.

Entirely different is anomic suicide out of a state of unregulated emotions or the disappointment following disturbances in regulation. These different social conditions can also affect the individual simultaneously and produce combined effects. Egoism and anomie have some affinity, cf. the egoist is detached from society and thus it has no sufficient hold upon her/him. Anomie can also be associated with altruism (e.g. the Jews after the fall of Jerusalem). Finally, egoism and altruism even can combine their influence, e.g. when people create an imaginary object which they attach themselves to .

The Social Element of Suicide

Suicide, then, is socially determined, independent of the individual. The collective tendencies that are responsible for suicide have a mind of their own; they are moral and social. Social life, then, is external to the individual. Murder and suicide, which seem alike, are not invariably related (e.g. wars lead to less suicide, yet more murder; anomie and altruistic suicide, on the other hand, are related; consequently, murder is social too and, since it has different causes, murder comes in different types). Since the indispensable conditions of life are useful, suicide is likely to occur. Indeed, social regulation and integration are needed in any society, and whether societies place high value on the individual or, on the contrary, constrain him heavily, there is suicide resulting from those social states (every morality produces its type of suicide).

However, the enormous increase in the number of suicides over the last century is due, not to progress, but to the particular conditions under which progress has actually occurred. These conditions are pathological (basically, a lack of regulation, due to the abruptness of the social changes, cf. Division of labour). Therefore, the current rate of suicide is pathological, not suicide as such!

The solution to the problem is not legislation, education, politics or family. The true solution is the professional group, to create a morality close enough to the individual.

Religion, Society and Knowledge

Durkheim studies religion in its most simple form to derive the basics, to find the universals of religion by tracking its indispensable properties. This also leads him to a theory of the origin of religion, and to postulate that religion is at the basis of all human thought (both sacred and profane), even of all the categories of human thought (e.g. space, time, causality). All of this, it will be shown, is essentially social: religious representations are collective representations which express collective realities. The categories of knowledge, because they are of religious origin, are therefore social too; e.g. spatial representations are universal because they are based on the fact that values are differentially attributed to different regions within any given civilization. Within that civilization, therefore, these values must be universal, i.e. they originated within that society (e.g. space is conceived the way a tribal area is divided). Since society is a reality sui generis, it representations which express it, must be supra-individual, it imposes itself upon the individual mind. Consequently, since these representations are so constraining, have such power over the individual, society is responsible for the necessity of the categories of thought as a reflection of the moral necessity of society. It will be shown that all representations come from religious representations as a social reality sui generis.

Therefore, religion has to be defined as a social fact: religion is a unified system of beliefs (states of opinion) and practices (modes of action) relative to sacred things, i.e. things set apart and forbidden; the beliefs and practices unite all those adhere to them into a single moral community, i.e. the church. The beliefs refer to representations of the sacred, but at once they identify the relations between different scared things and between the sacred and the profane. The practices are tied with the beliefs. Religious rites and beliefs, then, have a special object, i.e. they presuppose a classification of things into scared and profane, determined by the attitudes people have towards those things on the basis of their social reality.

Durkheim proceeds, on the basis of this definition, to refute other conceptions of religion. Animistic theories explain religion by reference to the worship of the soul which would be the result of dreams, of an illusion, of fantasy. This is nonsense since it is an individualistic interpretation, and because it cannot account for the fact that something which has sustained as long as religion it must have physical, concrete aspects. Likewise, naturalistic theories pose that religion comes from the fact that sacredness is attributed to sensuous experiences and the language by which reference is made to these phenomena. Again, this is nonsense since religion is again attributed to an illusion, namely the illusion of just names.

Totemic Beliefs

Durkheim proposes to study totemic religion among Australian tribes because it is a very simple society and it will therefore exhibit the original form of religion. The clan that worships the totem is of central significance: the clan is a bond of kinship united by name (not biology), and the totem of the clan is also the totem of the clan members. Another clan has another totem. Totems can be animals, vegetables and even ancestors. Clans are united by bonds of fraternity in phratries; these phratries also have a totem, and they relate to the different totems of the clans in a relation of subordination. Clan totems enjoy special status: some persons may not touch the totem, it is kept in a special place, it gives men special powers, and its loss is a disaster. Other things can be scared because they are in some way related to the totem. Note that totems are worshipped, not because the person has some sensation of it, but because it fulfils the need of representing ideas which are formed of it. (later Durkheim will of course seek to explain what these ideas are). There is also a marked parallelism between men and totems: the prohibitions regarding totems also apply to clan members (e.g. they have the same name).

Then Durkheim proceeds to show that the totemic classifications form the basis for the idea of social class. Men were first organized as men, in clans and phratries, and therefore they were able to organize things. The fundamental notions of the intellect are the product of social factors. The notion of class is not an ideal but a defined group of interrelated things. Human classification is based on social hierarchy.

Origin of Totemic Beliefs

After refuting a series of theories, Durkheim asserts that totems have an underlying idea of force. The force of the totem, its symbolic qualities of sacredness, must indeed have a referent (symbols refer to something). There must be something unifying in all that is worshipped in these totemic religions, and this unity lies in what is symbolized and not in the symbol. Here Durkheim argues that totems are forceful over and against the individual because they are an instance of the idea of force in general. This force derives from the strength of the clan, so that the totemic principle of force is in fact the clan under an empirically concrete form: if the totem's symbol is god and society, then god and society are identical.

Indeed, following from Durkheim's approach to sociology in general, it follows that the reality underlying religious thought cannot be representations of the individual or of the material environment. This external reality, Durkheim will contend, is society itself. Society alone is the moral authority which can exert such a powerful hold over man. Therefore, god or any other sacred object is a symbolic representation of society. The ideas of religious, then, are real in that they express something real, a real idea so to speak, or what Durkheim calls essential idealism.

Note how the soul can be seen from this perspective. The idea of the soul is universal to religion. The human body shelters a soul; body and soul are not the same, but they are closely related. The soul represents the sacred, it concerns moral ideas; while the body is in a sense profane, and represents the material world. The soul, Durkheim asserts, was created because it refers to something real, namely the relation between individual and society (body and soul).

Other religious ideas are also of social origin. The god, for instance, is an ancestor who gained a prominent place. All religious ideas of totem, souls, spirits, and gods, derive from the original form of the tribe: the tribal unity is expressed in the form of a god, it expresses the tribe conscious of itself.

Ritual Attitudes

Here Durkheim explains the origin of rituals in its most basic form. Cults are negative or positive. Negative cults prohibit or interdict (by means of taboo), in order to keep different sacred things apart or to separate sacred from profane. These interdictions can translate into the prohibition of contact with the scared, not speaking out the scared, and the territorial or temporal separation of sacred and profane. The positive cult worships something. In rites, something is awakened, then it is sacrificed.

These acts produce feelings of well-being, which itself becomes the justification of the rite. The ritual arouses sentiments, it affects the mental status of its participants. Note how the notion of causality is produced by rituals. Causality is a social force, external to the mind. Causality is the work of the group and not just an intellectual construction; it derives from the efficaciousness of ritual manipulations. Rituals tie the individual to the group. Religious rituals reaffirm the social group and strengthen the collectivity. Rituals of passage (e.g. burial) have the same function: when someone dies, the group is weakened, so the collective sentiments have to renewed, reaffirmed. This also explains the rise of civil religion, e.g. the worship of Fatherland, Reason and Liberty in the French revolution.

These simple religions which Durkheim studies, share essential elements with all religions. Specifically, the sentiments of the believers, unanimously shared, cannot be illusory, they have objective causes in a reality sui generis, i.e. society. Society produces religion, it can account for the sentiments involved, it is even society who makes the individual. To do this, society must come in action, it must make itself felt and it does this in the assembly of believers. By this form of common action, society takes consciousness of itself. It is the idea of society which is the soul of religion; and through religion, all the fundamental categories of thought were formed.

It could be objected that this 'society' at the origin of religion is an ideal version of society, that it is not real. No, it is real, but an idealization nonetheless; the idealization itself stems from the intensity of rituals, as a natural product of social life, i.e. as a condensed or concentrated version of that society. The idealized society is therefore not outside the real society but a part of it. The ideals of religion are thus an expression of the collective life: in the school of collective life, the person has learned to idealize. This is not to be confused with an historical-materialist argument.

Concepts are collective representations. They derive their more specific nature (their diversity) from the fact that clans and tribes are differentiated, and, at the same time, they derive their universal nature from the fact that every society is always part of a larger whole. Therefore, it is always society which furnishes the most general notions with which it should be represented. Society is the consciousness of consciousness, it is itself an individuality, of a superior status.

Division of Labour

In his review of the works of Marx and Durkheim, Alexander outlines Durkheim's theory of modern society as forming a hierarchy of processes and institutions ranging from the particularism of individual life to the universalism of culture. At the most general level, culture refers to the cognitive, moral and aesthetic representations of collective life that inform the rest of society. It refers to what Durkheim described as the "collective consciousness", society as it thinks of itself, the morality of society which regulates the social institutions as well as economic life. Beneath culture, the state and the law represent this universal culture in a more particularistic way and organize the lower levels of the educational, occupational and domestic institutions. The individual is at the bottom of the social hierarchy. Some central elements emerging out of this scheme are Durkheim's notion of culture and morality, state and politics, law and punishment, the corporation or occupational group, and the characteristics of modern economic life. Durkheim's ideas on these issues have undergone changes in the course of his work; basically in The Division of Labour he argued for a materialist interpretation, while in The Elementary Forms of the Religious Life he gives an idealist account. This presentation rests on his first major excursion in The Division of Labour in Society, but when necessary I will indicate if and how Durkheim's ideas have developed in his later works.

Labour and Its Causes

The purpose of Durkheim's work on the division of labour is to construct a positivistic science of morality and discover how social solidarity can be maintained despite the growing autonomy of the individual resulting out of the division of labour. Economic forces have lead not only to a functional differentiation of labour but also to differentiation processes in all other domains of society. Durkheim argues that this is the result of an evolution from mechanical to organic societies. Mechanical societies are composed of similar replicated parts (families, hordes, clans). The collective conscience, defined as "the totality of beliefs and sentiments common to the average members of a society", reflects this "solidarity by similarities": the collective practices and beliefs of the group are shared by all of its members, and any offense against the collective consciousness is perceived a threat to the entire social order. Durkheim argues that in the course of history organic society made progress in the proportion to which mechanical society has regressed. Organic societies are made up of functionally different organs, each performing a special role. The collective consciousness of this social type has a different hold on the individual: the bonds to tradition and family are loosened, but the individual now has the social duty to specialize and to concentrate his range of activities. The collective consciousness in modern societies still has a hold on individuals, if only to affirm their individuality.

The causes of this evolution to a society characterized by a functional division of labour are twofold. First, "It is because there occurs a drawing together of individuals who were separated from one another, or at least they draw more closely together than they had been.". Then social relations become more numerous since "they push out beyond their original boundaries on all sides". Durkheim calls this "drawing together and the active exchanges that result from it" dynamic or moral density. Second, the social volume also increases, that is, the total number of members of society becomes larger. More dense and more voluminous societies, Durkheim argues, necessitate the division of labour because the struggle for existence becomes more strenuous. As people are drawn together this will increase competition among them and when they have "ample space at their disposal, they will flee from one another. If they cannot go beyond set limits, they will begin to differentiate, but in a way so that they become still more dependent of one another". Therefore, "the division of labour unites at the same time it sets at odds; it causes the activities that it differentiates to converge; it brings closer that it separates".

The secondary factors that account for the development of the division of labour include, first, the greater independence of individuals in relation to the group. This means that the collective consciousness becomes progressively indeterminate as societies get larger: "Because they are spread over a much vaster area, the common consciousness is itself forced to rise above all local diversities, to dominate more the space available, and consequently to become more abstract". This trend is for instance demonstrated by the changing nature of the notion of divinity. Originally, the objects of religious devotion are sacred beings who derived their sacred character directly from the object with which they were identified (sacred plants or animals). Then develops the notion of spirits "who, whilst preferring this or that location, nevertheless exist outside the particular objects to which they are more especially attached...; they still exist in space". With the evolution to polytheism "the dwelling-place of the gods becomes more clearly distinct from that of man", and, finally, the god of Christianity "goes beyond space; His Kingdom is no longer of this world".

Another secondary factor in the evolution to organic societies is the weakening of the influence of tradition. This occurs because in modern societies "individuals are no longer restricted to their place of origin and free space is opened up, attracting them, they cannot fail to spread out over it". Especially the growth of the town demonstrates that "The more the group is spread out, although densely concentrated, the more the collective attention, dissipated over a wide area, becomes incapable of following the movements of each individual, because attention does not become more intense as the number of individuals increases. It must oversee too many points at one time to be able to concentrate on any single one. The surveillance is less careful, because there are too many people and things to watch. There is therefore a general decrease in social control because the individual's "more frequent journeys, the more active communications that he exchanges, the affairs with which he busies himself outside his own locality, etc., divert his gaze from what is taking place around him. The centre of his life and concerns is no longer to be found wholly in the place where he lives". Therefore, "collective surveillance is irrevocably relaxed, the common consciousness loses its authority... In short, for social control to be rigorous and for the common consciousness to be maintained, society must split up into moderately small compartments that enclose completely the individual. By contrast, both social control and the common consciousness grow weaker as such divisions fade".

Along with the division of labour, there is then a general trend for social life to become regulated in a different way (and not unregulated as some observers had thought). The economic order itself does not lead to order or disorder, it is the collective consciousness that accompanies it which determines the cohesion of society. The moralities of mechanical and organic societies fulfill the function of binding the individual, offering cohesion to the whole, albeit in different ways which are themselves the result of changed conditions in social density and volume.

Crime, Law and Punishment

In the Division of Labour, Durkheim conceives law as a manifestation of the collective consciousness. Hence he uses as a measure for the development from mechanical to organic societies the evolution from repressive to restitutive law. Repressive law is characteristic for simple and ancient societies. Law is essentially religious law and infractions against it are immediately punished because they threaten the existence of the collectivity itself. Crimes that are not religious are less severely punished. The moral beliefs and justifications on which law and punishment are based are specific but not explicitly specified since every member of society knows them (the collective consciousness is identical to the individual consciousness). In modern societies only criminal law is still repressive: it serves the unconscious function of strengthening social solidarity.

The nature of modern solidarity, however, changed and criminal law declined in favor of restitutive law. Punishment follows legal violations in a restitutive way so that the relations between individual and society are restored. Because individuals are more and more differentiated from one another (they have different professions), legal regulations are more abstract and general so they can still apply to all different individuals and provide the solidarity necessary for the cohesion of society: "That alone is rational that is universal. What defies the understanding is the particular and the concrete".

The growth of commercial law is an index of organic social solidarity: it indicates the need to maintain relations between differentiated parts (analogous to the specialized functions of the organs of the body), which are backed up by society. In contract law, for instance, every contract "assumes that behind the parties who bind eachother, society is there, quite prepared to intervene and to enforce respect for any undertakings entered into". In organic societies it is therefore the state which becomes the organ of priority to direct the other organs (like the brain). Violating the rules of a contract between individuals is an offense against the state as the representative body of modern collective conscience.

Political Society and State (I)

The evolution of political life, under normal conditions, corresponds to the growing indeterminacy of the collective consciousness in organic societies: "the place of the individual is becoming greater and governmental power less absolute". The modern state is more universal and less coercive and repressive, but this does not mean that it has become less in size. On the contrary, "the state's attributions become even more numerous and diverse as one approaches the higher types of society". The state's functions thus generally increase and specialize; "At the same time, it extends progressively over the whole area of its territory and ever more densely packed, complex network, with branches that are substituted for existing local bodies or that assimilate them". According to Durkheim, the state develops not as a counterbalance to but by mechanical necessity out of the division of labour. The government cannot regulate at any moment all the conditions of economic life since it is "too general to ensure the cooperation of the social functions, if such cooperation is not realized spontaneously". This "spontaneous consensus of its parts" is still necessary if society is to be held together and only the collective consciousness can provide this unity. Therefore, the state "is not the brain that creates the unity of the organism, but it expresses it, setting its seal upon it, [while] the parts must be already solidly linked to one another".

We already saw that Durkheim conceives the law as fulfilling the function of maintaining solidarity between the component parts in society, to secure the autonomy of different individuals while maintaining the relationships that hold them together. In a later work Durkheim modifies his view of law and outlines two laws of penal evolution. The first law stipulates that "the intensity of punishment is greater the more closely societies approximate to a less developed type-and the more the central power assumes an absolute character". Durkheim thus reaffirms what he earlier argued in The Division of Labour: the collective consciousness is stronger in mechanical societies, more loosened in organic societies. He now explicitly links this evolution with the religious or secular nature of law. In primitive societies, the collective consciousness is essentially religious and so are their laws. In organic societies, the law is secularized to refer to some human interest, not an individually held interest but to mankind in general (analogous to the development of the collective consciousness). Any offense is an offense against another human and "cannot arouse the same indignation as on offense of man against God". However, in the second part of the first law Durkheim states that the nature of political power also intervenes in the development of the intensity of punishment. The law does not always "automatically" represent the collective consciousness; it may be "distorted" by the political regime that determines its contents. An absolutist government which faces no counter-balancing social forces, in particular, may create and enforce laws which do not correspond to the collective consciousness: the laws may be repressive, even in a differentiated society characterized by a division of labour. However, Durkheim asserted, this is not "a consequence of the fundamental nature of society, but rather depends on unique, transitory, and contingent factors". The political society to be normal, therefore, should always be in concord with the development of the collective consciousness.

The other "law of law" refers to the fact that "deprivations of liberty, and of liberty alone, varying in time according to the seriousness of crime, tend to become more and more the normal means of social control". Durkheim refers to the lack of prisons in primitive societies where, he argues, imprisonment would not fulfill any need since crimes directly threaten the collectivity and should therefore also be punished collectively. When with the division of labour collective responsibility gradually declines, the individual comes to the focus of attention and the deprivation of his freedom is a natural consequence.

Social Regulation of Economic Life

With his study of the division of labour Durkheim wanted to show that the "cult of individualism" and the persistence of collective consciousness are not mutually exclusive, but on the contrary that the division of labour produces and necessitates a different kind of social solidarity. Under exceptional circumstances, however, Durkheim maintained that the division of labour often did not produce organic solidarity, because it was produced under conditions of an absence of rules regulating social relations (anomie), or forced under conditions of economic-material inequalities. Economic life as such is not normal or pathological, Durkheim contends, it is the (lack of) its regulation which should be dealt with. The intervention of the state Durkheim saw in this regard necessary but insufficient because the state is too far removed from the concrete lives of people and the specific needs of their different professions (the state is too general). Therefore, Durkheim proposed that a secondary groups placed between the individual and the state should take care of this function. He judged the corporation or professional group to be ideal in this regard.

Durkheim first discussed the professional group in some detail in his work Suicide. As a remedy to egoistic and anomic suicide, he argued that a restoration of man's attachment to, and regulation by, society is needed, and that this role should be taken up by the corporation. Political society is too far removed from the individual to affect him, religious society is generally in decline (secularization), and the family's duration is too brief (it has become a non-entity).

The corporation, on the other hand, could fulfill the function of investing society in the individual, because it has a strong cohesion and its influence on individuals is "not intermittent, like that of political society, but it is always in contact with them by the constant exercise of the function of which it is the organ and in which they collaborate". To take up this function the corporation has to become a definite and recognized organ of public life "instead of remaining a private group legally permitted, but politically ignored".

It has to be moved between the state and the individual to form "a cluster of collective forces outside the State, though subject to its action, whose regulative influence can be exerted with greater variety". The state remains important to fulfill the function of opposing "the need for organic equilibrium to the particularism of each corporation".

In the preface to the second edition of The Division of Labour and in the posthumously published Professional Ethics and Civic Morals further expands this idea. In the preface, he reasserts that a society "cannot be maintained unless, between the state and individuals, a whole range of secondary groups are interposed". Of these secondary institutions only the corporation can 'tame' the economy. The family can no longer take up this function since it has lost much of its integrative and regulatory force. Corporations should take over because the profession under conditions of the division of labour determines our life more and more. Such corporations already exist since, like other secondary institutions, "as soon as a certain number of individuals find they hold in common ideas, interests, sentiments and occupations which the rest of the population does not share in, it is inevitable that, under the influence of these similarities, they should be attracted to one another. They will seek one another out, enter into relationships and associate together". The existing corporations, however, should be reformed: they must set codes guiding each of the professions (regulatory) and they must be well-organized groups (integrative) constituting a moral force upon and not a servant of the economy.

Bibliography

Abbot, Andrew: *Time Matters: On Theory and Method*, Chicago, Chicago University Press, 2001.

Alexander, Jeffrey C.: *Theoretical Logic in Sociology: Presuppositions and Current Controversies*, London, Routledge and Kegan Paul, 1982.

Althusser, Louis: *Lenin and Philosophy and Other Essays*, London, New Left Books, 1971.

Archer, Margaret S.: *Realist Social Theory: The Morphogenetic Approach*, Cambridge: Cambridge University Press, 1995.

Bhaskar, Roy: *A Realist Theory of Science*, London, Verso, 1997.

Byrne, David: *Complexity Theory and the Social Sciences: An Introduction*, London, Routledge, 1998.

Cilliers, Paul: *Complexity and Postmodernism: Understanding Complex Systems*, London, Routledge, 1998.

Coleman, James S: *Foundations of Social Theory*, Cambridge, Mass.: Belknap Press of Harvard University Press, 1990.

Durkheim, Emile, and Lewis A. Coser: *The Division of Labor in Society*,.Free Press, New York, 1997.

Giddens, Anthony: *The Constitution of Society*, Cambridge: Polity Press, 1984.

Goldthorpe, John H.: *The Affluent Worker in the Class Sttructure*, Cambridge: Cambridge University Press, 1969.

Gould, Stephen Jay: *Wonderful Life: The Burgess Shale and the Nature of History*, London: Norton, 1989.

Jervis, Robert: *System Effects: Complexity in Political and Social Life*, Princeton: Princeton University Press, 1997.

Merton, Robert: *Social Theory and Social Structure*, London, The Free Press of Glencoe, 1957.

Index

A

Aesthetic Sphere, 167.
Approach, 5, 6, 7, 8, 10, 13, 28, 33, 39, 61, 67, 69, 79, 180, 245, 247, 250, 255, 266.
Association, 14, 17, 76, 183, 252.
Authority, 50, 60, 61, 88, 89, 97, 102, 103, 104, 105, 106, 107, 109, 120, 131, 138, 145, 158, 173, 174, 175, 176, 177, 188, 203, 204, 207, 247, 260, 262, 267, 271.

B

British Sociology, 248.

C

Capitalistic Spirit, 172.
Charismatic Authority, 176, 247.
Citizenship, 171.
Class Power, 251.
Classical Social Theory, 27.
Classical Sociological Theory, 249.
Commission, 78, 85, 199, 234.
Communication, 8, 30, 51, 52, 63, 64, 71, 90, 96, 105, 109, 114, 133, 182, 196.
Comprehensive Theory, 50, 71, 78, 79, 80.
Conflict Theory, 6, 7, 8, 29, 140.
Conscious Development, 83, 195.
Crisis of Social Theory, 32, 57.
Critical Ethnography, 62.
Critical Global Theory, 46, 49.
Cultural Transmission, 97.
Culture, 10, 13, 14, 29, 33, 35, 36, 37, 39, 41, 52, 58, 60, 62, 63, 64, 87, 98, 109, 142, 154, 155, 168, 169, 178, 180, 203, 238, 243, 269.

D

Developments, 30, 46, 48, 49, 56, 57, 75, 138, 232, 244, 245, 249.
Division of Labour, 33, 44, 107, 108, 161, 174, 264, 269, 270, 271, 273, 274, 275, 276.

E

Economic Sphere, 164, 180.
Emile Durkheim, 2, 3, 23, 28, 243, 246, 254.
Exercising of Power, 251.

F

Foundations, 23, 24, 56, 89, 111, 148, 158, 183.
Freedom, 33, 54, 60, 65, 89, 104, 116, 121, 127, 129, 170, 181, 207, 240, 242, 274.

G

German Sociology, 246.
Governments, 84, 86, 105, 107, 110, 142, 240.
Green Revolution, 74, 84, 85, 86, 87, 108, 113, 193.

I

Importance of Theory, 2.
Impression Management, 12.
Infrastructure, 71, 77, 79, 81, 82, 89, 100, 111, 112, 117, 126, 130, 131, 194, 195, 196, 197, 198, 199, 205, 206.
Integration Theory, 13.
Intellectual Sphere, 167.

L

Laws, 15, 20, 22, 24, 26, 29, 44, 87, 96, 97, 105, 107, 110, 111, 112, 137, 164, 170, 178, 195, 241, 247, 248, 249, 252, 258, 273, 274.
Legitimate Authority, 173.

M

Management, 11, 12, 72, 108, 115, 136, 179.
Max Weber, 20, 23, 28, 61, 147, 151, 243, 247, 250.
Measurement, 199, 200, 201, 202, 203, 216.

N

Natural Sciences, 14, 17, 25, 26, 61, 245.

O

Organization, 19, 21, 35, 48, 51, 52, 74, 76, 79, 81, 82, 85, 86, 87, 88, 96, 97, 98, 99, 100, 101, 102, 103, 104, 107, 108, 109, 110, 111, 112, 113, 114, 117, 118, 120, 121, 122, 124, 125, 126, 127, 129, 130, 131, 132, 133, 134, 135, 138, 139, 140, 154, 155, 157, 164, 169, 171, 174, 176, 181, 185, 253.

P

Paradigms in Sociology, 14.
Philosophy, 24, 26, 27, 28, 29, 30, 33, 35, 36, 37, 39, 40, 44, 50, 51, 53, 54, 58, 63, 64, 65, 66, 137, 157, 172, 243, 263, 273, 276.
Planned Development, 84, 86, 87, 92, 95.
Political Philosophy, 27.
Political Power, 30, 135, 171, 184, 274.
Political Society, 261, 274, 275.
Political Sphere, 165.
Possession of Power, 250.
Postmodern Critical Theory, 61.
Powers, 38, 41, 69, 77, 98, 103, 107, 137, 177, 184, 190, 223, 266.
Prominent Sociological Theories, 3.
Punishment, 106, 229, 255, 269, 272, 273, 274.

R

Rational Legal Authority, 173.
Relationship, 1, 2, 3, 8, 30, 61, 69, 101, 131, 134, 141, 150, 164, 174, 181, 195, 202, 228, 249, 251.

Role Theory, 10, 11.

S

Social Action, 8, 23, 147, 148, 150, 152, 153, 154, 252.
Social Activity, 26, 45, 69, 82, 97, 102, 132.
Social Constructionism, 12, 13.
Social Contract Theory, 27.
Social Development, 21, 22, 41, 68, 78, 84, 91, 106, 107, 111, 114, 115, 116, 118, 122, 127, 128, 129, 132, 137, 140, 144, 145, 192, 196, 216, 217, 218, 219, 220, 221, 223, 239, 242.
Social Integration, 27, 261.
Social Phenomena, 1, 3, 4, 14, 19, 20, 23, 24, 26, 46, 180, 245, 255.
Social Power, 129, 154, 194.
Social Preparedness, 87, 94.
Social Stratification, 250, 251.
Society, 3, 4, 5, 6, 7, 8, 9, 10, 13, 15, 17, 18, 19, 20, 21, 22, 23, 24, 26, 27, 28, 29, 30, 32, 33, 35, 36, 37, 38, 39, 41, 42, 43, 44, 45, 46, 47, 48, 49, 50, 51, 52, 53, 54, 55, 56, 57, 58, 59, 60, 62, 65, 68, 69, 70, 71, 72, 73, 75, 78, 79, 80, 81, 82, 83, 84, 85, 86, 87, 88, 90, 91, 92, 93, 94, 95, 96, 97, 98, 99, 100, 101, 102, 103, 104, 105, 106, 107, 108, 109, 110, 111, 112, 113, 114 116, 117, 118, 119, 12(121, 123, 124, 125, 12 127, 128, 129, 130, 13 132, 133, 134, 135, 13 137, 139, 141, 142, 15 167, 173, 191, 194, 195, 196, 197, 199, 203, 204, 205, 206, 213, 214, 225, 229, 239, 245, 246, 248, 249, 250, 251, 252, 254, 255, 256, 259, 260, 261, 262, 263, 264, 265, 266, 267, 268, 269, 270, 271, 272, 273, 274, 275, 276.
Sociological Explanation, 19, 259.
Sociological Method, 28, 254.
Sociological Paradigm, 17, 18, 19.
Symbolic Interactionism, 8, 9, 10, 64.

T

Technology, 54, 56, 71, 72, 74, 75, 76, 79, 81, 85, 86, 90, 94, 98, 100, 108, 112, 113, 114, 117, 122, 131, 134, 136, 137, 138, 139, 170, 172, 194, 240.
Theoretical Paradigms, 32.
Totemic Beliefs, 265, 266.
Traditional Authority, 175, 247.

W

Welfare, 145, 201.
Wisdom, 176, 195.

□□□